On Surface and Place

On Surface and Place is a rich and poetic exploration of surfaces which foregrounds their significance in our understanding and experience of place. Adopting weaving as its overarching metaphor, it departs from Gottfried Semper's discussion of correspondences between architecture and textiles, and emerges from the reading of photographs, a swatch of Harris Tweed and curtain wall façade juxtaposed. In juxtaposing the fabric of the city with the weave of Harris Tweed the book charts an original course across a range of connected ideas and questions, combining many different themes, writers and disciplines. It presents integrated and innovative rethinkings on a number of fundamental relationships, including correlations between body and building, word and image, and between the rural and the metropolitan, and the hand-crafted and the mass-reproduced. In doing so, it seeks to foreground the very interrelationship of surface and place, as it makes a claim for the relational nature of the world in which we live.

Peta Carlin is an artist and an essayist. She holds a PhD, along with a Bachelor degree in architecture, and an Honours and a Masters degree in fine art imaging. She is currently a Lecturer at the Department of Architecture, Xi'an Jiaotong-Liverpool University, Suzhou, P.R. China.

Studies in Architecture Series
Series Editor: Eamonn Canniffe, Manchester School of Architecture, Manchester Metropolitan University, UK

The discipline of Architecture is undergoing subtle transformation as design awareness permeates our visually dominated culture. Technological change, the search for sustainability and debates around the value of place and meaning of the architectural gesture are aspects which will affect the cities we inhabit. This series seeks to address such topics, both theoretically and in practice, through the publication of high quality original research, written and visual.

For a full list of titles in this series, please visit www.routledge.com/architecture/series/ASHSER-1324

Other titles in this series

Phenomenologies of the City
Studies in the History and Philosophy of Architecture
Edited by Henriette Steiner and Maximilian Sternberg

From Formalism to Weak Form
The Architecture and Philosophy of Peter Eisenman
Stefano Corbo

Forthcoming titles in this series

On Discomfort
Moments in a Modern History of Architectural Culture
Edited by Andrew Leach and David Ellison

Architecture, Death and Nationhood
Monumental Cemeteries of Nineteenth-Century Italy
Hannah Malone

Reconstruction and the Synthesis of the Arts in France, 1944–1962
Nicola Pezolet

On Surface and Place
Between Architecture, Textiles and Photography

Peta Carlin

LONDON AND NEW YORK

First published 2018
by Routledge
2 Park Square, Milton Park, Abingdon, Oxon OX14 4RN

and by Routledge
711 Third Avenue, New York, NY 10017

Routledge is an imprint of the Taylor & Francis Group, an informa business

© 2018 Peta Carlin

The right of Peta Carlin to be identified as author of this work has been asserted by her in accordance with sections 77 and 78 of the Copyright, Designs and Patents Act 1988.

All rights reserved. No part of this book may be reprinted or reproduced or utilised in any form or by any electronic, mechanical, or other means, now known or hereafter invented, including photocopying and recording, or in any information storage or retrieval system, without permission in writing from the publishers.

Trademark notice: Product or corporate names may be trademarks or registered trademarks, and are used only for identification and explanation without intent to infringe.

British Library Cataloguing-in-Publication Data
A catalogue record for this book is available from the British Library

Library of Congress Cataloging in Publication Data
Names: Carlin, Peta, author.
Title: On surface and place : between architecture, textiles and photography / Peta Carlin.
Description: New York : Routledge, 2017. | Series: Ashgate studies in architecture series | Includes bibliographical references and index.
Identifiers: LCCN 2016031517 | ISBN 9781472477644 (hardback : alk. paper) | ISBN 9781315598840 (ebook)
Subjects: LCSH: Surfaces (Philosophy) | Place (Philosophy)
Classification: LCC B105.S85 C37 2017 | DDC 114–dc23
LC record available at https://lccn.loc.gov/2016031517

ISBN: 9781472477644 (hbk)
ISBN: 9781315598840 (ebk)

Typeset in Sabon
by Out of House Publishing

For my mother, Marlene, and in loving memory of my father, Paul.

Contents

List of figures viii
List of epigraphs xi
Acknowledgements xiv

1 On | Opening 2

2 Appearing | Weaving 20

3 Wall | Face 44

4 Image | Word 64

5 Surface | Pattern 80

6 Place | Dressing 98

7 Ritual | Repetition 118

8 Text | Memory 136

9 On | Closing 154

Index 168

List of figures

On | Opening
1.1 Peta Carlin, *Untitled*, from *Urban Fabric: Greige*, 2007. Digital print on Belgian linen. Edition of 6. 152 × 96 cm. © Peta Carlin.   2
1.2 Peta Carlin, Unknown Weaver, *Swatch of Harris Tweed*, 2010. Digital image, variable dimensions. © Peta Carlin.   3

Appearing | Weaving
2.1 Anonymous, *Grid Photo, Grand Theatre of Liceu*, 1904. From *El Gran Teatre del Liceu: Reconstruction and Extension* (Barcelona: Actar, 1997), 56. Copyright unknown.   20
2.2 Anonymous, *Shuttle Coursing across a Loom*. From E. Ostick, *Textiles for Tailors: What You Should Know about Cloth* (London: Tailor and Cutter, n.d.), 18. Copyright unknown.   21

Wall | Face
3.1 Anonymous, *Cairo and the Banks of the Nile*, painted by Émile Wauters (1882), after its collapse in 1971, Brussels. Institut Royal du Patrimoine Artistique. © KIK-IRPA Brussels.   44
3.2 Heinz Hajek-Halke, *Erotik—Ganz Groß! (Erotic—In a Big Way!)*, 1930. Gelatin silver print. 11 9/16 × 9 5/16 in. (29.4 × 23.7 cm). The Museum of Fine Arts, Houston, Gift of Manfred Heiting, The Manfred Heiting Collection.   45

Image | Word
4.1 From Ralph Gibson, *Overtones: Diptychs and Proportions* (New York: Editions Stemmle, 1998). By kind permission of Ralph Gibson.   64

4.2 From Ralph Gibson, *Overtones: Diptychs and Proportions* (New York: Editions Stemmle, 1998). By kind permission of Ralph Gibson.   65

Surface | Pattern
5.1 S. Albany Newall, *Men Stretching and Rolling Up a Length of Harris Tweed*, c. 1920. From Francis Thompson, *Harris Tweed: The Story of a Hebridean Industry* (Newton Abbot: David and Charles, 1969). Copyright unknown.   80
5.2 Gisela Vogler, *Marion Campbell, Hanging Tweeds Out to Dry*, n.d. From Gisela Vogler, *A Harris Way of Life: Marion Campbell (1909–1996)* (West Tarbert: Harris Voluntary Service, 2002). By kind permission of Gisela Vogler.   81

Place | Dressing
6.1 Edward Burt, *Men Attired in the Feileadh Mhor*, c. 1720. From *Letters from a Gentleman in the North of Scotland to his Friend in London; Containing the Description of a Capital Town in that Northern Country, with an Account of Some Uncommon Customs of the Inhabitants; Likewise an Account of the Highlands, with the Customs and Manners of the Highlands. To which is added, a Letter, Relating to the Military Ways among the Mountains, Begun in the Year 1726.* © National Museums Scotland.   98
6.2 Eadweard Muybridge, *Animal Locomotion*, 1887, Plate 428, Detail. Copyright Public Domain. Image kindly supplied by The Boston Public Library.   99

Ritual | Repetition
7.1 Walter Blaikie, *Waulking, Eriskay*, 1899. © Gaidheil Alba / National Museums of Scotland. Licensor: www.scran.ac.uk.   118
7.2 Anonymous, *Weaving Shed at the Baltic Works, Dundee*, late nineteenth century. © Archive Services, University of Dundee. Licensor: www.scran.ac.uk.   119

Text | Memory
8.1 'The Abbey Memory System'. From Johann Horst von Romberch, *Congestorium artificiose memorie* (Venice: Melchiorre Sessa, 1533). By kind permission of Kislak Center for Special Collections, Rare Books and Manuscripts, University of Pennsylvania.   136

x List of figures

8.2 Ezra Stoller, *Seagram Building, Mies van der Rohe with Philip Johnson, New York, NY,* 1958. © Ezra Stollter/Etso. All rights reserved. 137

On | Closing
9.1 Anonymous, *Corset Hardware*, nineteenth century. From Bernard Rudofsky, *Are Clothes Modern: An Essay on Contemporary Apparel* (Chicago: Paul Theobald, 1947), 159. Copyright unknown. 154
9.2 Bill Brandt, *Shad Thames*, 1939. © Bill Brandt Archive. 155

Names | Topics
I.1 Sasha Stone, *Kartei* (Files), c. 1925–6. From Franz Roh and Jan Tschichold eds., *Foto-Auge: 76 Fotos der Zeit (Photo-Eye: 76 Photos of the Period)* (Stuttgart: Fritz Wedekind, 1929). By kind permission of the Estate of Franz Roh and Ernst Wasmuth Verlag. 164
I.2 I. G. Farbenindustrie, *Am Strande (Sur la Plage, Strand)*, before 1929. From Franz Roh and Jan Tschichold eds., *Foto-Auge: 76 Fotos der Zeit (Photo-Eye: 76 Photos of the Period)* (Stuttgart: Fritz Wedekind, 1929). By kind permission of the Estate of Franz Roh and Ernst Wasmuth Verlag. 165

End Image Peta Carlin, *Urban Fabric*, Proposed Installation View without Artefacts. Drawing Letó Tsolakis and Tina Atic, 2013 173

List of epigraphs

On | Opening
Ian Stephen, 'Fathom of Tweed', in Ian Stephen and Sam Maynard, *Malin, Hebrides, Minches* (Mudelstrup: Dangaroo Press, 1983), 26–7. By kind permission of Ian Stephen. 4

W. G. Sebald, *The Rings of Saturn*, trans. Michael Hulse (London: Harvill Press, 1999), 283. By kind permission of Random House. 5

Appearing | Weaving
Alfred North Whitehead, *Essays in Science and Philosophy* (New York: Philosophical Library, 1947), 83. By kind permission of Philosophical Library. 22

Indra Kagis McEwen, *Socrates' Ancestor: An Essay on Architectural Beginnings* (Cambridge, MA: MIT Press, 1993), 54. © 1993 by the Massachusetts Institute of Technology. By permission of the MIT Press. 23

Wall | Face
Samuel Beckett, *The Unnamable*, ed. Steven Connor (London: Faber and Faber, 2010), 100. By kind permission of Faber and Faber. *Excerpts* from 'Three Novels' by Samuel Beckett, English translation copyright © 1955 by the Estate of Patrick Bowles and the Estate of Samuel Beckett. Used by permission of Grove/Atlantic, Inc. Any third party use of this material, outside of this publication, is prohibited. 46

Georg Simmel, 'Bridge and Door', *Lotus: International* 47 (1985): 54. By kind permission of *Lotus International*. 47

xii List of epigraphs

Image | Word
Excerpt from 'Entrance' from *The Book of Images* by Rainer
Maria Rilke, translated by Edward Snow. Translation copyright ©
1991 by Edward Snow. Reprinted by permission of North Point
Press, a division of Farrar, Straus and Giroux, LLC.   66

Walter Benjamin, 'A Small History of Photography', in *One Way
Street and Other Writings*, trans. Edmund Jephcott and Kingsley
Shorter (London: NLB Books 1979). 243. By kind permission
of Verso.   67

Surface | Pattern
Clement Greenberg, 'On the Role of Nature in Modernist
Painting', in *Art and Culture: Critical Essays* (Boston, MA: Beacon
Press, 1971), 172. By kind permission of Beacon Press.   82

Friedrich Nietzsche, quoted and translated by Joseph Rykwert,
in 'The *Ecole des Beaux-Arts* and the Classical Tradition'. In *The
Beaux-Arts and Nineteenth-Century French Architecture*, ed.
Robin Middleton (London: Thames and Hudson, 1982), 17. By
kind permission of Joseph Rykwert.   83

Place | Dressing
Georges Poulet, *Proustian Space*, trans. Elliott Coleman
(Baltimore, MD: Johns Hopkins University Press, 1977), 26.
Originally published as *L'espace proustien*, Georges Poulet ©
Editions Gallimard, Paris, 1963. By kind permission of Editions
Gallimard.   100

Reprinted with the permission of Free Press, a Division of Simon
& Schuster, Inc., from *The Sociology of Georg Simmel* by Georg
Simmel, translated and edited by Kurt H. Wolff. Copyright © 1950
by The Free Press. Copyright renewed © 1978 by The Free Press.
All rights reserved.   101

Ritual | Repetition
Walter Benjamin: Selected Writings, Volume 2: Part 1, *1927–1930*,
translated by Rodney Livingstone and Others, edited by Michael
W. Jennings, Howard Eiland and Gary Smith. Copyright © 1999
by the President and Fellows of Harvard College.   120

Select Papyri, Volume 3: poetry, texts, translations, and notes by
D. L. Page, Loeb Classical Library Volume 360, first published
1941. Loeb Classical Library ® is a registered trademark of the
President and Fellows of Harvard College.   121

Text | Memory

Guillaume Apollinaire, excerpt from 'Shadows'. In *Calligrammes: Poems of War and Peace (1913–1916)*, trans. Anne Hyde Greet (Berkeley, CA: University of California Press, 1991), 136–7. 138

The Arcades Project by Walter Benjamin, translated by Howard Eiland and Kevin McLaughlin. Copyright © 1999 by the President and Fellows of Harvard College. Originally published as *Das Passagen-Werk*, edited by Rolf Tiedemann. Copyright © 1982 by Suhrkamp Verlag. 139

On | Closing

Gottfried Semper, *The Four Elements of Architecture and Other Writings*, translated by H. Francis Mallgrave and W. Herrmann (Cambridge: Cambridge University Press, 1989). 156

Roger Caillois, *The Writing of Stones*, translated by Barbara Bray (Charlottesville, VA: University of Virginia Press, 1985), 103–4. By kind permission of The University of Virginia Press. 157

Names | Topics

Excerpt from *The Life of the Mind*, Volume 2 by Hannah Arendt. Copyright © 1978 by Houghton Mifflin Harcourt Publishing Company. Reprinted by permission of Houghton Mifflin Harcourt Publishing Company. All rights reserved. 166

Edward S. Casey, *The Fate of Place: A Philosophical History* (Berkeley, CA: University of California Press, 1997), 290. By kind permission of The University of California Press. 167

Acknowledgements

Emerging from my art practice and in turn re-informing it, this book has slowly materialised over a number of years. Many people have lent their support and encouragement along the way, and while I am able to mention only a few here, I am grateful, nonetheless, to all who contributed for their generosity.

In particular, I would like to thank a number of teachers whose guidance and support is the legacy from which this book is born. Elizabeth Grosz introduced me to critical theory and cultural studies and encouraged me to bring my own interests to the task at hand. Ian Lobb and Les Walkling shared with me their passion for photography and demonstrated the value of its craft. And Mark Burry and Jeff Malpas believed in the project and stood by me. Their own work remains a touchstone for my thinking.

More recently I have benefited from the generosity of Katie Stewart and David Leatherbarrow, each of whom I hope to meet so that I can thank them in person.

The love and support of my family, Matthew, Ellen and Liam; Rowena; Jerome, Suzana, Nicholas and Oliver; Chantelle, and my cousins too, has sustained me throughout, along with that of my friends Elif Kendir, Letó Tsolakis, Tina Atic, Alison Bell, and Anna Nervegna and Toby Reed. I am especially indebted to Fiona Gunn and Greg Doolan, the dearest of friends, who I can't thank enough.

RMIT University and The British Council awarded funding in support of this research, with Bollinger + Grohmann and John Wardle Architects generously contributing to its realisation. I am also grateful to Pierre-Alain Croset and Gisela Loehlein at Xi'an Jiaotong-Liverpool University for their support.

A number of practitioners collaborated and contributed to the projects which underpinned my thinking and I am especially grateful to Spike Hibberd for his magnificent graphic design, to Ursuala Hill for her exquisite embroidery and to Frances Dunlop and *Sgioba Luaidh Inbhirchluaidh* for advice on and performances of waulking.

In the Outer Hebrides, my thanks go to Lorna Macauly, Donald Martin, Murdo Morrison and Kristina Macleod at the Harris Tweed Authority, for their interest and support, as well as to Ronnie MacKenzie at the Lewis Loom Centre, with especial thanks to Donald John and Maureen MacKay of Luskentyre Harris Tweed. My thanks also go to Louise Butler for facilitating a number of important exchanges.

Two of the book's essays have been previously published with my thanks to the editors and publishers for their inclusion. In the first instance, a near-similar version of 'Ritual | Repetition' appeared in *Textile: Journal of Cloth and Culture* 13, no. 1 (2015), © Taylor and Francis, available online: www.tandfonline.com/ DOI: 10.2752/175183515x14235680035386. And in the second instance, 'Place | Dressing' was published in another form in *Craft + Design Enquiry* 7 (2015), available online: http://press.anu.edu.au/wp-content/uploads/2015/11/ch053.pdf.

The support of Valerie Rose at Ashgate, and Louise Baird-Smith, Sadé Lee, Richard Skipper and Aoife McGrath at Routledge, was instrumental in the early stages of the publication of this book, and it benefited from Adam Guppy's experience and advice in bringing it to completion.

Finally, my thanks go to Joan Mitchell and Rob Willis, and the Scottish-Gaelic Society of Victoria. It is through their passion for the *Chlò Mhór* and Scottish-Gaelic culture that this project came to life and took form.

Tapagh Leibh
Suas leis a' Ghàidhlig agus leis a' Chlò Mhór!

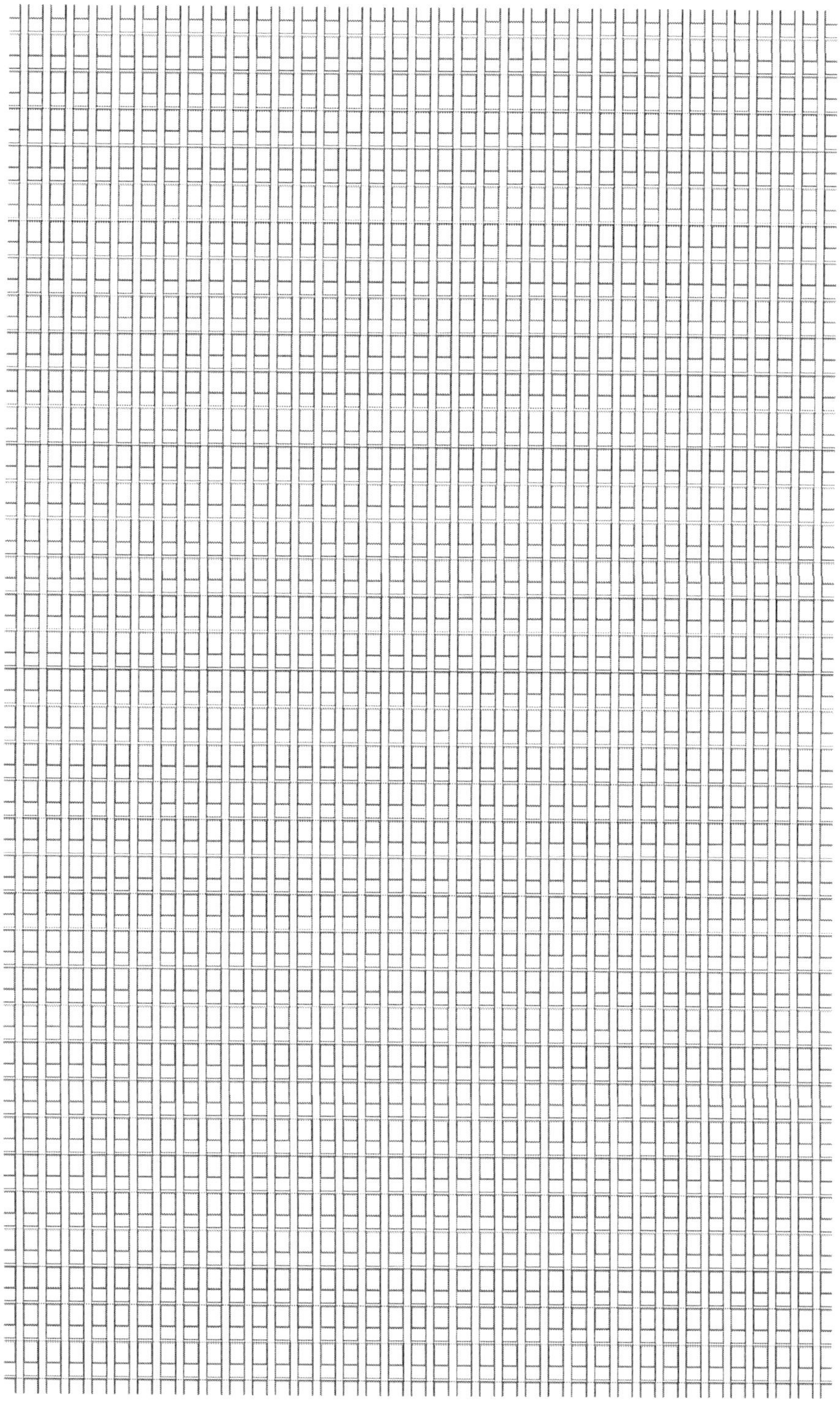

On

Figure 1.1 Peta Carlin, *Untitled*, from *Urban Fabric: Greige*, 2007.

Opening

Figure 1.2 Peta Carlin, Unknown Weaver, *Swatch of Harris Tweed*, 2010.

I sit before a moor of tweed:
a narrow gorge and fading folds.

Two ends must be finished
now I see neither, only
my fathom's reach of arms.

Though I seem to choose this task
there is a tyranny in the
needed eveness of the weave.

Ian Stephen

Weavers […] along with scholars and writers […] had much in common.
W. G. Sebald

6 On | Opening

In wandering through his home town of Berlin, Walter Benjamin (1892–1940) was once to recall the landscape of a far-off distant place travelled to years before, recounting in his city's chronicling that:

> the dunes of the Baltic landscape have appeared to me like a *fata morgana* here on Chauseestrasse, supported only by the yellow, sandy colours of the station building and the boundless horizon opening in my imagination behind its walls.[1]

So too in journeying through the streets of my own city Melbourne were the combination of hue and tone, the colours and patternations of its mid-twentieth-century façades to echo of travels long past, a voyage that still lingers, to the western isles of Scotland. For it was there that I took up the camera for the first time in earnest, astounded by the beauty of the landscape, its vastness and its variegated colouring, reminiscent of tartans and checks of curious, and prior to then, seemingly inharmonious admixtures, bathed in an almost mystical light, an ethereal light that contrasted so sharply with the harshness of the Australian sun that I had known. So moved, it was through photography that I sought to capture all this, to hold it, to prevent it from escaping my memory, to stop the colours fading over the passage of time, photography operating, in a way, as a kind of mordant.[2]

In journeying, it is said that:

> [t]here is even in the very experience of the voyage something more marvellous than in the memory; for memory joins only those things that resemble each other. On the contrary, travel makes neighbours of places without any likeness. It links sites that belong to different planes of existence.[3]

Through movement, between the past and the present, between here and there, we come to know the world, our journeying, it is said, enabling us to grasp it in its complexity, its cohesion built up out of fragmentary experiences, no longer kaleidoscopic, but through our very passage, ordered and composed. The body unified in its movement, its kinaesthetic synthesis operating at rest as in play, is reflected in its movement between destinations, finding itself in place, animate only in relation. Between the metropolis of Melbourne and the largely rural Hebridean Isles, the differences are pronounced, but despite such variances, associations were disclosed: distances and differences breached by the mediation of colour, their surfaces in correspondence.

For the nineteenth-century German architect and champion of the crafts Gottfried Semper (1803–79),[4] architecture, and by extension cities, are 'held in place and in play [...] by the work of colour',[5] his writings on architecture's four elements drawing inspiration from ancient civilisations and titled in one of its editions, *On Polychromy*.[6] Colour, according to Semper, provided 'the artist with a new way to throw the surface into relief [...] bring[ing] the eye back again to the natural way of seeing', a view which conceived of colour and form as one, further acknowledging the implicit and necessary interaction of the arts, of dialogues tacit or otherwise conveyed.[7] For Semper, we are told, did not distinguish between the fine arts and the crafts, between '*Kunst* and *Kunstgewerbe*', no distinction was to be discerned 'between the laws which govern[ed] the work of art and those of a product of the crafts';[8] all man-made artefacts regardless of scale were understood as ornaments, symbolically signifying 'analogical relations with the cosmos'.[9] The principles 'which govern[ed] the conception of [...] work[s] of art',[10] we are told, were to be premised upon the productive arts, with primacy given to textiles and the practices of weaving.[11]

Affiliations between architecture and textiles are long held, the ancient Greek philosopher Democritus (c. 460–c. 370 B.C.), it is said, comparing architecture and weaving with the building of nests by birds and webs by spiders,[12] with the Augustan architect Marcus Vitruvius Pollio (c. 80/70–c. 15 B.C.) later claiming that walls were once originally woven.[13] Semper was to extend the metaphor, in essence between body and building further, his interest in polychromy, lending itself to textiles, culminating in the vestiary arts, or *Bekleidung*, as he was to term it, conceived of as an all-encompassing fabric, an attire skilfully woven.

'Our culture', it is said, 'rests on Greek foundations, and weaving is as much a part of our conceptual scheme today as it was in the time of Homer',[14] the nature of fabrication inherent in the weave evident not only in the bonds and sense of cohesion that are basic to the establishment of societies, but of their cultures too, 'culture occur[ing] [only] in and through the formation of places',[15] reflected in the design and construction of its various fabrics, and realised through their very surfacing.

On Surface and Place takes weaving as its motif, as both its metaphor and model, logic and imagination necessarily entwined in the stitching together of diptychs from disparate disciplines, architectural and textile, their conjoining founded upon association. The book departs from a series of photographs, *Urban Fabric: Greige*, portraits of Melbourne's mid-twentieth-century corporate architectural façades, which exposed the latent image of Harris Tweed amidst the buildings' faces.[16] Operating from the intimate to the architectural, this study interweaves between the hand-crafted, geographically specific and culturally grounded fabric of Harris Tweed, and the global phenomenon of the mass-mediaised surface of the curtain glass wall. Arising out of the taking of photographs and the reading of them, it speculates on how allegiances between surfaces might contribute to our understanding and creation of place, the hyphantic potential of the photograph put to work in its making.

Image-based, the study is largely read through the lens of Walter Benjamin's scribings. For the writings of Benjamin, as it has often been commented, are 'inextricably bound up with [...] images',[17] his texts ascribing 'an incomparably greater significance to pictoriality than is usual in philosophy; [...] speak[ing] at length in, and even more out of, images;'[18] with a particular 'recourse to the language of photography',[19] 'the wonder of appearance' always central to his concerns.[20] The invocation of images in his texts relied upon an engagement with the world, with readings of it, often across the grain, the tactility of experience thus exposed. Such perusals plunged the depths of surface appearances, and were, by and large, deemed a matter of necessity.

> For the matter itself is only a deposit, a stratum, which yields only to the most meticulous examination what constitutes the real treasure hidden within the earth; the images, severed from all earlier associations, that stand – like precious fragments of torsos in a collector's gallery – in the prosaic room of our later understanding. True, for the successful excavation a plan is needed. Yet no less indispensible is the cautious probing of the spade in the dark loam, and it is to cheat one's self of the richest prize to preserve as a record merely the inventory of one's discoveries and not this dark joy of the place of the finding itself.[21]

But perhaps before proceeding any further, how Harris Tweed, the curtain wall and photography have come to be understood in the shaping of this enquiry should be discussed, along with the central themes of surface, place and weaving.

Semper was to extol the dyeing skills of the Celts, this skill also revealed in 'the art of pattern drawing originally practiced on their own skins', a natural precursor to the development of the 'multi-coloured check patterns that form the national dress of Scotland'.[22] Existing long before it became designated as Harris,[23] this Hebridean form of the twill weave, a living heritage, continues in this tradition to this day.[24] The 'big cloth', or *clò mhòr* as Islanders refer to Harris Tweed, is defined by a British Act of Parliament as a fabric that is made of pure virgin Scottish wool, dyed, spun and finished in the Outer Hebrides and hand-woven by weavers at their homes on these islands,[25] located off the north-west coast of Scotland. The activities of Catherine Herbert, Lady Dunmore (1814–86), widow of the sixth Earl of Dunmore, were to establish Harris Tweed; she was, in a sense, the first to commercialise it,[26] commissioning webs of the Murray tartan in 1846,[27] while also contributing to its future through philanthropic investments in the people and their crafts.[28]

Distinguishing between the solid and load-bearing masonry wall, *Mauer*, and the enclosing surface supported by a frame, *Wand*, Semper was to discern the fabrication of the weave in the light-framed structure's walls.[29] His writings were first translated into English by the architect John Wellborn Root, a partner of Dan Burnham, their *Reliance Building* (1890–5) having some claim, it is said, as the first curtain-walled building, as we understand it today;[30] the formulation of the curtain wall building at the end of the nineteenth century said to reference 'Semper's insistence on the conceptual priority of [the] textile art[s]'.[31] Once understood in military terms as a partition hung and tautened between two bastions or towers, from which the pending onslaught of enemies could be espied and surveyed, the curtain wall in its fortification of the enclosure is now consumed by and adorns the tower itself, a doubtless redoubt, the figure an exemplar of Modernism and its purported all-over ornamentation,[32] in a move to abstraction conceivably epitomised by the grid.

Pursued through the taking of photographs, these writings extend the moment of their taking, protracting the sense of wonder that caused them to be thus framed; the engagement of photography is largely conceptual, facilitating explorations of an idea, a certain correspondence between architecture and textiles, and their surface manifestations. If a photographic genre were to be ascribed to these images, it would be that of portrait photography, since these images are indeed of façades.

Recalling Aby Warburg's (1866–1929) proposition that 'the extremes of pure and applied art should be studied, as documents of expression, on an entirely equal footing',[33] photography operates as the medium of equivalence, the common denominator in the equation, with both surfaces, the architectural and the textile, inscribed onto a light-fixing substrate, rendered no longer material, but rather substituted as photographic. The sensoria of their surfaces, the concrete, glass and steel of the façade and the matted polychromatic web of the tweed are both reduced to the optical domain, trapped amidst the vitrine of emulsion or similarly, numerically ciphered behind the flat screen of digital print, for '[o]nly in an image', it is said, 'are we confronted with the surface and the aggregate state of things'.[34]

Like a skin or a membrane, the photograph can also conceivably be 'considered [as] a barrier or an interpolation between two forms rather than a form in its own right'.[35] And indeed, in the nineteenth century, the photograph was said to have operated as a 'kind of a hyphen' bridging between art and science,[36] and later when accepted as an art form in the mid-twentieth century, was seen to contest Modernism's formalist drive and self-referential predisposition, undermining the supposed isolation of the different art and design practices.[37] Worthy of note, the textile arts were once denoted by the term 'hyphantics'.

In his treatise on painting, the Renaissance polymath Leon Battista Alberti (1404–72), we are told, was 'concerned with visual *appearances*' and 'the extreme limit of things',[38] with outlines and in particular surfaces featuring, these often conceived of as a fabric or a skin, with 'lines, like threads, woven together in cloth, mak[ing] a plane'.[39] Knowledge then was based on information accrued by the senses, and it was the play of light on its surfaces, whether porous or produced by the loom, that enabled an object to be known and understood.

Some four hundred years later, the concept of the surface was to form the foundations of Semper's architectural speculations, predicated on his theory of dressing. Symbolic of planarity, the surface was to take form in floors, ceilings and walls, their articulation dependent on orientation, conveying a sense of directionality and movement, seeking harmony in their quest for unity. For:

> Covers are only the subservient, preparatory elements for a whole whose centre of reference is not the envelope or the cover, nor any outstanding part on its surface, but the thing that is deemed unified by the envelope or cover.[40]

Understood as a veiling, his discussion of the shrouding of structural elements, and of architecture in general, was essentially to 'overturn [...] the tectonic basis of nearly two thousand years of architectural theory'.[41]

While place has long been avowed as difficult to describe, it is conceived of as a unifying and unitary structure. Singular in nature,[42] it is nonetheless possessed of a 'mosaic heterogeneity'[43] which is offered 'only in terms of a multiplicity of reflections'.[44] Understood as the foundation of being, indeed necessary and inextricable from it, place is conceived of as more than simple location, as here or there, but is rather envisioned and experienced only *in relation* as boundless and binding.[45] It recalls Semper's conception of the surface, when he states: 'everything closed, protected, enclosed, enveloped, and covered presents itself *as unified*, as a collective; whereas everything bound reveals itself as articulated, as a plurality', unified through its very binding.[46]

Weaving, it is said, 'is primarily a process of structural organisation',[47] a generative act, emerging out of the orthogonal interlacing of threads, one known as the warp, the other the weft, 'the interrelation of the two' capable of enacting a 'subtle play [...] supporting, impeding or modifying' the very appearance of the strands composed in the making.[48] The resultant web can be read as a structure, surface or pattern, or often a combination of these, for the concept like a fabric is pliable and is given shape via deft manipulations. Engaged with throughout, weaving is sometimes literally employed and at other times metaphorically, and on occasion, the metaphor of weaving is literalised, a phenomenon which conveys the very fecundity inherent in the concept or term.

Indeed, the book itself is conceived of as a kind of wool-work, for *calanas*, as the Hebrideans refer to it:[49]

> includes [...] arts, which are divided in two according to whether they separate or combine: carding separates, spinning combines; and, significantly, weaving does both, given that the shuttle first *separates* warp and [weft], and later *combines* them into a fabric. It separates better to combine.[50]

Adopting a similar approach, here the themes are separated out from the work, and aligned anew through juxtaposition, the weaving between them taking place in the writing. The nature of juxtaposition is significant; the placement of one image beside the other enables correspondences to appear, the result of their adjacency and proximity. Two images, opposite and fragmentary, are thus brought 'nearer in such a way that both of them' are 'bounded in time as in extent, form[ing] a totality and a continuity', each image nonetheless maintaining its originality, foregoing only its perceived limitedness and exclusivity.[51] In a series of essays dialogues thus ensue, each text elucidating different aspects, and tied on, the one after the other, like webs of tweed, and pulled through the loom.

Like a *pteron*, a colonnade of webs traversed, the relational contexture between the curtain wall, Harris Tweed and photography shifts in the progression from one essay to the next, the texts understood as a series of webs in the weaving.[52] Manifesting as both 'action and artefact, process and product, becoming and being',[53] they seek to demonstrate the necessity of weaving in the pursuit of an understanding of the world and a place to create within it. For it has been said that 'like a poem, no way of life is given so transparently that it unambiguously declares its meaning. There can be no definitive statement of that meaning; it must be established, ever anew and precariously in interpretation',[54] transforming it, regardless of means, weaving all the same.

In reading, we are told, a relationship is woven between the author and the reader, interlacing between them like the warp and the weft, establishing a shared fabric that enshrouds them. The reading done, the cloth unravels, its threads only to be later recollected and drawn up again in the design and reading in of different patterns, as a weaver does in setting up the loom.

Notes

1 Walter Benjamin, 'Berlin Chronicle', trans. Edmund Jephcott, in *Selected Writings*, Volume 2, Part 2: *1931–1934*, ed. Michael W. Jennings, Howard Eiland and Gary Smith (Cambridge, MA: Belknap Press of Harvard University Press, 2005), 598.
2 As Belting observes: 'The collecting of photographs, their exchange, or their function as symbols of memory follow anthropological patterns for the use of the image that are far from new; namely, the use of the image as a means of taking possession of the world and making sense of it'. Hans Belting, 'The Transparency of the Medium: The Photographic Image', in *An Anthropology of Images: Picture, Medium, Body*, trans. Thomas Dunlap (Princeton, NJ: Princeton University Press, 2011), 145.
3 Georges Poulet, *Proustian Space*, trans. Elliott Coleman (Baltimore, MD: Johns Hopkins University Press, 1977), 74.
4 For an overview of Semper's life and work see, for example, Rosemary Haag Bletter, 'Gottfried Semper', in *Macmillan Encyclopaedia of Architects*, vol. 4, ed. Adolf K. Placzek (London: Free Press, 1982), 25–33; Wolfgang Herrmann, *Gottfried Semper: In Search of Architecture* (Cambridge, MA: MIT Press, 1984); Mari Hvattum, *Gottfried Semper and the Problem of Historicism* (Cambridge: Cambridge University Press, 2004); Harry Francis Mallgrave, *Gottfried Semper: Architect of the Nineteenth Century* (New Haven, CT: Yale University Press, 1996); and Joseph Rykwert, 'Gottfried Semper: Architect and Historian', in Gottfried Semper, *The Four Elements of Architecture and Other Writings*, trans. Harry Francis Mallgrave and Wolfgang Herrmann (Cambridge: Cambridge University Press, 1989), vii–xviii.
5 Andrew Benjamin, 'Surface Effects: Borromini, Semper, Loos', *Journal of Architecture* 11, no. 1 (2006): 19.
6 With reference to Leopold Ettlinger's *Gottfried Semper und die Antike*, see David van Zanten, *The Architectural Polychromy of the 1830's* (New York: Garland Publishing, 1977), 60; and Gottfried Semper, 'The Four Elements of Architecture: A Contribution to the Comparative Study of Architecture', in *The Four Elements of Architecture and Other Writings*, trans. Harry Francis Mallgrave and Wolfgang Herrmann (Cambridge: Cambridge University Press, 1989), 74–129.
7 See Gottfried Semper, 'Preliminary Remarks on Polychrome Architecture and Sculpture in Antiquity', in *The Four Elements of Architecture and Other Writings*, trans. Harry Francis Mallgrave and Wolfgang Herrmann (Cambridge: Cambridge University Press, 1989), 61.
8 Joseph Rykwert, 'Gottfried Semper and the Conception of Style', in *Gottfried Semper und die Mitte des 19.Jahrhunderts*. Conference Proceedings (Basel: Birkhäuser, 1976), 71.
9 Spyros Papapetros, 'World Ornament: The Legacy of Gottfried Semper's 1856 Lecture on Adornment', *Res: Journal of Anthropology and Aesthetics* 57/58 (2010): 310.
10 Rykwert, 'Semper and the Conception of Style', 71.

11 For Semper, textiles are 'the primordial art from which all other arts [...] borrowed their types and symbols'. Gottfried Semper, *Style in the Technical and Tectonic Arts: or, Practical Aesthetics*, trans. Harry Francis Mallgrave and Michael Robinson (Los Angeles: Getty Research Institute, 2004), 113.

12 See John Scheid and Jesper Svenbro, *The Craft of Zeus: Myths of Weaving and Fabric*, trans. Carol Volk (Cambridge, MA: Harvard University Press, 1996), 128.

13 See Vitruvius, *The Ten Books on Architecture*, trans. Morris Hickey Morgan (Cambridge, MA: Harvard University Press, 1914), 38.

14 Arthur C. Danto, 'Weaving as Metaphor and Model for Political Thought', in *Sheila Hicks: Weaving as Metaphor*, ed. Nina Stritzler-Levine (New Haven, CT: Yale University Press, 2006), 23. For a discussion of the formulation of weaving as a craft *and* a medium in the twentieth century see T'ai Smith, *Bauhaus Weaving Theory: From Feminine Craft to Mode of Design* (Minnesota, MN: University of Minnesota Press, 2014).

15 Jeff Malpas, 'Cultural Heritage in the Age of New Media', in Yehuda Kalay, Thomas Kvan and Jane Affleck (eds.), *New Heritage: New Media and Cultural Heritage* (London: Routledge, 2007), 16.

16 For a discussion on how the concept of 'urban fabric' or *tissu urbain* is understood in architectural and urban design terms, see Pierre Merlin and Françoise Choay, *Dictionnaire de l'Urbanisme et de l'Aménagement* (Paris: Presses Universitaires de France, 1988), 666–7. With my thanks to Joseph Rykwert for alerting me to this text. The subtitle of this work, 'greige', is a textile term and refers to their lack of finish.

17 Jeff Malpas, 'Heidegger in Benjamin's City', *Journal of Architecture* 12, no. 5 (2007): 489.

18 Rolf Tiedemann, *Walter Benjamin 1892–1940*, quoted in Samuel Weber, *Mass Mediauras: Form, Technics, Media* (Sydney: Power Publications, 1996), 78, n. 2.

19 Eduardo Cadava, *Words of Light: Theses on the Photography of History* (Princeton, NJ: Princeton University Press, 1997), xix.

20 Hannah Arendt, 'Introduction: Walter Benjamin: 1892–1940', in Walter Benjamin, *Illuminations: Essays and Reflections*, ed. Hannah Arendt and trans. Harry Zohn (New York: Schocken Books, 1969), 12.

21 Benjamin, 'Berlin Chronicle', 611.

22 Gottfried Semper, 'From "Concerning the Formal Principles of Ornament and Its Significance as Artistic Symbol"', in *The Theory of Decorative Art: An Anthology of European and American Writings, 1740–1940*, ed. Isabelle Frank and trans. David Britt (New Haven, CT: Yale University Press, 2000), 93.

23 For studies on the history of Harris Tweed see, for example, Janet Hunter, *The Islanders and the Orb: The History of the Harris Tweed Industry 1835–1995* (Stornoway: Acair, 2001); Francis Thompson, *Harris Tweed: The Story of a Hebridean Industry* (Newton Abbot: David and Charles, 1969), and Gisela Vogler, *A Harris Way of Life: Marion Campbell (1909–1996)* (West Tarbert: Harris Voluntary Service, 2002). For a largely pictorial and

sumptuous survey see Ian Lawson, *From the Land Comes the Cloth: Harris Tweed* (Penrith: Ian Lawson Books, 2011), along with Paul Strand's sublime black-and-white photographs taken some fifty years earlier, in *Tir A'Mhurain: The Outer Hebrides of Scotland* (New York: Aperture, 2002).

24 As Barber observes, the word 'tweed' is derived 'from the same root as *two*, *twice*, and *twin*'. E. J. W. Barber, *Prehistoric Textiles: The Development of Cloth in the Neolithic and Bronze Ages with Special Reference to the Aegean* (Princeton, NJ: Princeton University Press, 1991), 187. Emphasis in Barber. In terms of Scottish tweeds, Anderson notes that the term 'tweed' was derived either from a misreading of the Scottish word *tweel* or twill, or alternatively from the Tweed River in the Scottish Borders. See Fiona Anderson, 'Spinning the Ephemeral with the Sublime: Modernity and Landscape in Men's Fashion Textiles 1860–1900', *Fashion Theory* 9, no. 3 (2005): 286.

25 See London, United Kingdom. *Harris Tweed Act 1993*, Chapter xi, 20 July 1993. www.legislation.gov.uk/ukla/1993/11/introduction/enacted. Accessed 18 March 2016.

26 The genealogist and historian Bill Lawson commented on this in a lecture organised by him and his wife, Chrissie, which was accompanied by demonstrations of carding; spinning, both with a wheel and a spindle; and weaving, along with a waulking. Bill Lawson, 'Harris Tweed', Public Lecture (Tarbert, Isle of Harris: Harris Hotel, 3 July 2008).

27 The Harris Tweed Authority website gives 1846 as the date of the commissioning, but it would seem that the exact date is difficult to determine, it occurring sometime between 1839 and 1846. See *The Harris Tweed Authority*, www.harristweed.org/about-us/heritage-and-history/. Accessed 18 March 2016; Hunter, *Islanders and the Orb*, 28–43, and Thompson, *Harris Tweed*, 58.

28 See Thompson, *Harris Tweed*, 58–60, and Hunter, *Islanders and the Orb*, 27–46.

29 See Semper, 'Four Elements', 103.

30 See Joseph Rykwert, 'Architecture is All on the Surface: Semper and Bekleidung', *Rassegna* 73 (1998): 24. Merwood disputes the fact that the Reliance Building is the first curtain wall building, suggesting instead that it be understood as 'the representative example of a "protomodern" building in its use of steel-framed construction and in its blatantly non-structural employment of terra-cotta'. Joanna Merwood, 'The Mechanisation of Cladding: The Reliance Building and Narratives of Modern Architecture', *Grey Room* 4 (2001): 53.

31 Rykwert, 'Semper and the Conception of Style', 81.

32 '[Robert] Venturi argues that modern architecture, 'while rejecting explicit symbolism and frivolous appliqué ornament, has distorted the whole building into one big ornament"'. Mark C. Taylor, *Disfiguring: Art, Architecture, Religion* (Chicago: University of Chicago Press, 1992), 194.

33 Aby Warburg, quoted in Kurt W. Forster, 'Aby Warburg: His Study of Ritual and Art on Two Continents', trans. David Britt, *October* 77 (1996): 22.

34 Kurt W. Forster, 'The Sudden Incursion of Unreality into the Real World', trans. Ishbel Flett, in *Thomas Ruff: Surfaces, Depths*, ed. Cathérine Hug (Nuremburg: Verlag für moderne Kunst Nürnberg, 2009), 118.
35 James Elkins, *Pictures of the Body: Pain and Metamorphosis* (Stanford, CA: Stanford University Press, 1999), 36. Elkin's description here recalls the concept of the Epicurean *eidolon*, a skin or film emitted from an object and transferred to the eye.
36 See Ann Thomas, 'The Search for Pattern', in *Beauty of Another Order: Photography in Science*, ed. Ann Thomas (New Haven, CT: Yale University Press, 1997), 76–7.
37 See Douglas Crimp, quoted in Sarah Charlesworth and Barbara Kruger, 'Glossolalia', in *The Last Picture Show: Artists Using Photography 1960–1992*, ed. Douglas Fogle (Minneapolis, MN: Walker Art Centre, 2003), 260.
38 John R. Spencer, introduction to *On Painting*, by Leon Battista Alberti (New Haven, CT: Yale University Press, 1966), 17. Emphasis in Spencer.
39 Leon Battista Alberti, *On Painting*, trans. John R. Spencer (New Haven, CT: Yale University Press, 1966), 44.
40 Semper, *Style*, 138. As Ward notes: 'The word *surface*, like *superficies*, is derived from the Latin *super* (above) and *facies* (face, form, figure, appearance, visage).' Janet Ward, *Weimar Surfaces: Urban Visual Culture in 1920's Germany* (Berkeley, CA: University of California Press, 2001), 254, n. 1. Emphasis in Ward. For a further discussion of the surface, see, for example, Glenn Adamson and Victoria Kelley, eds. *Surface Tensions: Surface, Finish and the Meaning of Objects* (Manchester: Manchester University Press, 2013); Joseph A. Amato, Surfaces: A History (Berkeley, CA: University of California Press, 2013); and Giuliana Bruno, *Surface: Matters of Aesthetics, Materiality, and Media* (Chicago: University of Chicago Press, 2014).
41 Mallgrave, *Gottfried Semper*, 299–300.
42 See Jeff Malpas, 'Place and Singularity', in *The Intelligence of Place: Topographies and Poetics*, ed. Jeff Malpas (London: Bloomsbury, 2015), 65–92.
43 For Leatherbarrow, place, or what he refers to here as the 'topographical', is possessed of this heterogeneity and is 'paradoxical: manifestly latent, or given, not shown'. David Leatherbarrow, 'Topographical Premises', *Journal of Architectural Education* 57, no. 3 (2004): 70.
44 Jeff Malpas, 'A Taste of Madeleine: Notes toward a Philosophy of Place', *International Philosophical Quarterly* 34, no. 4, issue no. 136 (1994): 441, in light of this multiplicity, also refer to, for example, Edward S. Casey, *The Fate of Place: A Philosophical History* (Berkeley, CA: University of California Press, 1997); David Leatherbarrow, *Topographical Stories: Studies in Landscape and Architecture* (Philadelphia, PA: University of Pennsylvania Press, 2004); Jeff Malpas, ed., *The Intelligence of Place: Topographies and Poetics* (London: Bloomsbury, 2015); and Joseph Rykwert, 'Topo-philia and -phobia', in *Topophilia and Topophobia: Reflections on Twentieth-Century Human Habitat*, ed. Xing Ruan and Paul Hogben (London: Routledge, 2007), 12–22.

45 For Malpas: '[t]he concept of place is essentially the concept of a bounded, but open region *within which* a set of interconnected elements can be located'. J. E. Malpas, *Place and Experience: A Philosophical Topography* (Cambridge: Cambridge University Press, 1999), 170. Emphasis in Malpas.
46 Semper, *Style*, 123. Emphasis in Semper.
47 Anni Albers, 'The Pliable Plane: Textiles in Architecture', *Perspecta* 4 (1957): 36.
48 See Anni Albers, 'On Weaving', in *The Craft Reader*, ed. Glenn Adamson (Oxford: Berg, 2010), 29. As Albers notes, the right-angle composition distinguishes weaving from all other textile techniques.
49 See Thompson, *Harris Tweed*, 158.
50 With reference to Plato's *The Statesman*, see Scheid and Svenbro, *Craft of Zeus*, 26. Emphasis in Scheid and Svenbro.
51 See Poulet, *Proustian Space*, 80.
52 McEwen suggests that the *pteron* in its earliest form was created through the linking together of looms. See Indra Kagis McEwen, *Socrates' Ancestor: An Essay in Architectural Beginnings* (Cambridge, MA: MIT Press, 1993), 110–11.
53 Thomas K. Hubbard, 'Nature and Art in the Shield of Achilles', *Arion*, 3rd series, vol. 2, no. 1 (1992): 18.
54 Karsten Harries, *The Ethical Function of Architecture* (Cambridge, MA: MIT Press, 1998), 149.

Bibliography

Adamson, Glenn and Victoria Kelley, eds. *Surface Tensions: Surface, Finish and the Meaning of Objects*. Manchester: Manchester University Press, 2013.

Albers, Anni. 'The Pliable Plane: Textiles in Architecture', *Perspecta* 4 (1957): 36–41.

———. 'On Weaving'. In *The Craft Reader*. Edited by Glenn Adamson, 29–33. Oxford: Berg, 2010.

Alberti, Leon Battista. *On Painting*. Translated by John R. Spencer. New Haven, CT: Yale University Press, 1966.

Amato, Joseph A. Surfaces: A History. Berkeley, CA: University of California Press, 2013.

Anderson, Fiona. 'Spinning the Ephemeral with the Sublime: Modernity and Landscape in Men's Fashion Textiles 1860–1900', *Fashion Theory* 9, no. 3 (2005): 283–304.

Arendt, Hannah. 'Introduction: Walter Benjamin: 1892–1940'. In Walter Benjamin, *Illuminations: Essays and Reflections*. Edited by Hannah Arendt and translated by Harry Zohn, 1–55. New York: Schocken Books, 1969.

Barber, E. J. W. *Prehistoric Textiles: The Development of Cloth in the Neolithic and Bronze Ages with Special Reference to the Aegean*. Princeton, NJ: Princeton University Press, 1991.

Belting, Hans. 'The Transparency of the Medium: The Photographic Image'. In *An Anthropology of Images: Picture, Medium, Body*. Translated by Thomas Dunlap, 144–68. Princeton, NJ: Princeton University Press, 2011.

Benjamin, Andrew. 'Surface Effects: Borromini, Semper, Loos', *Journal of Architecture* 11, no. 1 (2006): 1–36.

Benjamin, Walter. 'Berlin Chronicle'. Translated by Edmund Jephcott. In *Selected Writings*, Volume 2, Part 2: *1931–1934*. Edited by Michael W. Jennings, Howard Eiland and Gary Smith, 595–637. Cambridge, MA: Belknap Press of Harvard University Press, 2005.

Bletter, Rosemary Haag. 'Gottfried Semper'. In *Macmillan Encyclopaedia of Architects*, vol. 4, ed. Adolf K. Placzek, 25–33. London: Free Press, 1982.

Bruno, Giuliana. *Surface: Matters of Aesthetics, Materiality, and Media*. Chicago: University of Chicago Press, 2014.

Cadava, Eduardo. *Words of Light: Theses on the Photography of History*. Princeton, NJ: Princeton University Press, 1997.

Casey, Edward S. *The Fate of Place: A Philosophical History*. Berkeley: University of California Press, 1997.

Charlesworth, Sarah and Barbara Kruger. 'Glossolalia'. In *The Last Picture Show: Artists Using Photography 1960–1992*. Edited by Douglas Fogle, 259–61. Minneapolis, MN: Walker Art Centre, 2003.

Danto, Arthur C. 'Weaving as Metaphor and Model for Political Thought'. In *Sheila Hicks: Weaving as Metaphor*. Edited by Nina Stritzler-Levine, 22–37. New Haven, CT: Yale University Press, 2006.

Elkins, James. *Pictures of the Body: Pain and Metamorphosis*. Stanford, CA: Stanford University Press, 1999.

Forster, Kurt W. 'Aby Warburg: His Study of Ritual and Art on Two Continents'. Translated by David Britt, *October* 77 (1996): 5–24.

———. 'The Sudden Incursion of Unreality into the Real World'. Translated by Ishbel Flett. In *Thomas Ruff: Surfaces, Depths*. Edited by Cathérine Hug, 116–34. Nuremburg: Verlag für moderne Kunst Nürnberg, 2009.

Harries, Karsten. *The Ethical Function of Architecture*. Cambridge, MA: MIT Press, 1998.

Herrmann, Wolfgang. *Gottfried Semper: In Search of Architecture*. Cambridge, MA: MIT Press, 1984.

Hubbard, Thomas K. 'Nature and Art in the Shield of Achilles', *Arion*, 3rd Series, vol. 2, no. 1 (1992): 16–41.

Hunter, Janet. *The Islanders and the Orb: The History of the Harris Tweed Industry 1835–1995*. Stornoway: Acair, 2001.

Hvattum, Mari. *Gottfried Semper and the Problem of Historicism*. Cambridge: Cambridge University Press, 2004.

Lawson, Bill. 'Harris Tweed', Public Lecture. Tarbert, Isle of Harris: Harris Hotel, 3 July 2008.

Lawson, Ian. *From the Land Comes the Cloth: Harris Tweed*. Penrith: Ian Lawson Books, 2011.

Leatherbarrow, David. 'Topographical Premises', *Journal of Architectural Education* 57, no. 3 (2004): 70–3.

———. *Topographical Stories: Studies in Landscape and Architecture*. Philadelphia, PA: University of Pennsylvania Press, 2004.

London, United Kingdom. *Harris Tweed Act 1993*, Chapter xi, 20 July 1993. www.legislation.gov.uk/ukla/1993/11/introduction/enacted. Accessed 18 March 2016.

McEwen, Indra Kagis. *Socrates' Ancestor: An Essay in Architectural Beginnings*. Cambridge, MA: MIT Press, 1993.

Mallgrave, Harry Francis. *Gottfried Semper: Architect of the Nineteenth Century*. New Haven, CT: Yale University Press, 1996.

Malpas, Jeff. 'A Taste of Madeleine: Notes Toward a Philosophy of Place', *International Philosophical Quarterly* 34, no. 4, issue no. 136 (1994): 433–51.

———. *Place and Experience: A Philosophical Topography*. Cambridge: Cambridge University Press, 1999.

———. 'Cultural Heritage in the Age of New Media'. In *New Heritage: New Media and Cultural Heritage*. Edited by Yehuda Kalay, Thomas Kvan and Jane Affleck, 13–26. London: Routledge, 2007.

——— 'Heidegger in Benjamin's City', *Journal of Architecture* 12, no. 5 (2007): 489–97.

——— 'Place and Singularity'. In *The Intelligence of Place: Topographies and Poetics*. Edited by Jeff Malpas, 65–92. London: Bloomsbury, 2015.

Malpas , Jeff, ed. *The Intelligence of Place: Topographies and Poetics*. London: Bloomsbury, 2015.

Merlin, Pierre and Françoise Choay. *Dictionnaire de l'Urbanisme et de l'Aménagement*. Paris: Presses Universitaires de France, 1988.

Merwood, Joanna. 'The Mechanisation of Cladding: The Reliance Building and Narratives of Modern Architecture', *Grey Room* 4 (2001): 52–69.

Papapetros, Spyros. 'World Ornament: The Legacy of Gottfried Semper's 1856 Lecture on Adornment', *Res: Journal of Anthropology and Aesthetics* 57/58 (2010): 309–29.

Poulet, Georges. *Proustian Space*, trans. Elliott Coleman. Baltimore, MD: Johns Hopkins University Press, 1977)

Rykwert, Joseph. 'Gottfried Semper and the Conception of Style'. In *Gottfried Semper und die Mitte des 19.Jahrhunderts*. Conference Proceedings, 67–83. Basel: Birkhäuser, 1976.

———. 'Gottfried Semper: Architect and Historian'. In Gottfried Semper, *The Four Elements of Architecture and Other Writings*. Translated by Harry Francis Mallgrave and Wolfgang Herrmann, vii–xviii. Cambridge: Cambridge University Press, 1989.

———. 'Architecture is All on the Surface: Semper and *Bekleidung*', *Rassegna* 73 (1998): 20–9.

———. 'Topo-philia and –phobia'. In *Topophilia and Topophobia: Reflections on Twentieth-Century Human Habitat*. Edited by Xing Ruan and Paul Hogben, 12–22, London: Routledge, 2007.

Scheid, John and Jesper Svenbro. *The Craft of Zeus: Myths of Weaving and Fabric*. Translated by Carol Volk. Cambridge, MA: Harvard University Press, 1996.

Semper, Gottfried. 'The Four Elements of Architecture: A Contribution to the Comparative Study of Architecture'. In *The Four Elements of Architecture and Other Writings*. Translated by Harry Francis Mallgrave and Wolfgang Herrmann, 74–129. Cambridge: Cambridge University Press, 1989.

———. 'Preliminary Remarks on Polychrome Architecture and Sculpture in Antiquity'. In *The Four Elements of Architecture and Other Writings*. Translated by Harry Francis Mallgrave and Wolfgang Herrmann, 45–73. Cambridge: Cambridge University Press, 1989.

———. 'From "Concerning the Formal Principles of Ornament and Its Significance as Artistic Symbol"'. In *The Theory of Decorative Art: An Anthology of European and American Writings, 1740–1940*. Edited by Isabelle Frank and translated by David Britt, 91–115. New Haven, CT: Yale University Press, 2000.

———. *Style in the Technical and Tectonic Arts: or, Practical Aesthetics*. Translated by Harry Francis Mallgrave and Michael Robinson. Los Angeles: Getty Research Institute, 2004.

Smith, T'ai. *Bauhaus Weaving Theory: From Feminine Craft to Mode of Design*. Minnesota, MN: University of Minnesota Press, 2014.

Spencer, John R. Introduction to *On Painting*, by Leon Battista Alberti, 1–28. New Haven, CT: Yale University Press, 1966.

Strand, Paul. *Tir A'Mhurain: The Outer Hebrides of Scotland*. New York: Aperture, 2002.

Taylor, Mark C. *Disfiguring: Art, Architecture, Religion*. Chicago: University of Chicago Press, 1992.

Thomas, Ann. 'The Search for Pattern'. In *Beauty of Another Order: Photography in Science*. Edited by Ann Thomas, 76–119. New Haven, CT: Yale University Press, 1997.

Thompson, Francis. *Harris Tweed: The Story of a Hebridean Industry*. Newton Abbot: David and Charles, 1969.

van Zanten, David. *The Architectural Polychromy of the 1830's*. New York: Garland Publishing, 1977.

Vitruvius. *The Ten Books on Architecture*, translated by Morris Hickey Morgan. Cambridge, MA: Harvard University Press, 1914.

Vogler, Gisela. *A Harris Way of Life: Marion Campbell (1909–1996)*. West Tarbert: Harris Voluntary Service, 2002.

Ward, Janet. *Weimar Surfaces: Urban Visual Culture in 1920's Germany*. Berkeley, CA: University of California Press, 2001.

Weber, Samuel. 'Mass Mediauras, or: Art, Aura and Media in the Work of Walter Benjamin'. In *Mass Mediauras: Form, Technics, Media*, 76–107. Sydney: Power Publications, 1996.

Appearing

Figure 2.1 Anonymous, *Grid Photo, Grand Theatre of Liceu*, 1904.

Weaving

Figure 2.2 Anonymous, *Shuttle Coursing across a Loom*, n.d.

There is no [independent] mode of existence. Every entity is only to be understood in terms of the way in which it is interwoven with the rest of the universe.

Alfred North Whitehead

It is the woven cloth, or perhaps its very weaving, that makes earth, with all its variegated, scintillating patterns, appear.

Indra Kagis McEwen

24   *Appearing | Weaving*

In pre-classical Greece, it is said, *dēmioergoi*, craftsmen, defined a certain citizenry composed of those such as heralds, doctors and magistrates as well as craftsmen as we understand the term today. Existing as a social order they worked in the service of the public, enabling the city, the *polis*, to emerge; its surface the consequence of the interweaving of their activity in its continual remaking, a ceaseless Penelopean enterprise.[1] Through the craftsmanship of these people's activities, the gods were able to appear, their 'coming-to-light' not so much the result of mastery, artisanal or otherwise, but rather that its pursuit provided the place in which divinity was allowed to manifest.

For up until the fourth century B.C., the ancient Greeks did not understand or worship divinity in the manner that monotheistic faiths operate today.[2] Their religion, so to speak, was not founded upon the veneration of a singular omnipresent and all-powerful being, rather multiple 'forms of worship' prevailed in a society whose very existence and experience of life recognised the confluence of spiritual dimensions, the ebb and flow of the sacred, its shifting and varying forms in the midst of the everyday.[3] The sacred, as such, was seen to suffuse 'the routines and places of daily life', so much so that the 'appearance [of the gods] conceivably graced every meaningful occasion'.[4] For each god was associated with a realm,[5] with the mountains and the streams in nature, the threshold and hearth of domestic life, and the roads and intersections that delineated the public ambit.[6] Moreover, each god was a world unto itself, embodying not a unique virtue but, rather, each was replete with a manifold of qualities; their dominion not set, their presence instead permeating existence, both shaping and illuminating it, vibrant in its totality.[7] Through private rituals and public festivities, the gods were celebrated, sharing briefly with mortals a certain splendour through their coming together in communion.[8]

In general, a god was said to become apparent when events or objects, either natural or man-made, or certainly even a person, provoked and inspired wonder and awe. Experienced as an intensity, a manifest power,[9] the force of the apparition, its be-stilling presence was such that it was seen to be more than human. Its qualities endured beyond the lifetime of its maker, or its participants and audiences; so much so that it could always be reassembled and configured, the circumstances re-enacted, only to be experienced again.

Daidalon was the term used to describe an object that possessed such phenomenal qualities, the expression acknowledging the activities of the first mythical architect, Daedalus, designer of the labyrinth at Knossos, amongst numerous other creations.[10] *Daidalon* was often translated in the epics of Homer as 'cunningly crafted' and 'curiously wrought',[11] and in the later texts of Hesiod, the term became increasingly bound with textiles; the craft evident in their tight, harmonious weaves, the pattern not latterly applied but woven; intrinsic to the very luminosity of their surfaces. For the word most often used to describe *daidala* was *poikilon*, and while it has sometimes been translated as 'embroidered', the lambent patternation of textiles or *daidala*, in general, was not applied to an existing surface, but was rather native to it, essential in its coming to be.[12] *Poikilon* is indicative not only of the richness and diversity of design,[13] but also pertains to 'anything variegated, complex or shifting'.[14] As such, all *daidala* were referred to as 'a wonder to behold', *thauma idesthai*, each encompassing in their well-crafted dimensions animate yet impalpable divinity which glimmered *on* their surfaces. Woven or otherwise shaped, such artefacts were described as polychrome[15] because of the use of a variety of materials,[16] and indeed, so well crafted were their seamless and harmonious joints that they were considered to be woven.[17]

In ancient Greek, the crafting of the web, the term for the plying of the loom, was *hyphainein*; weaving hence meant literally 'to bring to light', and consequently, to make visible. It was not a matter of mere conspicuousness, but rather of coming to be. It is perhaps not surprising then that the word for surface, *epiphaneia*, bares testament not only to 'appearance' but also corresponds to the very activity that made it possible.[18] As such, the craft of weaving was considered to be foundational, both literally and metaphorically, and was further exalted by Athena's dominion over both her city and this craft.[19] Aside from the weaving of cloth, it operated as the model and metaphor for political order,[20] in as much as it was seen to underpin the striation of the settlement grids, the orthogonal warp and weft of their streets and roads;[21] and was further witnessed in the accompaniment of loom and hearth in the establishment of the home; and more publicly, in the consecration of civic life, apparent in the *pteron*, the colonnade that circumscribed the temples, representative of the symbolic linking together of looms in the formation of community.[22] Ritual processions, itineraries, marked out by the shuttling back and forth from city centre to sanctuaries located on the outskirts, only to return again, created a web that defined the terrain, otherwise known as *chora*,[23] one of the archaic Greek terms along with *topos*, for place.[24]

The domain of the outermost sanctuaries, *chōra*, was 'a place of mediation between [man] and the gods who were together attached to this particular territory', a threshold girdling the realm, a signature of human presence and of the very *polis*.[25] Derived from the dance floor, *choros*, designed by Daedalus, *chora* was an enclosed space, the site of revelry and festivity, the wellspring from which chorus and choreography naturally arise.[26] *Chora* too denotes enclosure, derived, as some have said, from the very linking together of hands,[27] and by extension, *chros*, the

26 *Appearing | Weaving*

vital body (as opposed to *soma* understood as the corpse) and hence skin, and in addition, *chroma*, colour.[28] Enclosure, colour and skin suggest that *chora* was invested in the surface manifestations of place, united through their binding.

Understood as a matrix, 'the Receptacle' and 'nurse of all becoming'[29] and change, *chora* as a beholding vessel, we are told, 'is not that "out of which" [*ex hou*] things are made; it is that "in which" [*en hō*] qualities appear, as fleeting images are seen *in* a mirror'.[30] *Chora*, too, was also imbued with a sense of cultivation, related, as it is, to gardens, orchards and farmyards apparent in the Latin, *hortus*.[31] It was a fostered domain, of lifecycles ordered by the seasons, of tending and human investment, and it was the realm in which the *dēmioergoi* operated[32] together, collectively,[33] enabling it to appear.

Harris Tweed is inextricably bound with place, beyond its parliamentary edict; a fabric embedded in tradition, a tradition that remains thoroughly alive, and as the years have shown, changeable. Produced by weavers, for centuries at their homes, their crofts striating the landscape, the one beside the other, like the warp threads that traverse the loom, the Islanders' activities weave their communities, patterning them together, once finding fullest expression in the festivities associated with the waulking of the cloth, and *ceilidhs* or visits, now performed on occasion at Mòds.[34] With the exception perhaps of Stornoway, these rural communities do not constitute a city or town *per se*,[35] but are necessarily bound through their interactivities that invariably revolve around the tweed, for it is the *clo mhor* that continues to perpetuate the Scottish-Gaelic language and culture.[36]

The tweed itself exists as a blend of colours; from afar, its surface reminiscent of the spongy peaty moors of Barvas that extend across the Isle of Lewis, the yarn (not dyed but rather composed of different colours carded together and spun) already incandescent prior to its further combination in the weave. The woven surface upon closer inspection reveals those fragments of individual colours that compose the mix; softly Pollock-esque[37] and intermittently pronounced in composition. The polychromatic surface of the tightly woven weave possesses a vapoury density, the tangle of fibres ignited by eruptions of individual colour, illuminated by the mellow light, its lack of contrast revealing the intensity of the colour in its saturated depth.[38] To the hand, the surface is almost coarse and somewhat hirsute, the cloth's density, reassuring of warmth, reiterated by the occasional wafting of its scent; uncertain, but distinctly rural.[39]

'The archaic world', we are told, 'was a world that appeared through the things people made', the relationship between 'craft and community' necessarily 'indissoluble' in its making.[40] The appearing surface of a woven cloth, as such, was akin to the *polis*, and like the cloth 'of all the traces of material culture, one of the most perishable – ha[s] to be mended or made to appear'.[41] Cloth and *polis*, it could be said, are always under construction, and are inextricably bound with weaving.

At the turn of the twentieth century, however, the interweaving, the collective pursuit that enabled the Greek *polis* to appear, was seemingly no longer in operation, for the *polis*, it is said, was not so much the physical city-state, but operated through a form of 'organised remembrance', premised upon exchange, 'ris[ing] [...] out of acting together, the "sharing of words and deeds"', the unique value of each man acknowledged in participation.[42] In the modern city, by comparison, man had been reduced to a mere variant, largely indistinguishable, one among the many, a constituent of the masses. In the thriving metropolis labour had replaced work; labour sempiternal and unceasing, repetitive without variation,[43] work ascribing to a different rhythm altogether, its product finite, yet enduring until eroded by wear.[44] The public place in the ancient world, the *agora*, was distinguished not only by discussion and debate, but also, we are told, by conspicuous production, the displaying *and* crafting of wares admired and exchanged,[45] the modern city, conversely, replete with its arcades and avenues artificially illuminated, showcasing conspicuous consumption, production hidden, fuelling, nonetheless, another kind of spectacle, expenditure taking form in commodity fetishism.[46]

This schism between labour and work was to find a dissenting voice, however, in direct reference to weaving, Engels critical of the alienation of the labourer from his work as evidenced in the mechanised textile mills of Leeds and Manchester,[47] mills that replaced the hand-crafting of textiles,[48] such wholesale 'progress', by and large, stymied and denied in the Outer Hebrides.[49] Prescient of the rift between the fine arts and the crafts, this divide was perhaps first witnessed as a spectacle in the Great Exhibition (1851),[50] a 'cross-section of cultural science',[51] housed in the iron and glass construction of the Crystal Palace, works installed under the banners of raw materials, machinery and manufactures; Harris Tweed figuring under the rubric of manufactures,[52] with photography featuring, too new to be yet classified,[53] regardless, cloth and print were housed in a prototype of the curtain glass wall.[54] Here, the relationship once focused on the maker and his artefact was transformed, and was now directed toward a new kind of rapport concentrated instead on the relationship between spectator and object, making no longer experienced or part of the visual domain.[55]

By the century's end the rift between the arts and crafts had become categorically entrenched; and in the early years of the twentieth century *Sachlichkeit*, or objectivity,[56] became the catch-cry of a *Zeitgeist* increasingly invested in a profusion of 'the new': 'the "New Man", the "New Architecture", the "New Typography", and the "New Photography"',[57] mechanisation taking command, facilitated by advances in technological reproducibility. Style was promoted as a generalised phenomenon, with ever-newer modes increasingly accommodating a mass ideal, spurning the outdated, the previously most recent abhorred and deemed to be obsolescent.[58] The diversity of attires and wares fashioned, in accordance, cycled at increasingly accelerated speeds, commodities accessible in number, modes readily adopted[59] as the perceived value of the crafted artefact and its associated customs diminished.

> But, of what we call handicraft – which because of its utilitarian purpose appeals to a diversity of men – we request a more general and more typical articulation […] which make it possible for handicraft to be incorporated into the life systems of a great many different individuals. It is the greatest mistake to think that, because it always functions as the adornment of an individual, it must also be an individual work of art. Quite the contrary: because it is to serve the individual, it may not itself be of an individual nature – as little as the piece of furniture on which we sit, or the eating utensil which we manipulate, may not be individual works of art. The work of art cannot, in principle, be incorporated into another life – it is a self-sufficient world. […] The essence of stylisation is precisely this dilution of individual poignancy, this generalisation beyond the uniqueness of personality.[60]

Surfaces in general thus proliferated, though rendered wan and grey,[61] a lifeless facing preferred to the luminance native to the handcrafted artefact, traditional investment no longer preferred, the value inherent to it no longer esteemed.[62] Innovations in production methods and techniques were streamlined, with greater efficiencies and systemisations facilitating their distribution, usurping ritual and time-honoured means of manufacture and exchange.

The curtain wall was a prime exemplar of the modern age, its components prefabricated *en masse*, with its assemblage process delineated however disdainful of any lineage. Detached from tradition and its domain, the wall was no longer associated with a situatedness or place, as a sense of placelessness and disenchantment prevailed. Composed of concrete, glass and steel, a mere 'veneer for the corporate activities of "enlightened" capitalism',[63] these surfaces issued forth, the International Style donned as corporate attire in cities across the world, largely indistinguishable and ignorant of their site specificity.[64] While several companies were housed in buildings clad in the very 'materials representative of the industry to which the corporation belonged',[65] the gridded format of the garb, nonetheless, possessed an unceasingly variable repertoire of patterns, not unlike that of the Hebridean Tweed, symbolic textile origins renounced, however, in the face of functionalist ratiocination and expedience, so perceived. 'Variety within standardisation'[66] was the norm with components prefabricated and mass-reproduced, a frank formula readily replicated[67] with sections available off the rack; what was once tailored and suited to measure now subjected to Taylorising principles.[68]

Understood as a model for society designed by human relations engineers,[69] the curtain-walled building was said to speak increasingly of 'an inescapable collective destiny',[70] individuality subject to 'pseudo-personalisation',[71] internal differentiation, systematised, introjected and absorbed, the grid operating as a device at a range of scales which:

> gather[ed] together heterogeneous components, standardised production formats, the open-ended 'deep space' of the fluorescent-lit, air-conditioned office, mass-produced monoliths and plazas, the flux of the city and of the workplace – into a single, organised complex.[72]

The curtain wall thus projected a reductive and singular image, an identity incorporated, 'collaps[ing] near and far, inside and outside onto its surfaces',[73] these surfaces decried and disclaimed as 'façades of anonymity'.[74] As a mass-mediaised surface, the curtain wall assumed the form of a screen, a surface 'to be *watched* in passing rather than looked at [...] channel[ling] flows, patterns of patterns',[75] not of meaning, but of data, objective and abstracted.[76] Metaphoric relations were thus occluded, though the punch card of the Jacquard loom was appropriated and engaged,[77] weaving calculations in a world careering toward digitalisation, recalling Semper's claim that:

> In general it can be assumed that those patterns that pass through the loom most easily are also those that unfurl and unfold most attractively – but in our day everything passes through the loom easily, and thus this test of style no longer holds true.[78]

By the turn of the twentieth century, in the recognition of patterns, modern man's capacity to discern 'the magical correspondences and analogies that were familiar to ancient peoples'[79] had waned; however, despite such limitations, the search for pattern endured, photography, along with the cinematic arts seen to revolutionise vision. While a certain loss was invariably experienced as a result of reproductive means, new modes of media and communication complicit, these technologies, nonetheless, possessed the potential to reinvest in the very presence of things, giving them form, bringing them nearer, rather than distracting us from their value and significance. For in arresting 'the patterned interplay of light',

30 *Appearing | Weaving*

the split-second opening of the camera's aperture was to precisely capture the object of its focus, acutely delineating it, the power of the lens enlarging and decontextualising its features, exposing its traits at a speed not typically registered, at a scale not normally seen, revealing aspects hitherto concealed, 'bringing (optically) something entirely new into the world',[80] expanding our knowledge of what is seemingly routine and mundane.

> By close-ups of the things around us, by focusing on hidden details of familiar objects, by exploring commonplace milieus under the ingenious guidance of the camera, [it] extends our comprehension of the necessities which rule our lives; [and] it manages to assure us of an immense and unexpected field of action.[81]

Through the manipulations of the camera, its concertinaed bellows aligning façade with lens and film, portraits of Melbourne's mid-twentieth-century corporate faces were magnified and viewed from a seemingly disembodied standpoint, the dermis of the architectural façade transformed into a textile landscape, reflecting the colours of the place of its making, a topography seemingly alien and distant from the one in which it was momentarily uncovered and shown.

Place, it is said, is hidden, and '[a]ny and every place retains its own obscurity, its own hiddenness';[82] it is by nature apocryphal, in the earliest sense of the word, clandestine and mysterious, the camera recalling the Receptacle of old, capable of 'captur[ing] fleeting and secret images',[83] enantiomorphous and concealed,[84] nestled within the folds, cachéd away in pockets, like memories enveloped, an aperture opening up to these worlds, once infinitesimal, unobserved or unseen, 'strat[a] of material, the alluvi[a] of the recent past'[85] brought to light and laid bare, *topoi*[86] exposed, capable of being deciphered in the superficial sheen of its prints. For through photography, it is said, 'a world of particular secret affinities' is exposed, 'a world in which things enter into "the most contradictory communication"',[87] extending beyond their commonplace parameters and limits, a spatial tension, indeed, a distension, necessary for such mirroring to occur.

For, long ago, we are told that '[w]hatever will exist will have to be in itself something with extension (*augmen*), whether large or small, so long as it exists',[88] the camera expanding the range, the concept of extension deriving from the ancient Greek, *diastēma*. *Dia*, it is said, means through, *stēma* drawing from *stēmon*, the archaic Greek word for thread,[89] suggesting a passing through, over and under, indeed, in between, the lens given the task of making discoveries, enabling us to forge connections, initiating patterns in the weaving.

Appearing | Weaving 31

In the façades of Melbourne's mid-twentieth-century curtain walls, the latent image of Harris Tweed was exposed, bringing to light relationships between the handcrafted and the machine-made, drawing a living history and a history premised on progress alone closer, as passages between the Outer Hebrides and Melbourne were paved, a gridded fabric, one malleable, warm and enshrouding, the other cold, hard and rigid, a negligible screen, similarly attiring both body and wall, surfaces appearing in correspondence, a consequence of the weave. For within new means of production, we are told, lie analogous images, images in which the new and old are entwined, 'every epoch see[ing] in [its] images the epoch which is to succeed it', in which the future appears bound with the past, such interactions productive, giving rise to new ideals, which leave their traces in a thousand configurations of life, from permanent buildings to ephemeral fashions,[90] in the seemingly outmoded, in curtain walls and Harris Tweed, physiognomic thinking, premised on the task of teasing out vestiges and residues,[91] threads lingering with which to weave.

While modernity, we are told, means '"now, just now, recently", designat[ing] not [only] that which is new, but that which is present, current [and] contemporary'[92] with the one who speaks, it was also to be experienced in 'fragments borne forward from the past [as] shards of a vanished whole',[93] in the eternal drawn from the transitory;[94] the modern artefact, itself, interlaced with this very possibility. For despite its proclaimed renunciation of history, modernity was an epoch in which 'the energies which [were] at work' in it reverberated,[95] resounding between surfaces opening up to a place enclosed, 'bring[ing] it close[r] to antiquity',[96] unleashing potential, an immanence as yet unseen, 'the will to connect […] becom[ing] a shaping of things',[97] the role of the camera, upon reflection, critical in amplifying the exchange.[98]

For 'certain twilights and certain places', it is said, 'all want to tell us something'.[99]

Notes

1 See Richard Sennett, *The Craftsman* (New Haven, CT: Yale University Press, 2008), 22. As Casey observes, the Greek term *dēmios* means 'belonging to the people' and 'appears to derive from the […]*dem-* stem' which 'is the ultimate etymon of IndoEuropean words connoting "building", "house", "domestic", etc. The "demi" of Demiurge is thus not to be construed as "half" (the latter *demi* derives from the Latin *dimidium*).' Edward S. Casey, *The Fate of Place: A Philosophical History* (Berkeley: University of California Press, 1997), 356, n. 78.

2 The fourth century B.C. marked a revolution of sorts in Greek thinking, culture and associated practices. The gods were no longer worshipped or recognised in anthropomorphised form, rather they were 'identif[ied] […]

with the unchanging forces that govern the working of the universe'. Martin West, 'Early Greek Philosophy', in *The Oxford History of the Classical World*, ed. John Boardman, Jasper Griffin and Oswyn Murray (Oxford: Oxford University Press, 1986), 116. Theory too, by this stage, was no longer invested with its sacred or political dimensions. See William McNeill, *The Glance of the Eye: Heidegger, Aristotle and the Ends of Theory* (New York: State University of New York Press, 1999), 268.

3 Vernant following Vegetti suggests that 'forms of worship' is a more apt representation of Greek devout practices rather than the overarching concept offered by 'religion'. Jean-Pierre Vernant, Introduction to *The Greeks*, ed. Jean-Pierre Vernant and trans. Charles Lambert and Teresa Lavender Fagan (Chicago: University of Chicago Press, 1995), 9.

4 Mario Vegetti, 'The Greeks and their Gods', in *The Greeks*, ed. Jean-Pierre Vernant and trans. Charles Lambert and Teresa Lavender Fagan (Chicago: University of Chicago Press, 1995), 254.

5 Vernant, Introduction, *The Greeks*, 6.

6 Here the coupling of Hestia and Hermes, in particular, comes to mind: the 'immovable goddess of the hearth' embodied in Hestia and 'the mobile god of transitions, exchanges, movements', taking the form of Hermes, together contributing to the nature of place via their differences *and* partnership. See Jean-Pierre Vernant, 'Greek Religion, Ancient Religions', in *Mortals and Immortals: Collected Essays*, ed. Froma I. Zeitlin (Princeton, NJ: Princeton University Press, 1991), 278.

7 See Walter F. Otto, *The Homeric Gods: The Spiritual Significance of Greek Religion*, trans. Moses Hadas (London: Thames and Hudson, 1979), 160–1.

8 See Vernant, Introduction, *The Greeks*, 7.

9 See Vegetti, 'Greeks and their Gods', 259. Interestingly, the word 'craft' springs from 'the Saxon word for power, force or strength'. See Esther Leslie, 'Walter Benjamin: Traces of Craft', *Journal of Design History* 11, no. 1 (1998): 11.

10 See Sarah P. Morris, *Daidalos and the Origins of Greek Art* referred to in Indra Kagis McEwen, *Socrates' Ancestor: An Essay in Architectural Beginnings* (Cambridge, MA: MIT Press, 1993), 76. For a further discussion on Daedalus see Alberto Pérez-Gómez, 'The Myth of Daedalus', *AA Files* 10 (1985): 49–52.

11 The shield of Achilles crafted by Hephaestus and Anaximander's *pinax*, the tablet displaying the map of the world, were produced using the technique of toreutics, an ancient form of making that relied on the crafting of disparate materials in the construction of an artefact. So well crafted, they were considered to be woven. See McEwen, *Socrates' Ancestor*, 28 and 63; and David van Zanten, *The Architectural Polychromy of the 1830's* (New York: Garland Publishing, 1977), 19–20.

12 See McEwen, *Socrates' Ancestor*, 53–4.

13 John Scheid and Jesper Svenbro, *The Craft of Zeus: Myths of Weaving and Fabric*, trans. Carol Volk (Cambridge, MA: Harvard University Press, 1996), 58.

14 Anne Carson, *Eros the Bittersweet* (Champaign, MA: Dalkey Archive Press, 1998), 24.
15 van Zanten credits the Neo-classical scholar Antoine-Chrysostome Quatremère de Quincy (1755–1849) with the coining of the term 'polychromy', first used in his encyclopaedic study of ancient Greek sculpture, in particular, *Olympian Zeus*. See van Zanten, *Architectural Polychromy*, 17.
16 van Zanten, *Architectural Polychromy*, 19–20.
17 See McEwen, *Socrates' Ancestor*, 28 and 63. As Pérez-Gómez has commented: '*harmonia* initially had nothing to do with mathematics; it was a quality of embodiment (perfect adjustment) with the ultimate aim of love. *Harmonia* originally meant "joining", "a joint", "agreement"; only later did it signify a concordance of sounds and the more general "combination or adaptation of parts, elements, or related things, so as to form a consistent and orderly whole".' Alberto Pérez-Gómez, *Built upon Love: Architectural Longing after Ethics and Aesthetics* (Cambridge, MA: MIT Press, 2006), 35.
18 McEwen notes that: 'The word for weaving, or plying the loom, is *hyphainein*, which literally means to bring to light, or make visible, and the word for surface […], is *epiphaneia*', further observing that '*epiphaneia* […] has only a secondary relationship to conspicuousness. *Epiphaneia* has to do with appearing, visibility being the evidence for existence: *epiphaneia* is visible surface, and testifies to coming-to-light.' McEwen, *Socrates' Ancestor*, 54 and 87–8.
19 As Bérard remarks: 'Athena is 'the tutelary goddess of the city, [and] a divinity of work. She has the epithet *Ergane*, the worker. She is invoked as the goddess of the skilful hands, the lady of the spindle and the distaff.' Claude Bérard, 'The Order of Women', in Claude Bérard et al., *A City of Images: Iconography and Society in Ancient Greece*, trans. Deborah Lyons (Princeton, NJ: Princeton University Press, 1989), 90. McEwen also points out that the classical philologist Károly Kerényi (1897–1973) proposes that Athena's name refers to vessels or receptacles so-called, used by the land's earlier pre-Greek settlers. See McEwen, *Socrates' Ancestor*, 91.
20 See Arthur C. Danto, 'Weaving as Metaphor and Model for Political Thought', in *Sheila Hicks: Weaving as Metaphor*, ed. Nina Stritzler-Levine (New Haven, CT: Yale University Press, 2006), 22–37.
21 See McEwen, *Socrates' Ancestor*, 84–6.
22 See McEwen, *Socrates' Ancestor*, 107–13.
23 See McEwen, *Socrates' Ancestor*, 81.
24 For discussions on the relationship between *chora* and *topos*, see Casey, *Fate of Place*, 23–102; McEwen, *Socrates' Ancestor*, 81–3; Jeff Malpas, 'Putting Space in Place: Philosophical Topography and Relational Geography', *Environment and Planning D: Society and Space* 30 (2012): 232–7; and Joseph Rykwert, 'Topo-philia and -phobia', in *Topophilia and Topophobia: Reflections on Twentieth-Century Human Habitat*, ed. Xing Ruan and Paul Hogben (London: Routledge, 2007), 12–22.
25 See François de Polignac, *Cults, Territory, and the Origins of the Greek City-State*, trans. Janet Lloyd (Chicago: University of Chicago Press, 1995),

20–2. Also of interest is the fact that the French term 'to walk', *marcher*, derives from *marches*, places situated at the edges of a domain. See Gilles A. Tiberghien, 'Nomad City', in Francesco Careri, *Walkscapes: Walking as an Aesthetic Practice*, trans. Steve Piccolo and Paul Hammond (Barcelona: Gustavo Gili, 2001), 15.

26 McEwen, *Socrates' Ancestor*, 63.
27 Rykwert, 'Topo-philia and -phobia', 12.
28 Indra Kagis McEwen, 'Instrumentality and the Organic Assistance of Looms', in *Chora 1: Intervals in the Philosophy of Architecture*, ed. Alberto Pérez-Gómez and Stephen Parcell (Montreal: McGill University Press, 1994), 137.
29 With reference to Plato's *Timaeus*, see Casey, *Fate of Place*, 32–3.
30 Francis MacDonald Conford, *Plato's Cosmology: The Timaeus of Plato with a Running Commentary*, quoted in Casey, *Fate of Place*, 33.
31 See Rykwert, 'Topo-philia and -phobia', 12.
32 See Joseph Rykwert, *The Dancing Column: On Order in Architecture* (Cambridge, MA: MIT Press, 1996), 386.
33 McEwen, *Socrates' Ancestor*, 74.
34 The waulking of the cloth is now only performed in demonstration, or at music festivals known as *Mòds*, the Harris Tweed Authority awarding a prize for the best waulking performance. To view a contemporary re-enactment, see Bannal, *Bho Dhòrn gu Dòrn* (DVD and CD). Portree, Isle of Skye: Macmeanmna, 2006.
35 Simmel notes that: 'The ancient *polis* [...] seems to have had the very character of a small town.' Georg Simmel, 'The Metropolis and Mental Life', in *The Sociology of Georg Simmel*, trans. and ed. Kurt H. Wolff (Glencoe, IL: Free Press, 1950), 417.
36 Ian Angus Mackenzie, former chairman of the Harris Tweed Authority discussing Harris Tweed in the radio documentary, Leslie Campbell, *The Battle of the Tweed*, prod. Peter McManus (Glasgow: BBC Radio 4, 6 February 2009).
37 It has been said of Pollock's work '[t]hat an imaginary grid seemed always in operation'. Brian O'Doherty quoted in Hannah B. Higgins, *The Grid Book* (Cambridge, MA: MIT Press, 2009), 122.
38 Here it is perhaps interesting to note that for the scientist Michel-Eugène Chevreul (1786–1889), Director of Dyes at the Gobelins Tapestry Works in Paris (1824–83) was not concerned with the classification of colours so much as the heightening of their vibrancy generated by the juxtaposition of fragments of pure hues. See van Zanten, *Architectural Polychromy*, 69.
39 Part of the allure of Harris Tweed was the aroma of the peat fire, which until the early twentieth century at least, permeated the very fibres of its web, so much so that imitators developed a 'synthetic essence which exactly copies the smell of peat smoke' which at additional cost could be imbued into its offshore forgeries. With reference to an article in *The Scottish Daily Express* (20 December 1933), see Janet Hunter, *The Islanders and the Orb: The History of the Harris Tweed Industry 1835–1995* (Stornoway: Acair, 2001), 116.

40 See McEwen, *Socrates' Ancestor*, 130.
41 McEwen, *Socrates' Ancestor*, 82–3.
42 Hannah Arendt, *The Human Condition* (Chicago: University of Chicago Press, 1958), 198.
43 As McCann has noted rather sardonically: 'another day, another dolor'. Colum McCann, *Let the Great World Spin* (London: Bloomsbury, 2009), 4.
44 See Arendt's discussion of durability in *Human Condition*, 136–9.
45 See Arendt, *Human Condition*, 160.
46 As Schwartz has observed: 'Benjamin [...] sets the commodity in motion and grants it a life that enthrals the urban dweller, the consumer, and the poet. He calls this world of the commodity, along with Adorno, the "phantasmagoria." But his point is that the experience of the city, of capitalism, of modernity is mediated by commodity; his goal was a theory of *experience* and a critique of *culture*.' Frederick J. Schwartz, 'Form Follows Fetish: Adolf Behne and the Problem of *Sachlichkeit*', *Oxford Art Journal* 21, no. 2 (1998): 64. Emphasis in Schwartz.
47 See Friedrich Engels, *The Condition of the Working-Class in England in 1844*, trans. Florence K. Wischnewetzky (New York: Cosimo Books, 2008), 135–7.
48 As Carlyle commented: 'On every hand the living artisan is driven from his workshop to make room for the speedier, inanimate one. The shuttle drops from the fingers of the weaver and falls into iron fingers that ply it faster.' Thomas Carlyle, 'Signs of the Times', quoted in Glenn Adamson, 'Craft and the Industrial Revolution', in *The Craft Reader*, ed. Glenn Adamson (Oxford: Berg Publishers, 2010), 43.
49 William Hesketh Lever, 1st Viscount Leverhulme (1851–1925), Proprietor of the Isle of Lewis (1918–23), and later Harris (1919–25), sought to introduce more technologically advanced forms of mechanisation into the production of Harris Tweed, his efforts, with the exception of the carding and spinning mills already established by Kenneth Mackenzie and S. A. Newall in 1906, constantly ignored and rebuffed by the Islanders, though the Hattersley loom was over time adopted. See Hunter, *Islanders and the Orb*, 88–9. Leverhulme's heirs, Lever Brothers, it should be noted, commissioned one of the earliest curtain wall buildings in New York, Lever House (1950–2), designed by Gordon Bunshaft for Skidmore Owings and Merrill. For a discussion of this building, see for example Carol Herselle Krinsky, *Gordon Bunshaft of Skidmore, Owings and Merrill* (Cambridge, MA: MIT Press, 1988), 18–46.
50 Semper was involved in the design of the exhibitions for Turkey, Canada, Sweden and Denmark, which afforded him the opportunity to reflect on the variety of wares, industrial and handcrafted, presented by the different nations. He was also to review the event, his text 'Science, Industry and Art' serving both as a critique of the objects displayed as well as foundational to his own reformative pedagogical beliefs. See Gottfried Semper, 'Science, Industry and Art: Proposals for the Development of a National Taste in Art at the Closing of the London Industrial Exhibition', in *The Four Elements*

of Architecture and Other Writings, trans. Harry Francis Mallgrave and Wolfgang Herrmann (Cambridge: Cambridge University Press, 1989), 130–67.

51 Semper quoted in Harry Francis Mallgrave, introduction to *Style in the Technical and Tectonic Arts: or, Practical Aesthetics*, by Gottfried Semper (Los Angeles: Getty Research Institute, 2004), 15. Semper was to refer to the Crystal Palace as 'a glass covered vacuum'. See Gottfried Semper, *Style in the Technical and Tectonic Arts: or, Practical* Aesthetics, trans. Harry Francis Mallgrave and Michael Robinson (Los Angeles: Getty Research Institute, 2004), 47.

52 A plaid from St Kilda and a web from the Isle of Lewis dated 1768 illustrating the development of the craft over the preceding decades were exhibited, as well as knitting from the Isles, featuring as part of Donald MacDougall of Inverness's stand. See *The Great Exhibition of Works of Industry and All Nations, 1851: Official Descriptive and Illustrated Catalogue* (Cambridge: Cambridge University Press, 2011), 105.

53 Photography did not properly feature at a Great Exhibition until 1855. See Walter Benjamin, 'Paris: Capital of the Nineteenth Century: Exposé of 1935' (1935), in *The Arcades Project*, trans. Howard Eiland and Kevin McLaughlin (Cambridge, MA: Belknap Press of Harvard University Press, 2004), 6.

54 The interior of the Crystal Palace was designed by Owen Jones (1809–74), its colour scheme derived from Chevreul's 'Law of Simultaneous Colour Contrasts'. See Joseph Masheck, 'The Carpet Paradigm: Critical Prolegomena to a Theory of Flatness', *Arts Magazine* 5 (1976): 84.

55 See Joseph Rykwert, 'Gottfried Semper and the Conception of Style', in *Gottfried Semper und die Mitte des 19. Jahrhunderts*. Conference Proceedings (Basel: Birkhäuser, 1976), 78–80.

56 For a discussion of the term *Sachlichkeit* see Schwartz, 'Form Follows Fetish', especially p. 48. Here it is perhaps interesting to note that the word for 'lens' in French is *objectif*, a nuance lost in its English translation.

57 Herbert Molderings, 'The Modernist Cause: New Vision and New Objectivity 1919–1945', in *Collection Photographs: A History of Photography through the Collections of the Centre Pompidou, Musée National d'Art Moderne* (Paris: Centre Pompidou and Göttingen: Steidl, 2007), 106.

58 As Jauss has remarked, with fashion serving as his model: '*Modern* marks the dividing line between that which is newly produced and that which the newly produced has sidelined, between what was still in yesterday and what is already out today. [...] Crossing over into the modern is the process by which whatever was only just now current not only loses all value but is abruptly remanded to the mask-like vizier of the outmoded, without the gradual decay of organic processes.' Hans Robert Jauss, 'Modernity and Literary Tradition', trans. Christian Thorne, *Critical Inquiry* 31, no. 2 (2005): 332. Emphasis in Jauss.

59 See Georg Simmel, 'Adornment', in *The Sociology of Georg Simmel*, ed. and trans. Kurt H. Wolff (Glencoe, IL: Free Press, 1950), 341.

60 Simmel, 'Adornment', 341–2.

Appearing | Weaving 37

61 See Simmel, 'The Metropolis and Mental Life', 414. Here Gerhard Richter's *Spiegel, Grau* (1991) is recalled, a uniform grey canvas, covered in a sheet of glass, *Der Spiegel* being the German word for mirror, as well as the name of one the country's largest newspapers.
62 As Benjamin observed: 'The more industry progresses, the more perfect are the imitations which it throws on the market. The commodity is bathed in a profane glow; this glow has nothing in common with the glow that produces its "theological capers", yet it is of some importance to society. In a speech about trademarks Chaptal said on 17 July 1824: "Do not tell me that in the final analysis a shopper will know about the different qualities of a material. No, gentlemen, a consumer is no judge of them he will go only by the appearance of the commodity. But are looking and touching enough to determine the permanence of colours, the fineness of a material, or the quality and nature of its finish?" In the same measure as the expertness of a customer declines, the importance of his taste increases – both for him and for the manufacturer.' Walter Benjamin, 'The Paris of the Second Empire in Baudelaire', in *Selected Writings: 1938–1940*, vol. 4, ed. Howard Eiland and Michael W. Jennings (Cambridge, MA: Belknap Press of Harvard University Press, 2006), 64.
63 Colin Rowe, introduction to *Five Architects: Eisenman Graves Gwathmey Hejduk Meier*, quoted in Reinhold Martin, 'Atrocities. Or, Curtain Wall as Mass Medium', *Perspecta* 32 (2001): 68.
64 The modern curtain wall's genesis emerged with the Chicago School and the commercial architecture of the 1880s and 1890s, the Chicago Frame, a three-dimensional grid, alleviating the wall from its load-bearing function. For a discussion of the frame, see Colin Rowe, 'Chicago Frame', in *Mathematics of the Ideal Villa and Other Essays* (Cambridge, MA: MIT Press, 1982), 89–117.
65 Reinhold Martin, *The Organizational Complex: Architecture, Media and Corporate Space* (Cambridge, MA: MIT Press, 2003), 102.
66 Martin, *Organizational Complex*, 105.
67 See Manfredo Tafuri and Francesco Dal Co, *Modern Architecture*, vol. 2, trans. Robert Erich Wolf (New York: Rizzoli, 1986), 312.
68 Curtain walls were available as an off-the-shelf system in 1956. See Martin, *Organizational Complex*, 99.
69 See Martin, *Organizational Complex*, 103.
70 Tafuri and Dal Co, *Modern Architecture*, vol. 2, 339.
71 Theodor W. Adorno, 'Television and the Patterns of Mass-Culture', quoted in Martin, *Organizational Complex*, 120.
72 Martin, 'Atrocities', 71.
73 Martin, 'Atrocities', 71.
74 The architect Jose Luis Sert (1902–83) described the proliferation of the curtain wall thus, and is quoted in David Leatherbarrow and Mohsen Mostafavi, *Surface Architecture* (Cambridge, MA: MIT Press, 2002), 203.
75 Martin, *Organizational Complex*, 6.
76 As Baudelaire was once to proclaim: 'All is number. Number is all. Number is in the individual. Ecstasy is a number.' Charles Baudelaire, *Fusées*,

38 *Appearing | Weaving*

quoted in Jean-François Chevrier, 'Urban *Photogénie*', trans. Pierre Bouvier, in *Spectacular City: Photographing the Future*, ed. Emilano Gandolfi (Rotterdam: NAi, 2006), 174, n. 6.

77 See Martin, *Organizational Complex*, 159–60.

78 Semper, *Style*, 119. Emphasis in Semper. Semper here conceivably refers to the Jacquard loom, which operated as a model for Charles Babbage's protocomputers and machines.

79 Walter Benjamin, 'On the Mimetic Faculty', in *One-Way Street and Other Writings*, trans. Edmund Jephcott and Kingsley Shorter (London: Verso, 1998), 161.

80 See László Moholy-Nagy, 'How Photography Revolutionises Vision', trans. Morton Shand, *The Listener* (November 1933): 688.

81 Benjamin, 'Work of Art', 236.

82 Jeff Malpas, 'Repetitions', in *Repetitions*, exhibition catalogue (Hobart: Plimsoll Gallery, University of Tasmania, 2008), 6.

83 Walter Benjamin, 'Little History of Photography', trans. Edmund Jephcott and Kingsley Shorter, in *Selected Writings*, Volume 2, Part 2: *1931–1934*, ed. Michael W. Jennings, Howard Eiland and Gary Smith (Cambridge, MA: Belknap Press of Harvard University Press, 2005), 527.

84 An enantiomorph is 'a form which is related to another as an object is related to its image in a mirror; a mirror-image', the term most often used in relation to optics and crystallography. See *The Oxford English Dictionary*, www.oed.com/view/Entry/61555. Accessed 24 May 2012.

85 Rolf Tiedemann, 'Dialectics at a Standstill: Approaches to the *Passagen-Werk*', trans. Gary Smith and André Lefevere, in Walter Benjamin, *The Arcades Project*, trans. Howard Eiland and Kevin McLaughlin (Cambridge, MA: Belknap Press of Harvard University Press, 2004), 933. Didi-Huberman comments with reference to nineteenth-century Paris, and to Benjamin and Baudelaire, that the city 'was as much the capital of an *archaeology* as it was that of a *modernity*'. Georges Didi-Huberman, 'The Drapery of the Sidewalks', in *Herzog and De Meuron: Natural History*, ed. Philip Ursprung (Basel: Lars Müller Publishers, 2002). 270. Emphasis in Didi-Huberman.

86 One of the meanings associated with *topos*, the other archaic Greek term for place, is that it is something hidden. 'In medicine, it signifies the diseased points of the body as well as its secret places.' Rykwert, 'Topo-philia and -phobia', 12.

87 Tiedemann, 'Dialectics at a Standstill', 934.

88 Lucretius, *De rerum natura*, quoted in Casey, *Fate of Place*, 84. Casey also notes elsewhere that for the Neo-Platonic philosopher Philoponus (490–570 A.D.) 'every physical body "longs for a spatial extension not because of this extension, but because of its relation to other bodies"'. Philoponus, *In Aristotelis physicorum libros quinque posteriora commentaria*, quoted in Casey, *Fate of Place*, 136.

89 Casey, *Fate of Place*, 84. Barber notes that *stēmōn* was understood as the warp thread, and derives from the same root for 'stand', and is also associated with the word for the standing loom. See E. J. W. Barber, *Prehistoric*

Textiles: The Development of Cloth in the Neolithic and Bronze Ages with Special Reference to the Aegean (Princeton, NJ: Princeton University Press, 1991), 272–3.

90 See Walter Benjamin, 'Paris: Capital of the Nineteenth Century: Exposé of 1935', in *The Arcades Project*, trans. Howard Eiland and Kevin McLaughlin (Cambridge, MA: Belknap Press of Harvard University Press, 2002), 4–5.
91 See Benjamin, 'Paris: Capital of the Nineteenth Century', 13.
92 With reference to Hans Robert Jauss's *Toward an Aesthetic of Reception*, see Elvire Perego, 'The Urban Machine: Architecture and Industry', in *A New History of Photography*, ed. Michel Frizot (Cologne: Könemann, 1998), 201.
93 James Salter, *Light Years* (London: Penguin Books, 2007), 187.
94 See Charles Baudelaire, 'The Painter of Modern Life', in *The Painter of Modern Life and Other Essays*, ed. and trans. Jonathan Mayne (London: Phaidon Press, 1964), 12.
95 Benjamin, 'The Paris of the Second Empire in Baudelaire', quoted in Hans Robert Jauss, 'Reflections on the Chapter "Modernity" in Benjamin's Baudelaire Fragments', trans. Jim Gussen, in *On Walter Benjamin: Critical Essays and Recollections*, ed. Gary Smith (Cambridge, MA: MIT Press, 1988), 179.
96 Benjamin, 'Paris of the Second Empire in Baudelaire', 49.
97 Georg Simmel, 'Bridge and Door', trans. Mark Ritter, *Theory, Culture & Society* 11, no. 5 (1994): 6.
98 As Belting notes: 'We […] use photography to recognise yet another medium in its mirror.' Hans Belting, 'The Transparency of the Medium: The Photographic Image', in *An Anthropology of Images: Picture, Medium, Body*, trans. Thomas Dunlap (Princeton, NJ: Princeton University Press, 2011), 151.
99 Jorge Luis Borges, 'The Wall and the Books', in *The Total Library: Non-Fiction 1922–1986*, ed. Eliot Weinberger and trans. Esther Allen, Suzanne Jill Levine and Eliot Weinberger (London: Penguin Books, 2001), 346.

Bibliography

Adamson, Glenn. 'Craft and the Industrial Revolution'. In *The Craft Reader*. Edited by Glenn Adamson, 43–7. Oxford: Berg, 2010.

Arendt, Hannah. *The Human Condition*. Chicago: University of Chicago Press, 1958.

Bannal. *Bho Dhòrn gu Dòrn*. (DVD and CD). Portree, Isle of Skye: Macmeanmna, 2006.

Barber, E. J. W. *Prehistoric Textiles: The Development of Cloth in the Neolithic and Bronze Ages with Special Reference to the Aegean*. Princeton, NJ: Princeton University Press, 1991.

The Battle of the Tweed. Glasgow: BBC Radio 4. 6 February, 2009.

Baudelaire, Charles. 'The Painter of Modern Life'. In *The Painter of Modern Life and Other Essays*. Edited and translated by Jonathan Mayne, 1–40. London: Phaidon Press, 1964.

Belting, Hans. 'The Transparency of the Medium: The Photographic Image'. In *An Anthropology of Images: Picture, Medium, Body*. Translated by Thomas Dunlap, 144–68. Princeton, NJ: Princeton University Press, 2011.
Benjamin, Walter. 'The Work of Art in the Age of Mechanical Reproduction'. In *Illuminations: Essays and Reflections*. Edited by Hannah Arendt and translated by Harry Zohn, 217–52. New York: Schocken Books, 1969.
———. 'On the Mimetic Faculty'. In *One-Way Street and Other Writings*. Translated by Edmund Jephcott and Kingsley Shorter, 160–3. London: Verso, 1998.
———. 'Paris: Capital of the Nineteenth Century: Exposé of 1935' (1935). In *The Arcades Project*. Translated by Howard Eiland and Kevin McLaughlin, 3–13. Cambridge, MA: Belknap Press of Harvard University Press, 2002.
———. 'Little History of Photography'. Translated by Edmund Jephcott and Kingsley Shorter. In *Selected Writings*, Volume 2, Part 2: *1931–1934*. Edited by Michael W. Jennings, Howard Eiland and Gary Smith, 505–30. Cambridge, MA: Belknap Press of Harvard University Press, 2005.
———. 'The Paris of the Second Empire in Baudelaire'. In *Selected Writings: 1938–1940*, Volume 4. Edited by Howard Eiland and Michael W. Jennings, 3–92. Cambridge, MA: Belknap Press of Harvard University Press, 2006.
Bérard, Claude. 'The Order of Women', in *A City of Images: Iconography and Society in Ancient Greece*. Edited by Claude Bérard, Christiane Bron, Jean-Louis Durand, Françoise Frontisi-Ducroux, Francoise Lissarrague and translated by Deborah Lyons, 88–107. Princeton, NJ: Princeton University Press, 1989.
Borges, Jorge Luis. 'The Wall and the Books'. In *The Total Library: Non-Fiction 1922–1986*. Edited by Eliot Weinberger and translated by Esther Allen, Suzanne Jill Levine and Eliot Weinberger, 344–6. London: Penguin Books, 2001.
Carson, Anne. *Eros the Bittersweet*. Champaign, MA: Dalkey Archive Press, 1998.
Casey, Edward S. *The Fate of Place: A Philosophical History*. Berkeley: University of California Press, 1997.
Chevrier, Jean-François. 'Urban *Photogénie*'. Translated by Pierre Bouvier. In *Spectacular City: Photographing the Future*. Edited by Emilano Gandolfi, 173–7. Rotterdam: NAi, 2006.
Danto, Arthur C. 'Weaving as Metaphor and Model for Political Thought'. In *Sheila Hicks: Weaving as Metaphor*. Edited by Nina Stritzler-Levine, 22–37. New Haven, CT: Yale University Press, 2006.
de Polignac, François. *Cults, Territory, and the Origins of the Greek City-State*. Translated by Janet Lloyd. Chicago: University of Chicago Press, 1995.
Didi-Huberman, Georges. 'The Drapery of the Sidewalks'. In *Herzog and De Meuron: Natural History*. Edited by Philip Ursprung, 271–8. Montreal: Canadian Centre for Architecture and Baden: Lars Müller, 2002.
Engels, Friedrich. *The Condition of the Working-Class in England in 1844*. Translated by Florence K. Wischnewetzky. New York: Cosimo Books, 2008.
The Great Exhibition of Works of Industry and All Nations, 1851: Official Descriptive and Illustrated Catalogue. Cambridge: Cambridge University Press, 2011.

Higgins, Hannah B. *The Grid Book*. Cambridge, MA: MIT Press, 2009.
Hunter, Janet. *The Islanders and the Orb: The History of the Harris Tweed Industry 1835–1995*. Stornoway: Acair, 2001.
Jauss, Hans Robert. 'Reflections on the Chapter "Modernity" in Benjamin's Baudelaire Fragments'. Translated by Jim Gussen. In *On Walter Benjamin: Critical Essays and Recollections*. Edited by Gary Smith, 176–84. Cambridge, Massachusetts: MIT Press, 1988.
———. 'Modernity and Literary Tradition'. Translated by Christian Thorne, *Critical Inquiry* 31, no. 2 (2005): 329–64.
Krinsky, Carol Herselle. *Gordon Bunshaft of Skidmore, Owings and Merrill*. Cambridge, MA: MIT Press, 1988.
Leatherbarrow, David and Mohsen Mostafavi. *Surface Architecture*. Cambridge, MA: MIT Press, 2002.
Leslie, Esther. 'Walter Benjamin: Traces of Craft', *Journal of Design History* 11, no. 1 (1998): 5–13.
McCann, Colum. *Let the Great World Spin*. London: Bloomsbury, 2009.
McEwen, Indra Kagis. *Socrates' Ancestor: An Essay in Architectural Beginnings*. Cambridge, MA: MIT Press, 1993.
———. 'Instrumentality and the Organic Assistance of Looms'. In *Chora 1: Intervals in the Philosophy of Architecture*. Edited by Alberto Pérez-Gómez and Stephen Parcell, 123–42. Montreal: McGill University Press, 1994.
McNeill, William. *The Glance of the Eye: Heidegger, Aristotle and the Ends of Theory*. New York: State University of New York Press, 1999.
Mallgrave, Harry Francis. Introduction to *Style in the Technical and Tectonic Arts: or, Practical Aesthetics*, by Gottfried Semper. Translated by Harry Francis Mallgrave and Michael Robinson, 1–67. Los Angeles: Getty Research Institute, 2004.
Malpas, Jeff. 'Repetitions'. In *Repetitions*, Exhibition Catalogue, 6–20. Hobart: Plimsoll Gallery, University of Tasmania, 2008.
———. 'Putting Space in Place: Philosophical Topography and Relational Geography', *Environment and Planning D: Society and Space* 30 (2012): 226–42.
Martin, Reinhold, 'Atrocities: Or, Curtain Wall as Mass Medium', *Perspecta*, no. 32 (2001): 67–75.
———. *The Organizational Complex: Architecture, Media and Corporate Space*. Cambridge, MA: MIT Press, 2003.
Masheck, Joseph. 'The Carpet Paradigm: Critical Prolegomena to a Theory of Flatness', *Arts Magazine* 51 (1976): 82–109.
Moholy-Nagy, László. 'How Photography Revolutionises Vision'. Translated by Morton Shand, *The Listener* (November, 1933): 688–90.
Molderings, Herbert. 'The Modernist Cause: New Vision and New Objectivity 1919–1945'. In *Collection Photographs: A History of Photography through the Collections of the Centre Pompidou, Musée National d'Art Moderne*, 97–114. Paris: Centre Pompidou and Göttingen: Steidl, 2007.
Otto, Walter F. *The Homeric Gods: The Spiritual Significance of Greek Religion*. Translated by Moses Hadas. London: Thames and Hudson, 1979.

Perego, Elvire. 'The Urban Machine: Architecture and Industry'. In *A New History of Photography*. Edited by Michel Frizot, 197–223. Cologne: Könemann, 1998.

Pérez-Gómez, Alberto. 'The Myth of Daedalus', *AA Files* 10 (1985): 49–52.

———. *Built upon Love: Architectural Longing after Ethics and Aesthetics*. Cambridge, MA: MIT Press, 2006.

Rowe, Colin. 'Chicago Frame'. In *Mathematics of the Ideal Villa and Other Essays*, 89–117. Cambridge, MA: MIT Press, 1982.

Rykwert, Joseph. 'Gottfried Semper and the Conception of Style'. In *Gottfried Semper und die Mitte des 19. Jahrhunderts*. Conference Proceedings, 67–83. Basel: Birkhäuser, 1976.

———. *The Dancing Column: On Order in Architecture*. Cambridge, MA: MIT Press, 1996.

———. 'Topo-philia and –phobia'. In *Topophilia and Topophobia: Reflections on Twentieth-Century Human Habitat*. Edited by Xing Ruan and Paul Hogben, 12–22. London: Routledge, 2007.

Salter, James. *Light Years*. London: Penguin Books, 2007.

Scheid, John and Jesper Svenbro. *The Craft of Zeus: Myths of Weaving and Fabric*. Translated by Carol Volk. Cambridge, MA: Harvard University Press, 1996.

Schwartz, Frederic J. 'Form Follows Fetish: Adolf Behne and the Problem of *Sachlichkeit*', *Oxford Art Journal* 21, no. 2 (1998): 45–77.

Semper, Gottfried. 'Science, Industry and Art: Proposals for the Development of a National Taste in Art at the Closing of the London Industrial Exhibition'. In *The Four Elements of Architecture and Other Writings*. Translated by Harry Francis Mallgrave and Wolfgang Herrmann, 130–67. Cambridge: Cambridge University Press, 1989.

———. *Style in the Technical and Tectonic Arts: or, Practical Aesthetics*. Translated by Harry Francis Mallgrave and Michael Robinson. Los Angeles: Getty Research Institute, 2004.

Sennett, Richard. *The Craftsman*. New Haven, CT: Yale University Press, 2008.

Simmel, Georg. 'Adornment'. In *The Sociology of Georg Simmel*. Edited and translated by Kurt H. Wolff, 338–44. Glencoe, IL: Free Press, 1950.

———. 'The Metropolis and Mental Life'. In *The Sociology of Georg Simmel*. Edited and translated by Kurt H. Wolff, 409–24. Glencoe, IL: Free Press, 1950.

———. 'Bridge and Door'. Translated by Mark Ritter, *Theory, Culture & Society* 11, no. 5 (1994): 5–10.

Tafuri, Manfredo and Francesco Dal Co. *Modern Architecture*, Volume 2. Translated by Robert Erich Wolf. New York: Rizzoli, 1986.

Tiberghien, Gilles A. 'Nomad City'. In Francesco Careri, *Walkscapes: Walking as an Aesthetic Practice*. Translated by Steve Piccolo and Paul Hammond, 10–17. Barcelona: Gustavo Gili, 2001.

Tiedemann, Rolf. 'Dialectics at a Standstill: Approaches to the *Passagen-Werk*'. Translated by Gary Smith and André Lefevere. In Walter Benjamin, *The Arcades Project*. Translated by Howard Eiland and Kevin McLaughlin, 927–45. Cambridge, MA: Belknap Press of Harvard University Press, 2004.

van Zanten, David. *The Architectural Polychromy of the 1830's*. New York: Garland Publishing, 1977.
Vegetti, Mario. 'The Greeks and their Gods'. In *The Greeks*. Edited by Jean-Pierre Vernant and translated by Charles Lambert and Teresa Lavender Fagan, 254–84. Chicago: University of Chicago Press, 1995.
Vernant, Jean-Pierre. 'Greek Religion, Ancient Religions'. In *Mortals and Immortals: Collected Essays*. Edited by Froma I. Zeitlin, 269–89. Princeton, NJ: Princeton University Press, 1991.
———. Introduction to *The Greeks*. Edited by Jean-Pierre Vernant and translated by Charles Lambert and Teresa Lavender Fagan, 1–22. Chicago: University of Chicago Press, 1995.
West, Martin. 'Early Greek Philosophy'. In *The Oxford History of the Classical World*. Edited by John Boardman, Jasper Griffin and Oswyn Murray, 113–23. Oxford: Oxford University Press, 1986.

Wall

Figure 3.1 Anonymous, *Cairo and the Banks of the Nile*, painted by Émile Wauters (1882), after its collapse in 1971, Brussels. © KIK-IRPA Brussels.

Face

Figure 3.2 Heinz Hajek-Halke, *Erotik—Ganz Groß! (Erotic—In a Big Way!)*, 1930.

… perhaps that's what I am, the thing that divides the world in two,
on the one side the outside, on the other the inside, that can be as thin
as foil, I'm neither one side nor the other, I'm in the middle, I'm the partition,
I've two surfaces and no thickness …

Samuel Beckett

The wall is mute. But the door speaks.
Georg Simmel

In ancient Greece, we are told, a married woman was rendered conspicuous by a veil drawn across her face, distinguishing her from slaves who walked around more freely though bare-faced. This shrouding operated as a symbol and outward sign of social standing, defining the woman as wife as it concealed her, a screen from the untoward gaze and unwelcomed advances of strangers.[1] Similarly revetted were cities, curtained by fortified walls, this facing differentiating all that lay beyond from that enclosed within, shielding them from the perceived and ever-imminent onslaught of enemies.[2] In the interplay between concealment and disclosure, by a turn of phrase, so to speak, an image of a woman's head-binding, *krēdemnon*, is revealed in the curtain wall,[3] costuming by wall and veil conveying both possession and purity, their limitation and containment, qualities capable of inspiring wonder and fear.[4]

Once synonymous with the law in defining limitations and establishing boundaries, the wall enabled the formation of political communities and the establishment of the public realm, further providing for the conditions of family life, in order that it be sheltered and sheathed.[5] The nature of government, and by analogy the wall, we are told, 'is the principle ... by which it is made to act ... the human passions which set it in motion', in establishing a certain rapport.[6]

Communicative and communitarian, the theatre was 'a place to view [and] to behold';[7] it was the realm in which the *polis* and its citizens were re-presented to themselves, a spectacle wherein the relationship between the audience and dramatic action functioned as a reproduction of the extant community and its political will in operation, reconsolidating them through participation in performance.[8] Tragedy performed in Athens before the fifth century B.C., it is said, occurred on an *orkhēstra*, a dance floor, located in the public meeting place, the *agora*, temporary wooden structures effecting a theatrical space, thereafter finding a sense of permanence on the southern face of the Acropolis.[9] The presentation of Greek tragedy, we are told, always took place before a door, entrances and exits being central to the unfurling of the narrative.[10] Passage from one realm to the next, from outside to within, from an exterior to an interior world, and vice versa was hence enabled, entry and egress 'dramatis[ing] a coming-to-order',[11] the threshold a realm of transformation and catharsis.[12] Distinct from the edge or boundary, the threshold is a means of access, a zone which one cannot inhabit nor remain in, a site awash with movement, vacillation and change,[13] 'of approach or withdrawal, anticipation or remembrance, [of a] coming-to-be or passing-away'.[14]

Setting the scene, the city's dramatic structuring, enacted by the embrasure of its walls, provided the arena in which the activities of daily life were performed. A consequence of gathering and enclosing, motifs expressed both literally and figuratively in the textile arts, the wall 'makes visible the enclosed space', and '[e]stablishes [...] boundaries within which cultural order can take place'.[15] The permeation of these walls through doors and gates was hence subject to a sense of theatricality, of unmediated decoration and display, the buildings contained within, on a more diminutive scale, playing a role, operating as background, contributing, nonetheless, to civic pride and sense of ceremony during the course of festivities.[16]

For Semper, the festival, a spectacle and theatrical event, provided the pre-architectural impetus for monumental architecture, its civic role celebratory as a place of consensus.[17] The physical construct of openings, of doors and windows, however, barely features in his writings and are only discussed in brief with particular reference to their framing. The frame, we are told, enabled doors and windows to be understood as eurhythmic enclosures, 'very similar to picture frames, except that the framed content is the person who enters or looks out',[18] for without a frame no image, nor its scale, could be determined, the frame 'where art and architecture' are said to have 'first intersected'.[19] Eurhythmy, as such, was understood as contributing to the lyrical make-up of a surface, enclosures which embraced 'laws of repetition, with cadence and caesuras, with elevations and depressions from which, when interlinked, the closed figure emerge[d]',[20] a form clothed in a fabric orchestrated for the eyes.

The Renaissance architect and polymath Leon Battista Alberti (1404–72), however, was to place some emphasis on openings, some for light and ventilation, others for entry and exits, as well as 'those through which water and smoke may pass in or out, such as wells, drains, the mouths, as it were, of fireplaces, oven doors and vents', referring to them as *apertio*.[21] Distinct from 'aperture', rare but more common in architectural parlance, *apertio*, it is said, is associated with baptism, *apertionis mysterium*, a rite of passage, not only from wretchedness into Christendom, but one in which the senses of smell and hearing are said to be initiated and released, enabling life and its sensations to be fully experienced, the transformation of an individual into a fully sentient being enabled, a promise of the afterlife as well as recollection revealed.[22]

Alberti, too, we are told, was also given some credence in the formulation of the façade, the concept however absent from his treatise, *On the Art of Building in Ten Books*.[23] This volume, nonetheless, was to make regular use of the term *facies*, the Latin term containing within it the memory of the face; however, 'the entire aspect of a building [was] envisaged as much in plan as in elevation, never only the front[al] plane'. *Facies*, it is said, is related to the word for making, *faciendo*, while also corresponding to *factura*, or the make-up of something,[24] the term coming to be associated with the quality of the execution of a surface, with emphasis on painting, the expression alluding to the concept of features.[25] The term *fabrica* is also a correlate, denoting both the artefact and the place of its making.[26]

Doors and windows were central to the composition of the façade, and were likened to the orifices and openings of the face: the door to the mouth, the lips opening and shutting in order to express or receive, with the eyes likened to windows allowing light in while providing views outward, these features also enabling access to the innermost depths of the soul. For:

> Doors permit passage to the inside, vitalising the building with living bodies, windows light interiors and enable views. Likewise, the mouth accepts things from without, above all the breath of life that animates the soul, eyes see the pictures of the world, brightening the mind with sensible reality.[27]

Passage was hence enabled, doors and windows facilitating participation in the ebb and flow of life, their opening and closing permeating solid walls, perforating their divide, demonstrating 'how separating and connecting are only two faces of one and the same action'.[28]

Fronting the enclosure, the façade as distinct and separate component of a building did not become entrenched as a concept in architectural theory, it is said, until the late Renaissance, 'loosen[ing] itself from the built fabric [...] it fronts', becoming 'clothing or dress for the building's body',[29] it's character thus relayed, 'oscillat[ing] between display and dissimulation', a prelude to modernity.[30] The concept of costume, we are told, was to precede what we understand today as expression and was said to cloak a man, with particular reference to the face, the brow featuring prominently in its formulation.

> The *costumi*, then, expose our soul and the thoughts which, although in themselves they cannot be expressed in any material [substance], leave traces that easily enable us, as Petrarch says, 'to read the heart from the forehead'.[31]

This dressing enabled a direct discernment of character, its constancy bearing the marks of fleeting emotions, man's moral fibre and along with his passions rendered legible, featuring on his face.

During the course of the Renaissance, the theory of expression, we are told, was to undergo a shift, gestures and movement no longer critical to the reading of the body, the emphasis focusing increasingly on the face,[32] its surface bearing the 'outward signs of inner character',[33] a movement later reflected in architectural theory, the building no longer conceived merely as a body in plan, its façade envisaged, so to speak.

'As a means for distinguishing the stigmata of vice from the shining marks of virtue',[34] physiognomy, the study of the face, we are told, derives from the compounding of the Greek *phusis* or nature and *gnomos*, interpretation or law,[35] and came to be understood, it is said, as the 'the art of judging someone by his physical appearance',[36] the face representative of 'one's entire countenance', encapsulating *in toto* 'one's movements, [...] passions, and mores'.[37] Known since antiquity, its formulation was attributed to Aristotle,[38] and 'provided the basis for a scientific psychology and physiology as well as a diagnostic technique for medical practice',[39] its association with astrology during the course of the Middle Ages allying it with the practices of divination. In the sixteenth century, Aristotelian themes were further elaborated upon, with medieval and Renaissance treatises cogently systematised, the publication of *De Humana Physiognomonia* in 1586 by Giambattista della Porta (1535–1615) exerting considerable influence, reprinted on numerous occasions during the seventeenth and eighteenth centuries, thereafter 'shift[ing] the course of physiognomy from divinatory uses to the study of passions and expressions'.[40]

In France during the course of the eighteenth century, *architecture parlante*, literally 'speaking architecture', was to engage with theories of physiognomics, architecture conceived of as capable of expressing emotions, correspondences between the contours of a face and the profile of a building thus conferred, with the entire volume of a building later envisaged as an indication of character. Knowledge of line forms and an understanding of standard expressions were said to enable the architect to compose edifices evocative of emotion, a building skilfully enacted capable of resonating with its audience, architecture's language understood, then, as symbolic.[41] Thought to be socially reformative, the external envelope of a building, like that of a mask and its role in dramatic performance, hence communicated its functions literally, the sum of its 'surfaces and profiles a comprehensive site of representation'.[42] The concept of character, it is said, has always been integral to architectural theory from its inception, existing well in advance of the Enlightenment '"psychologisation" of the individual'.

> From Vitruvius' analogy between the orders and human 'types' through the Renaissance interest in the relationship between the cosmological and the biological, character finally became fully anthropomorphic and sexualised in the classical age.[43]

With the Cartesian edict, however, body and mind were severed and architecture's miscellaneous costumings were increasingly decried, its rich symbolic patois becoming progressively attenuated. The experiencing of the world and its measures was no longer founded upon an 'order resonant with the body's own', but instead accorded with the rational and the objective, 'philosophy and cosmology' eschewed in favour of the self-referential logic of mathematics.[44] Architecture, as such, was no longer conceived of as an art, its elements becoming censored and standardised as innumerable schematic designs proliferated, their compositions the result of permutation and combination, premised on a methodological framework enacted by the grid, a system tabulated and devised by the 'revolutionary architect' Jean-Louis-Nicolas Durand (1760–1834).[45] Efficiency and functionalism were henceforth upheld as veritable measures and means. By the turn of the twentieth century such economies had become entrenched, and deceit and duplicity were to be discerned in the very concept of façadism:

> For those who are only capable of visualising the surface of architecture – the façade, so to speak – all remains façade. This term has become the figurative expression for the veiling of makeshifts and doubtful moral characteristics, in respect of individuals, firms, and political parties. The expression 'façade' has already been adopted [...] in the sense of disguise, a mask, intended to conceal personality, as if to say, the wolf in sheep's clothing.[46]

A new face then was said to be revealed, 'or, rather, scarcely a face but [one] "transparent and faceless"',[47] the curtain wall emblematic of this new guise. Indeed, with the advent of modernity, the façade, and the threshold as a consequence, were deemed to have disappeared, the 'analytical grid of "character"' applied but unable to discern any trace of countenance, confronted instead by its dearth.[48] 'The maximum of formal structurality [was] matched by the maximum absence of images',[49] the grid, once conceivably registering as a *fenestra locutaria*, literally a speaking window or grille through which the outside world was engaged, was no longer rendered *parlante*, but mute, incapable of conveying meaningful expression, of participating in productive exchange. For '[v]oice', it is said, 'assumes mouth, eye, and finally face, a chain that is manifest in [...] the name, *prosopon poien*, to confer a mask or a face'.[50]

While the photograph was seen to 'efface the contours of [an] object's "history"',[51] in taking on a face, openings, then again, might be exposed, murmurings issuing forth, susurrations from the past resounding, dreamlike and eidetic, the vestiges of these latent callings inscribed upon its surface.[52] For:

> It is through photography that we first discover the existence of this optical unconscious, just as we discover the instinctual unconscious

through psychoanalysis. Details of structure, cellular tissue, with which technology and medicine are normally concerned – all this, in its origins, more native to the camera than the atmospheric landscape or the soulful portrait; photography reveal[ing] in this material physiognomic aspects, image worlds, which dwell in the smallest things.[53]

The camera, as such, was not amenable to scientific discovery alone, memory and reverie were to be unearthed from the patinaed depths of its prints, passions once repressed and concealed, revealed through association. For the reading of photographs like the interpretation of the face seeks to recognise constancy, traits particular to it, analyses requiring a process of abstraction freezing the event or animated face, transforming 'constant flux into a state of immutability',[54] judgements and comparisons possible only 'after the soul's emotions and passions have cooled'.[55] For:

> When we say that a face is similar to another, that means that certain features of the second face appear to us in the first, without the first ceasing to be what it was. ... For, everything is in it: face, everything has the degree of physical presence, that enables, as in a face, the search for the apparition of traits.[56]

In portraits of Melbournian mid-twentieth-century curtain walls, amidst their various features openings were disclosed, the camera, its Medusan gaze intervening, its prints porous and skin-like assuming the form of a mask.[57] In 'turning away from [their] iconic environment', however, in order to address us, these prints are said to be apostrophied, and in an about face, turning again,[58] calling out to, gesturing unexpectedly to plaids of Harris Tweed, the façades echoing with waulking songs, a barely perceptible screed.[59] Taking place, correspondences thus occur in the crossing of gazes, façade and cloth both in dialogue through the ground-glass lattice of the camera. In this convoluted performance, commonplace surfaces are brought to light, such illumination akin to the flash of magnesium flare, however seared, neither cloth nor wall is changed, rather it is in the encountering, participation in the midst, that a certain truth is revealed. For true experience, we are told, is invested in a gaze returned, eyes upwelling in the witnessing of these occasional exchanges, our experiencing of the world, as a consequence, changed.

Quotidian experience, as such, is interrupted and overturned as the long *durée* is exposed, in the confrontation between what is seemingly run of the mill and familiar with its radical otherness. In the photographic sundering, curtain wall and Harris Tweed are thus yoked together cheek by jowl, similarities becoming manifest, their features brought nearer and rendered recognisable, legible in the liminal interval in between, opening up to the fullness of time, the now-time in which the eternal erupts, interpellating the present, an instant prolonged where a sense of place prevails.

The ultimate fullness of time, of due measure, proportionate and opportune, was once designated as *kairos* by an ancient poet,[60] such qualities attributed to the classical in art, those distinguished by endurance.[61] Imbued with a sense of place, *kairos* in archaic Greece was understood as a target or mark, the place in which a weapon could most easily penetrate the body, the temple, prior to any association with temporality, distinguished, as it was, from linear time or *chronos*.[62] Over time, it came to be understood not so much as a mark which was aimed at, but even more so, we are told, as 'a penetrable opening, an aperture, or passage[way]', a threshold exposed, enabling connections to be made. Integral to the ancient practice of weaving, *kairos* was also the momentary parting of the warp threads, the creation of a shed, so that the shuttle could be shot through, facilitating the very weaving.[63] Like the lifting of the heddles of the loom, the camera's aperture enables passage, *chairou achme*, the present punctuated, past and future aligned,[64] the photograph's hyphantic potential realised, a consequence of its coursing the in-between.

Whatsoever comes to be, it is said, must 'come to be in a certain place', a place interlaced with a 'moving *image* of eternity'.[65] In an opening, and through it, whether bounded by proscenium, 'lashless eye of Zeiss'[66] or loom, place emerges in the intermittent spectacle of this curious weave, space intertwined with time, 'the timeless that happens in time',[67] and in this place all façades dissolve as the image of our own face is confronted,[68] at the still point, that 'brief, decisive moment which marks a turning',[69] a rite of passage through which our being is exposed, brought to light as part of a shared fabric, marking a return once and again 'to the world in which we always already belong'.[70]

Notes

1 As Carson observes: 'A chaste wife like Penelope in Homer's *Odyssey* "holds her veil up on either side of her face (XVI.416, XVIII.210) when confronting suitors, while Medea's decision to abandon chastity for Jason is indicated by "holding her veil aside" (*A Rhod*. 3.444–45).' Anne Carson, *Eros the Bittersweet* (Champaign, MA: Dalkey Archive Press, 1998), 22.

2 See F. A. Wright, 'A Note on the Word ΚΡΗΔΕΜΝΟΝ', *Classical Review* 28, no. 2 (1914): 49.

3 *Krēdemnon* literally means 'veil', but in the plural possesses a metaphorical dimension in Homer's epics as '"battlements" which "crown" a city's walls

(*Illiad*, XVI, 100 and *Odyssey*, XIII, 388)', specifically those of Troy; as well as the cover or lid of a vessel. See Lucinda Buck Alwa, 'Veil and Citadel in Homer', *International Journal of Humanities* 6, no. 8 (2008): 135. On this basis, then, we could say that the origin of the concept of the curtain wall is to be found in ancient Greek epic poetry. Here, Semper's English contemporary, John Ruskin's (1819–1900) discussion of the wall-veil also comes to mind. See John Ruskin, *The Stones of Venice: The Foundations* (New York: John Wiley, 1851), 298–308.

4 See Anne Carson, 'Notes', in Sappho, *If Not, Winter: Fragments of Sappho*, trans. Anne Carson (New York: Alfred A. Knopf, 2002), 372, n. 98a.3.

5 See Hannah Arendt, *The Human Condition* (Chicago: University of Chicago Press), 63–4.

6 Charles-Louis de Secondat, Baron de La Brède et de Montesquieu, *De Esprit des lois*, quoted in Arendt, *Human Condition*, 190–1, n. 17. As Arendt observes, Montesquieu understood laws in terms of *rapports* in distinction from the usual conception of them as boundaries or limits. In calling for a theoretical history of the surface to be written, philosopher Andrew Benjamin conceivably echoes Montesquieu's concerns when he states: 'that such a form of production will give rise to a conception of the surface [...] which will have an effect rather than simply being the consequence of the process of its creation'. Andrew Benjamin, 'Surface Effects: Borromini, Semper, Loos', *Journal of Architecture* 11, no. 1 (2006): 3.

7 Harry Francis Mallgrave, introduction to *Style in the Technical and Tectonic Arts: or, Practical Aesthetics*, by Gottfried Semper (Los Angeles: Getty Research Institute, 2004), 50.

8 See Oddone Longo, 'The Theatre of the *Polis*', trans. John J. Winkler, in *Nothing to Do with Dionysos? Athenian Drama in Its Social Context*, ed. John J. Winkler and Froma I. Zeitlin (Princeton, NJ: Princeton University Press, 1990), 13.

9 See Longo, 'Theatre of the *Polis*', 16, n. 7.

10 See Ruth Padel, 'Making Space Speak', in *Nothing to Do with Dionysos? Athenian Drama in Its Social Context*, ed. John J. Winkler and Froma I. Zeitlin (Princeton, NJ: Princeton University Press, 1990), 355. Here Francis Bacon's 'Triptych Inspired by *The Oresteia* of Aeschylus' (1981) comes to mind.

11 Peter Kohane and Michael Hill, 'The Decorum of Doors and Windows, from the Fifteenth to the Eighteenth Century', *Architectural Research Quarterly* 10, no. 2 (2006): 142.

12 As Pérez-Gómez notes: '*Kartharsis* meant a purification or a reconciliation between the darkness of personal destiny and the light of the divine *dike*, as expressed in the tragedy.' Alberto Pérez-Gómez, 'The Space of Architectural Representation', in *Chora 1: Intervals in the Philosophy of Architecture*, ed. Alberto Pérez-Gómez and Stephen Parcell (Montreal: McGill University Press, 1994), 12.

13 See Walter Benjamin, *The Arcades Project*, trans. Howard Eiland and Kevin McLaughlin (Cambridge, MA: Belknap Press of Harvard University Press,

2004), [O2a,1]. Casey establishes an analogous relationship between edge and threshold, and in a discussion of landscape provides an elucidating taxonomy of edge/threshold conditions. See Edward S. Casey, 'The Edge(s) of Landscape: A Study in Liminology', in *The Place of Landscape: Concepts, Contexts, Studies*, ed. Jeff Malpas (Cambridge, MA: MIT Press, 2011), 91–109.

14 Jeff Malpas, 'At the Threshold: The Edge of Liminality', in *Liminal*, exhibition catalogue (Hobart: Hobart City Council, 2008), n.p.

15 Mari Hvattum, *Gottfried Semper and the Problem of Historicism* (Cambridge: Cambridge University Press, 2004), 71.

16 See David Leatherbarrow, *Uncommon Ground: Architecture, Technology, and Topography* (Cambridge, MA: MIT Press, 2000), 73–5. Here Leatherbarrow discusses the intermittent nature of festivals in light of pre-Renaissance architecture, distinguishing between sacred architecture and the more prosaic secular buildings, in terms of frontality and image.

17 See Gottfried Semper, *Style in the Technical and Tectonic Arts: or, Practical Aesthetics*, trans. Harry Francis Mallgrave and Michael Robinson (Los Angeles: Getty Research Institute, 2004), 249.

18 See Semper, *Style*, 86.

19 Kurt W. Forster, 'Pieces for Four and More Hands', in *Herzog and De Meuron: Natural History*, ed. Philip Ursprung (Montreal, Canadian Centre for Architecture and Baden: Lars Müller, 2002), 51.

20 Semper, *Style*, 86.

21 Leon Battista Alberti, *On the Art of Building in Ten Books*, trans. Joseph Rykwert, Neil Leach and Robert Tavenor (Cambridge, MA: MIT Press, 1988), 28–31.

22 See Werner Oechslin, 'Leon Battista Alberti's *apertio*: The Opening Absolute', in *The Architecture of the Window*, ed. Vittorio Magnano Lampugnani (Tokyo: YKK Architectural Products Inc., 1995), 24. The senses were subject to a hierarchical order during the Renaissance, sight given primacy with touch the lowliest. They were also related to the elements and participated in the image of the cosmic body, sight a correlate of light and fire, hearing related to air, smell associated with vapours, taste with water, and touch with the earth. See Juhani Pallasmaa, 'An Architecture of the Seven Senses', in Steven Holl, Juhani Pallasmaa and Alberto Pérez-Gómez, *Questions of Perception: Phenomenology of Architecture* (San Francisco: William Stout, 2006), 29.

23 See Charles Burroughs, 'The Building's Face and the Herculean Paradigm: Agendas and Agency in Roman Renaissance Architecture', *Res: Journal of Anthropology and Aesthetics* 23 (1993): 9–10.

24 See Burroughs, 'Building's Face', 10.

25 See *The Oxford English Dictionary*, www.oed.com/view/Entry/67534. Accessed 14 April 2011.

26 See Joseph Rykwert, 'Body and Mind', in *Storia delle Idee: Problemi e Prospettive*, Conference Proceedings, ed. Paul Dibdon and M. Bianchi (Rome: Edizioni dell' Ateneo, 1989), 159–60.

27 Kohane and Hill, 'Decorum of Doors and Windows', 150–1. In seventeenth-century optics, metaphoric relationships between eye and window were further developed, the pupil viewed as a window, the optic nerve the messenger, the lens a mirror, the curtaining of this ensemble provided by the eyelid. See Victor I. Stoichita, *The Self-Aware Image: An Insight into Early Modern Meta-Painting*, trans. Anne-Marie Glasheen (Cambridge: Cambridge University Press, 1997), 290, n. 61.
28 Georg Simmel, 'Bridge and Door', *Lotus International* 47 (1985): 54.
29 With reference to the Italian author Pietro Aretino (1502–56), see Charles Burroughs, *The Italian Renaissance Palace Façade: Structures of Authority, Surfaces of Sense* (Cambridge: Cambridge University Press, 2002), 4.
30 Burroughs, *Italian Renaissance Palace Façade*, 32.
31 Francesco Bocchi, *Eccellenza della statua del San Giorgio di Donatello*, quoted in Moshe Barasch, 'Character and Physiognomy: Bocchi on Donatello's *St George*, a Renaissance Text on Expression in Art', *Journal of the History of Ideas* 36, no. 3 (1975): 419. As Barasch notes, Bocchi's concept of the costume draws from Aristotle's *Poetics* and his discussion of *ethos* (characteristic moral qualities) and *pathos* (transient emotion), 416–17. The reading of the forehead was known as metoposcopy.
32 See Burroughs, *Italian Renaissance Palace Façade*, 32.
33 Allan Sekula, 'The Body and the Archive', *October* 39 (1986): 11.
34 Sekula, 'Body and the Archive', 12.
35 See Patrizia Magli, 'The Face and the Soul', trans. Ughetta Lubin, in *Zone 4: Fragments for a History of the Human Body*, Part 2, ed. Michael Feher, Ramona Naddaff and Nadia Tazi (New York: Zone Publications, 1989), 87.
36 Jean-François Bédard, 'The Measure of Expression: Physiognomy and Character in Lequeu's *Novelle Méthode*', in *Chora 1: Intervals in the Philosophy of Architecture*, ed. Alberto Pérez-Gómez and Stephen Parcell (Montreal: McGill University Press, 1994), 54, n. 25.
37 Giambattista della Porta, *De Humana Physiognomonia*, quoted in Magli, 'Face and the Soul', 90.
38 Aristotle's treatise was based on the discernment of physical similarities between men and animals which hence enabled the nature of human character to be judged. See Aristotle, 'Physiognomics', in *Minor Works: On Colours, On Things Heard, Physiognomics, On Plants, On Marvellous Things Heard, Mechanical Problems, On Indivisible Lines, Situations and Names of Winds, On Melissus, Xenophanes, and Gorgias*, trans. W. S. Hett (Cambridge, MA: Harvard University Press, 1936), 83–137. Hett notes, however, that 'it is almost certainly not the work of Aristotle'.
39 Joseph Rykwert, *The Dancing Column: On Order in Architecture* (Cambridge, MA: MIT Press, 1996), 36. For a further discussion of physiognomy in light of architecture, refer to pp. 36–56.
40 See Bédard, 'Measure of Expression', 54–5, n. 25. Bédard further notes that with the publication of *De Humana Physiognomonia* this systemisation of earlier treatises also signalled their demise.

41 See David Leatherbarrow and Mohsen Mostafavi, *Surface Architecture* (Cambridge, MA: MIT Press, 2002), 9–10. The architects usually associated with *architecture parlante* include: Germain Boffrand (1667–1754), Jacques-François Blondel (1705–74), Nicolas Le Camus de Mézières (1721–89), Étienne-Louis Boullée (1728–99) and Claude-Nicolas Ledoux (1736–1806), with particular emphasis on Boullée and Ledoux.

42 Leatherbarrow and Mostafavi, *Surface Architecture*, 10.

43 Bédard, 'Measure of Expression', 47. The 'classical age' discussed by Bédard refers to Foucault's nomenclature for the Enlightenment.

44 Alberto Pérez-Gómez, *Architecture and the Crisis of Modern Science* (Cambridge, MA: MIT Press, 1983), 1–2.

45 Bédard, 'Measure of Expression', 50. Rykwert suggests that Durand was 'the only *true* Revolutionary architect'. See Joseph Rykwert, 'In the Nature of Materials: A Rational Theory of Architecture', in *Solitary Travellers* (New York: Cooper Union, 1980), 99. Emphasis in Rykwert.

46 Bruno Taut, *Modern Architecture*, quoted in Mark Wigley, *White Walls, Designer Dresses: The Fashioning of Modern Architecture* (Cambridge, MA: MIT Press, 2001), 382, n. 72.

47 Walter Benjamin, 'Brecht's Threepenny Novel', in *Reflections: Essays, Aphorisms, Autobiographical Writings*, ed. Peter Demetz and trans. Edmund Jephcott (New York: Schocken Books, 1986), 196. As Leatherbarrow observes, '*[e]levations* came to replace façades'. Leatherbarrow, *Uncommon Ground*, 76. Emphasis in Leatherbarrow.

48 'The *physionorègle* was a grid used by eighteenth century draughtsmen to situate correctly the different parts of the human face.' Bédard, 'Measure of Expression', 37 and 53, n. 11.

49 Manfredo Tafuri and Francesco Dal Co, *Modern Architecture*, vol. 2, trans. Robert Erich Wolf (New York: Rizzoli, 1986), 312.

50 Paul de Man, 'Autobiography as De-Facement', *MLN* 94, no. 5 (1979): 926.

51 Siegfried Kracauer, 'Photography', in *The Mass Ornament: Weimar Essays*, ed. and trans. Thomas Y. Levin (Cambridge, MA: Harvard University Press, 1995), 58.

52 Benjamin conceived of physiognomics as an 'eidetic way of observing phenomena', as opposed to 'an historical one'. See Walter Benjamin, 'Curriculum Vitae III', trans. Rodney Livingstone, in *Selected Writings*, Volume 2, Part 1: *1927–1930*, ed. Michael W. Jennings, Howard Eiland and Gary Smith (Cambridge, MA: Belknap Press of Harvard University Press, 2005), 78. Purloining a quote from Victor Hugo's *Notre Dame de Paris*, Benjamin was to also wryly observe: 'On the wall of the Farmers-General, under Louis XVI: "The mur ‹wall› by which Paris is immured makes Paris murmur".' Benjamin, *Arcades Project*, [P4a,2].

53 Walter Benjamin, 'Little History of Photography', trans. Edmund Jephcott and Kingsley Shorter, in *Selected Writings*, Volume 2, Part 2: *1931–1934*, ed. Michael W. Jennings, Howard Eiland and Gary Smith (Cambridge, MA: Belknap Press of Harvard University Press, 2005), 510–11.

54 Magli, 'Face and the Soul', 90.

55 della Porta, *De Humana Physiognomonia*, quoted in Magli, 'Face and the Soul', 90.
56 Walter Benjamin, quoted in Eduardo Cadava, *Words of Light: Theses on the Photography of History* (Princeton, NJ: Princeton University Press, 1997), 123.
57 '[S]ight of the invisible is possible when a simulacrum replaces it [...] it becomes a bearable sight because it is an *eikon*', an image or mask. Françoise Frontisi-Ducroux, 'The Gorgon, Paradigm of Image Creation', trans. Seth Graebner, in *The Medusa Reader*, ed. Marjorie Garber and Nancy J. Vickers (New York: Routledge, 1993), 264. Vernant further notes that frontality and monstrosity are the two fundamental features of Gorgon iconography. See Jean-Pierre Vernant, 'Death in the Eyes: Gorgo Figure of the *Other*', in *Mortals and Immortals: Collected Essays*, ed. Froma I. Zeitlin (Princeton, NJ: Princeton University Press, 1991), 114.
58 See Frontisi-Ducroux, 'The Gorgon', 263.
59 As Frontisi-Ducroux notes in relation to the myth of Medusa, 'an aural dimension is emphasised by the literary texts'. Françoise Frontisi-Ducroux, 'In the Mirror of the Mask', in *A City of Images: Iconography and Society in Ancient Greece*, ed. Claude Bérard et al. and trans. Deborah Lyons (Princeton, NJ: Princeton University Press, 1989), 159. Casey also observes that 'there is no commemoration without calling'. Edward S. Casey, *Remembering: A Phenomenological Study*, 2nd ed. (Bloomington, IN: Indiana University Press, 2000), 232.
60 See Hesiod, *Work and Days*, quoted in Phillip Sipiora, 'Introduction: The Ancient Concept of *Kairos*', in *Rhetoric and Kairos: Essays in History, Theory and Praxis*, ed. Phillip Sipiora and James S. Baumlin (New York: State University of New York Press, 2002), 2.
61 As Tiedemann notes, the French art historian Henri Focillon (1881–1943) 'defined the classical in art as "*bonheur rapide*," as the "*chairou achme*" of the Greeks, and Benjamin wanted to use that definition for his own concept of messianic standstill'. Rolf Tiedemann, 'Dialectics at a Standstill: Approaches to the *Passagen-Werk*', trans. Gary Smith and André Lefevere, in Walter Benjamin, *The Arcades Project*, trans. Howard Eiland and Kevin McLaughlin (Cambridge, MA: Belknap Press of Harvard University Press, 2004), 945.
62 See Thomas Rickett, 'Invention in the Wild: On Locating *Kairos* in Space-Time', in *The Locations of Composition*, ed. Christopher J. Keller and Christian R. Weisser (Albany, NY: State University of New York Press, 2007), 72; and Sipiora, introduction to *Rhetoric and Kairos*, 2.
63 See Rickett, 'Invention in the Wild', 73. The origins of the word 'shuttle' derive from the same origins as 'to shoot', recalling what one indeed does with a camera. See *The Oxford English Dictionary*, www.oed.com/viewdictionaryentry/Entry/179072. Accessed 11 October 2011.
64 Barthes's concept of *punctum* is seemingly implicit in the concept of *kairos*, related, as it is, to the concept of piercing. See Roland Barthes, *Camera Lucida*, trans. Geoff Dyer (New York: Hill and Wang, 2010), 27.

60   Wall | Face

65   Plato, *Timaeus*, quoted in Edward S. Casey, *The Fate of Place: A Philosophical History* (Berkeley, CA: University of California Press, 1997), 32. Emphasis in Casey. Casey notes that Cornford's translation reads: 'an everlasting image moving according to number'.
66   Salvador Dali, 'Photography: Pure Creation of the Mind', quoted in Dawn Ades, 'Little Things: Close-Up in Photo and Film 1839–1963', in Dawn Ades and Simon Barker, *Close-Up: Proximity and Defamiliarisation in Art, Film and Photography*, exhibition catalogue (Edinburgh: Fruitmarket Gallery, 2008), 44.
67   David Leatherbarrow, *The Roots of Architectural Invention: Site, Enclosure, Materials* (New York: Cambridge University Press, 1993), 220.
68   Here the dissolution of the fourth wall which characterises theatrical performances is alluded to, the audience recognising itself in the presentation occurring on stage. As Gadamer observes: 'Thus it is not really the absence of a fourth wall that turns the play into a show. Rather, openness toward the spectator is part of the closedness of the play. The audience only completes what the play as such is.' Hans-Georg Gadamer, *Truth and Method*, 2nd ed. rev., trans. Joel Weinsheimer and Donald G. Marshall (London: Continuum, 2004), 109.
69   The art historian Erwin Panofsky (1892–1968) describes *kairos* thus. See Erwin Panofsky, *Studies in Iconology: Humanistic Themes in the Art of the Renaissance*, quoted in Carolyn R. Miller, foreword to *Rhetoric and Kairos: Essays in History, Theory and Praxis*, ed. Phillip Sipiora and James S. Baumlin (New York: State University of New York Press, 2002), xii.
70   Jeff Malpas, 'Beginning in Wonder: Placing the Origin of Thinking', in *Philosophical Romanticism*, ed. Nikolas Kompridis (London: Routledge, 2005), 296.

Bibliography

Ades, Dawn. 'Little Things: Close-Up in Photo and Film 1839–1963'. In Dawn Ades and Simon Barker, *Close-Up: Proximity and Defamiliarisation in Art, Film and Photography*. Exhibition Catalogue, 8–59. Edinburgh: Fruitmarket Gallery, 2008.

────── and Simon Barker. *Close-Up: Proximity and Defamiliarisation in Art, Film and Photography*. Exhibition Catalogue. Edinburgh: Fruitmarket Gallery, 2008.

Alberti, Leon Battista. *On the Art of Building in Ten Books*. Translated by Joseph Rykwert, Neil Leach and Robert Tavenor. Cambridge, MA: MIT Press, 1988.

Alwa, Lucinda Buck. 'Veil and Citadel in Homer', *International Journal of Humanities* 6, no. 8 (2008): 135–44.

Arendt, Hannah. *The Human Condition*. Chicago: University of Chicago Press, 1958.

Aristotle. 'Physiognomics'. In *Minor Works: On Colours, On Things Heard, Physiognomics, On Plants, On Marvellous Things Heard, Mechanical Problems, On Indivisible Lines, Situations and Names of Winds, On Melissus, Xenophanes, and Gorgias*. Translated by W. S. Hett, 83–137. Cambridge, MA: Harvard University Press, 1936.

Barasch, Moshe. 'Character and Physiognomy: Bocchi on Donatello's *St George*, a Renaissance Text on Expression in Art', *Journal of the History of Ideas* 36, no. 3 (1975): 413–30.

Barthes, Roland. *Camera Lucida*. Translated by Geoff Dyer. New York: Hill and Wang, 2010.

Bédard, Jean-François. 'The Measure of Expression: Physiognomy and Character in Lequeu's *Nouvelle Méthode*'. In *Chora 1: Intervals in the Philosophy of Architecture*. Edited by Alberto Pérez-Gómez and Stephen Parcell, 35–56. Montreal: McGill University Press, 1994.

Benjamin, Andrew. 'Surface Effects: Borromini, Semper, Loos', *Journal of Architecture* 11, no. 1 (2006): 1–36.

Benjamin, Walter. 'Brecht's Threepenny Novel'. In *Reflections: Essays, Aphorisms, Autobiographical Writings*. Edited by Peter Demetz and translated by Edmund Jephcott, 193–202. New York: Schocken Books, 1986.

———. *The Arcades Project*. Translated by Howard Eiland and Kevin McLaughlin. Cambridge, MA: Belknap Press of Harvard University Press, 2002.

———. 'Curriculum Vitae III'. Translated by Rodney Livingstone. In *Selected Writings*, Volume 2: Part 1: *1927–1930*. Edited by Michael W. Jennings, Howard Eiland and Gary Smith, 77–9. Cambridge, MA: Belknap Press of Harvard University Press, 2005.

———. 'Little History of Photography'. Translated by Edmund Jephcott and Kingsley Shorter. In *Selected Writings*, Volume 2, Part 2: *1931–1934*. Edited by Michael W. Jennings, Howard Eiland and Gary Smith, 505–30. Cambridge, MA: Belknap Press of Harvard University Press, 2005.

Burroughs, Charles. 'The Building's Face and the Herculean Paradigm: Agendas and Agency in Roman Renaissance Architecture', *Res: Journal of Anthropology and Aesthetics* 23 (1993): 7–30.

Cadava, Eduardo. *Words of Light: Theses on the Photography of History*. Princeton, NJ: Princeton University Press, 1997.

Carson, Anne. *Eros the Bittersweet*. Champaign, MA: Dalkey Archive Press, 1998.

Casey, Edward S. *The Fate of Place: A Philosophical History*. Berkeley: University of California Press, 1997.

———. *Remembering: A Phenomenological Study*, 2nd ed. Bloomington: Indiana University Press, 2000.

———. 'The Edge(s) of Landscape: A Study in Liminology'. In *The Place of Landscape: Concepts, Contexts, Studies*. Edited by Jeff Malpas, 91–109. Cambridge, MA: MIT Press, 2011.

Forster, Kurt W. 'Pieces for Four and More Hands'. In *Herzog and De Meuron: Natural History*. Edited by Philip Ursprung, 41–62. Montreal: Canadian Centre for Architecture and Baden: Lars Müller, 2002.

Frontisi-Ducroux, Françoise. 'In the Mirror of the Mask'. In *A City of Images: Iconography and Society in Ancient Greece*. Edited by Claude Bérard, Christiane Bron, Jean-Louis Durand, Francoise Frontisi-Ducroux, Francoise Lissarrague and translated by Deborah Lyons, 151–65. Princeton, NJ: Princeton University Press, 1989.

———. 'The Gorgon, Paradigm of Image Creation'. Translated by Seth Graebner. In *The Medusa Reader*. Edited by Marjorie Garber and Nancy. J. Vickers, 262–6. New York: Routledge, 1993.

Gadamer, Hans-Georg. *Truth and Method*, 2nd ed. rev. Translated by Joel Weinsheimer and Donald G. Marshall. London: Continuum, 1989.

Hvattum, Mari. *Gottfried Semper and the Problem of Historicism*. Cambridge: Cambridge University Press, 2004.

Kohane, Peter and Michael Hill. 'The Decorum of Doors and Windows, from the Fifteenth to the Eighteenth Century', *Architectural Research Quarterly* 10, no. 2 (2006): 141–56.

Kracauer, Siegfried. 'Photography'. In *The Mass Ornament: Weimar Essays*. Edited and translated by Thomas Y. Levin, 46–63. Cambridge, MA: Harvard University Press, 1995.

Leatherbarrow, David. *The Roots of Architectural Invention: Site, Enclosure, Materials*. New York: Cambridge University Press, 1993.

———. *Uncommon Ground: Architecture, Technology, and Topography*. Cambridge, MA: MIT Press, 2000.

——— and Mohsen Mostafavi. *Surface Architecture*. Cambridge, MA: MIT Press, 2002.

Longo, Oddone. 'The Theatre of the Polis'. Translated by John J. Winkler. In *Nothing to Do with Dionysos? Athenian Drama in Its Social Context*. Edited by John J. Winkler and Froma I. Zeitlin, 12–19. Princeton, NJ: Princeton University Press, 1990.

Magli, Patricia. 'The Face and the Soul'. Translated by Ughetta Lubin. In *Zone 4: Fragments for a History of the Human Body*, Part 2. Edited by Michael Feher, Ramona Naddaff and Nadia Tazi, 87–127. New York: Zone Publications, 1989.

Mallgrave, Harry Francis. Introduction to *Style in the Technical and Tectonic Arts: or, Practical Aesthetics*, by Gottfried Semper. Translated by Harry Francis Mallgrave and Michael Robinson, 1–67. Los Angeles: Getty Research Institute, 2004.

Malpas, Jeff. 'Beginning in Wonder: Placing the Origin of Thinking'. In *Philosophical Romanticism*. Edited by Nikolas Kompridis, 282–98. London: Routledge, 2005.

———. 'At the Threshold: The Edge of Liminality'. In *Liminal*. Exhibition Catalogue. Hobart: Hobart City Council, 2008. n.p.

Man, Paul de. 'Autobiography as De-Facement', *MLN* 94, no. 5 (1979): 919–30.

Miller, Carolyn R. Foreword to *Rhetoric and Kairos: Essays in History, Theory and Praxis*. Edited by Phillip Sipiora and James S. Baumlin, xi–xiii. New York: State University of New York Press, 2002.

Oechslin, Werner. 'Leon Battista Alberti's *apertio*: The Opening Absolute'. In *The Architecture of the Window*. Edited by Vittorio Magnano Lampugnani, 24–33. Tokyo: YKK Architectural Products, 1995.

Padel, Ruth. 'Making Space Speak'. In *Nothing to Do with Dionysos? Athenian Drama in Its Social Context*. Edited by John J. Winkler and Froma I. Zeitlin, 336–65. Princeton, NJ: Princeton University Press, 1990.

Pallasmaa, Juhani. 'An Architecture of the Seven Senses'. In Steven Holl, Juhani Pallasmaa and Alberto Pérez-Gómez, *Questions of Perception: Phenomenology of Architecture*, 26–37. San Francisco: William Stout, 2006.

Pérez-Gómez, Alberto. *Architecture and the Crisis of Modern Science*. Cambridge, MA: MIT Press, 1983.

———. 'The Space of Architectural Representation'. In *Chora 1: Intervals in the Philosophy of Architecture*. Edited by Alberto Pérez-Gómez and Stephen Parcell, 1–34. Montreal: McGill University Press, 1994.

Rickett, Thomas. 'Invention in the Wild: On Locating *Kairos* in Space-Time'. In *The Locations of Composition*. Edited by Christopher J. Keller and Christian R. Weisser, 71–89. Albany, NY: State University of New York Press, 2007.

Ruskin, John. *The Stones of Venice: The Foundations*. New York: John Wiley, 1851.

Rykwert, Joseph. 'In the Nature of Materials: A Rational Theory of Architecture'. In *Solitary Travellers*, 97–116. New York: Cooper Union, 1980.

———. 'Body and Mind'. In *Storia delle Idee: Problemi e Prospettive*. Conference Proceedings, edited by Paul Dibdon and M. Bianchi, 157–68. Rome: Edizioni dell' Ateneo, 1989.

———. *The Dancing Column: On Order in Architecture*. Cambridge, MA: MIT Press, 1996.

Sappho. *If Not, Winter: Fragments of Sappho*. Translated by Anne Carson. New York: Alfred A. Knopf, 2002.

Sekula, Allan. 'The Body and the Archive', *October* 39 (1986): 3–64.

Semper, Gottfried. *Style in the Technical and Tectonic Arts: or, Practical Aesthetics*. Translated by Harry Francis Mallgrave and Michael Robinson. Los Angeles: Getty Research Institute, 2004.

Simmel, Georg. 'Bridge and Door', *Lotus International* 47 (1985): 52–6.

Sipiora, Phillip. 'Introduction: The Ancient Concept of *Kairos*'. In *Rhetoric and Kairos: Essays in History, Theory and Praxis*. Edited by Phillip Sipiora and James S. Baumlin, 1–22. New York: State University of New York Press, 2002.

Stoichita, Victor I. *The Self-Aware Image: An Insight into Early Modern Meta-Painting*. Translated by Anne-Marie Glasheen. Cambridge: Cambridge University Press, 1997.

Tafuri, Manfredo and Francesco Dal Co. *Modern Architecture*, vol. 2. Translated by Robert Erich Wolf. New York: Rizzoli, 1986.

Tiedemann, Rolf. 'Dialectics at a Standstill: Approaches to the *Passagen-Werk*'. Translated by Gary Smith and André Lefevere. In Walter Benjamin, *The Arcades Project*. Translated by Howard Eiland and Kevin McLaughlin, 927–45. Cambridge, MA: Belknap Press of Harvard University Press, 2004.

Vernant, Jean-Pierre. 'Death in the Eyes: Gorgo Figure of the *Other*'. In *Mortals and Immortals: Collected Essays*. Edited by Froma I. Zeitlin, 111–38. Princeton, NJ: Princeton University Press, 1991.

Wigley, Mark. *White Walls, Designer Dresses: The Fashioning of Modern Architecture*. Cambridge, MA: MIT Press, 2001.

Wright, F. A. 'A Note on the Word ΚΡΗΔΕΜΝΟΝ', *Classical Review* 28, no. 2 (1914): 49.

Image

Figure 4.1 From Ralph Gibson, *Overtones: Diptychs and Proportions*, 1998.

Word

Figure 4.2 From Ralph Gibson, *Overtones: Diptychs and Proportions*, 1998.

And you have made the world. And it is huge
and like a word which grows ripe in silence.

Rainer Maria Rilke

Immerse yourself in such a picture long enough and you will realise
to what extent opposites touch.

Walter Benjamin

In days long past, it is said, no one could refuse the invitation to a waulking, the fulling and thickening of the cloth, the work performed voluntarily by women, numbering ten or so.[1] The waulking, as such, was an occasion for 'the exercise of all possible hospitality', with feasts prepared and attention to dress paid, the visit of the tailor and of the waulking women two occasions in which those not native to the family were admitted into the domestic realm, an old proverb observing that cheeks reddened in the presence of these guests.[2]

In one telling, when the waulking was done, the ceremony was not yet complete, with two women then standing, rolling the cloth from opposite ends, meeting in the middle, wherein four fell upon the bolt, beating it in time to tune, flattening out the creases. One standing would then cry, 'The rhymes, the rhymes!', the others responding, 'three rhymes, four rhymes, five and a half rhymes', the vestiges of a forgotten rite. The cloth unrolled then tightly rewound again, the women would all rise and stand in reverence, the lead singer placing her hand on the bale,[3] intoning an ancient blessing, an easy mixture of folkloric and Christian traditions:

> Let not the Evil Eye afflict, let not be mangled
> The man about whom thou goest, for ever.
>
> When he goes into battle or combat
> The Protection of the Lord be with him.[4]

Only then, we are told, could the cloth be said to be finished and fulled.[5] While the one to wear the cloth was not always known, goodwill and benevolence were regardless bestowed upon him revested in the tweed.

By 1887, however, it was commented that the waulking was, even then, 'one of the institutions of the past',[6] and by the early twentieth century the practice had almost entirely waned. While always the very fabric of the Isles, in modern times Harris Tweed's circulation beyond its shores obliged the establishment of 'the Orb', a mark and mercantile means, verifying its craft and authenticity,[7] affording the cloth a protection of its own, subject, as it was, in the late 1800s to profligate forgery.[8] With the formation of the Harris Tweed Association in 1909, and the subsequent registration of a trademark the following year, the fabric was to bear an imprint on its obverse from that time onward, stamped twice on every metre.[9] The label on the inner breast pocket of a sports coat, its most common vestiary form, was also encoded with a numerical cipher, this notation enabling the tweed to be traced back to its weaver, with enquiries to this day still forthcoming, despite the passing years, so that something of the cloth's story might be told, or in addition, the pattern rewoven again.[10]

Acts of goodwill and hospitality are one story, those of commodification an altogether different tale, Harris Tweed embodying a strange mix of both, the former sense of gestening, recalling 'guest-friendship' or *xenia*, which operated in ancient Greece. Premised upon the exchange of gifts, this economy, so to speak, was understood as inextricable from the formation of a social fabric incessant in its weaving, the elements of which were manifest in non-economic transactions including 'kinship, marriage, hospitality, artistic patronage and ritual friendship', establishing customs in which a common sense of reciprocation and personal indebtedness prevailed, the concept of profit an anathema to its functioning, though gifts were sometimes weighed.[11]

One such custom was the *symbolon*, 'a token of remembrance', from which our word symbol derives, a gesture of camaraderie shared, a bone split, halves held by both host and guest, the word *xenos* signifying the visitor and receiver, as well as 'stranger', 'outsider', 'alien', emblematic of bonds forged upon the rhythms of reciprocity, the accommodation of these meanings within a single term conveying the unitary nature of the relationship.[12] A keepsake, the *symbolon* was the mutual embodiment of identity and obligation, and should a descendent of the guest or host happen to cross the threshold years later, the one or the other visiting again, 'the two pieces could be fitted together […] to form a whole in an act of recognition', replenishing the friendship.[13] The significance of the *symbolon*, like a web of Harris Tweed, is that 'the history of the giver [is carried] into the life of the receiver and continues […] there', giving it a form of currency, a presence, replete with a sense of relay and return, the possibility of renewal, still lingering.[14]

The bone that was severed in the creation of a *symbolon*, we are told, was usually the knuckle, a joint, like a hinge, facilitating the movement of the hand, its gestures of pointing, of opening and closing, of beckoning and dismissing, releasing and grasping; harmonious joints, it is said, the miraculous means through which life is capable of being reproduced, well-crafted and manufactured. For '[t]he hand is there', it is said, 'making its presence known in the joining of the limbs, in the energetic calligraphy of a face, [and] in the profile of a walled city blue in the atmosphere'.[15]

A 'species of symbol', metaphor is one of three types of words, ordinary and strange its other variants once designated by an ancient philosopher.

> Strange words simply puzzle us;
> ordinary words convey what we already know;
> it is from metaphor that we can get hold of something new and fresh.[16]

Metaphor functions by means of transference, giving 'names to nameless things', those 'kindred or similar in appearance',[17] altering in our minds their relation, performing a 'semantic shift', enabling a change in proximity, bringing two seemingly unrelated things into alignment, revealing their filiation. *Epiphora* enables this appearance of a nearness affecting emanation and release,[18] this movement toward intimacy fuelled by imagination, the dynamic, 'living power and prime agent of all human perception',[19] novelty occurring through the establishment of correspondences.

Fragmentary and incomplete, seemingly unrelated and ill-disposed, an image of a curtain wall is juxtaposed with a swatch of Harris Tweed, their incongruities exposed, as new associations are made, such imaginings recognising shared allegiances despite discrepancies and other deviations. To the hand, the surface of the fabric is malleable, slightly matted and dense, its fibres seemingly impossible to entirely tame, the visibility of the alt or grain of the cloth largely diminished as the result of its finishing, the cloth regardless still exuding a vitality and warmth; the surface of the façade, by comparison, is cold, hard and unyielding, composed of concrete, glass and steel, the one dressing a body, the other cladding a building, the differences in scale and sensation considerable. Performative, however, metaphor, as a *'fabricated image'*,[20] dresses both building and cloth alike, attiring them anew, 'as new clothes envelop a man',[21] the building costumed, the cloth inhabited *en masse*, each transformed and rendered sensuous, capable of becoming artefacts, artefacts emergent with the foundations of community, symbolic of their binding.

Metaphor's significance, it is said, lies in its embodiment of both a routine and a new meaning, a 'literal sense *and* a novel sense, the ordinary, descriptive reference *and* a novel reference',[22] movements in between defamiliarising what is seemingly commonplace to us. A metamorphosis of our everyday experience, as such, occurs, creating an:

> unusual [image] of a familiar object, an [image] different from those that we are accustomed to see, unusual and yet true to nature, and for that reason doubly impressive to us because it startles us, makes us emerge from our habits and at the same time brings us back to ourselves by recalling to us an earlier impression.[23]

For within the meaning that metaphor conveys is a strangeness which embodies all manner of proximity, of 'distance and nearness, indifference and involvement', conveying a form of objectivity devoid of 'passivity and detachment'.[24] Always understood in relation, strangeness establishes a rapport between heterogeneous things, those proverbial and those less familiar to us, compelling them into a union. Two things, as such, are extracted from the world in order to differentiate them, and are as a result brought nearer and related to each other; but this relationship is also subject to a distancing, this selection equally not unique to these

Image | Word 71

two elements alone, but applicable to all things perceived as different, hence what is far is conceivably near, the unity of nearness and remoteness wavering.[25] For 'we experience as connected', it is said, 'only what we have previously isolated in some way'.[26]

Reconfigured and rejoined, metaphors as a split reference mark a return; they 'are the means by which the oneness of the world is [recognised and] poetically brought about'.[27] Lending a dimensionality to seeing, they enrich the fullness of experience, for 'to see', we are told, 'is to forget the name of the thing one sees', only so that new names can be ascribed, the world re-envisioned and re-made anew again.[28]

In the early years of the twentieth century, however, the medium of photography was seen to be endemic of a sense of disconnectedness and remove, '[t]he blizzard of photographs', it is said, 'betray[ing] an indifference to what [...] things mean'.[29] Subject to a 'rapid crowding of changing images', man experienced 'sharp discontinuit[ies] in the grasp of a single glance', synthesis seemingly unachievable in the face of an 'unexpectedness of onrushing impressions', this torrent emblematic of metropolitan life and new means of reproduction.[30] The photograph's source, its connection to its subject or event and their situatedness, the relationship between memory and experience, and the very possibility of knowledge was thus undermined, the consequence of its reproducibility. Images, as such, took on reductive form, mere information enervating but without story, one image seemingly indistinguishable from the other, mass-reproduced, their dissemination and dispersal anonymous, without trace, man's capacity to discern blunted and blasé, contemplation prohibited, or so it would seem, by immensity in number and pace. '[T]he passionate inclination of [the] masses', the compulsion 'to bring things spatially and humanly "closer"', in the form of a photograph, a reproduced image, was, by and large, to expose an inherent aporia, the revelation of events mediated, their transit, however, curtailed.[31] The fixity of points of reference, as such, was no longer assured; the relational nature of nearness and farness, of palpable proximity, was rendered indeterminable, the horizon blurred, if not erased.

Notes and coins, surfaces printed and impressed, circulated similarly, all values reduced to diminished tokens of quantity, arbitrary determinants, the means and measure of the money exchange.

> Money, with all its colourlessness and indifference, becomes the common denominator of all values; irreparably it hollows out the core of things, their individuality, the specific value, and their incomparability. All things float with equal specific gravity in the constantly moving stream of money. All things lie on the same level and differ from one another only in the size of the area which they cover.[32]

Objects once admired and passed on from hand to hand thus lost their status in taking on the form of a commodity, reduced to surface value and stripped of their iridescence, their craft and the time of their making abstracted and reduced to two dimensions, not a web skilfully executed, nor a vase well-formed, all qualities reduced to pecuniary worth, people no longer connecting in the ritual of exchange, the circulation of goods coursing without rhyme, under the premise of mere accumulation. Nominally assigned a single value, an object, like its photograph when substituted as its proxy, was denied its inherent richness and multiplicity, rendering the artefact as fixed and immutable, seemingly as is, 'arrested in the approximate',[33] such a limited point of view thwarting the potential of its abundant prospects and presentations, impeding any passage, its significance as a material with which to make variegated patterns renounced.

But if the image is perceived not as singular, but rather as constituent of a radiant multiplicity, it possesses the potential for the presencing of the very multiplicity inherent in the artefact. For the image like the photograph is never singular, 'tiny sparks of contingency' lie within, possibilities for connecting immanent, capable of drawing things closer. Through the photograph, it has been observed, 'we encounter something new and strange', an evocation of the photograph's metaphoric potential, image worlds erupting, uncanny experiences unexpectedly emerging amidst the ordinary and everyday.[34] By means of the lens, changes in aperture and depth of field, the camera exposes a range of proximities hitherto concealed, optical rather than physical, bringing things nearer, 'produc[ing] new, as yet unfamiliar relationships'.[35]

> With the close-up, space expands; with slow motion, movement is extended. The enlargement of a snapshot does not simply render more precise what in any case was visible, though unclear: it reveals entirely new structural formations of the subject.[36]

Reduced dimensions operating at the other end of the spectrum also facilitated novel techniques, diminution enabling a degree of mastery over works of art which could not otherwise be achieved, recontextualisations possible, art works and objects in general now malleable in positioning, application and scale.

'[W]ithout image', the curtain wall is understood as representative of a 'language of absence',[37] its metrical scansions devoid of poetry, reduced to economic and functionalist imperatives, columns and spandrels all tallying. But through manipulations of photographs, exacted by scalar shifts and equivalence in frame, coupled with their composition side by side, semblances are conveyed; through the patternation of the tweed's weave composed of warp and weft, and the arrangement of the walls' spandrels and mullions similarly interlocking, the metaphoric potential of these surfaces is revealed, as textile adherences are brought to light through the play of photography. Amplified Harris Tweed thus takes on architectural proportions, the curtain wall, by turn, diminished, becoming cloth for the enshrouding of the body, associations proliferating, in light of a different nature made accessible through the camera, rather than the naked eye.

Eliciting a shock, memory is the site of such indelible images, their traces an awakening to the past suddenly illuminated and contemporaneous. 'The trace', we are told, 'is the appearance of a nearness, however far removed the thing that left it behind may be. [...] In the trace, we gain possession of the thing',[38] amidst the distraction of quotidian existence. Like the ancient precursor to the photograph, the Epicurean *eidolon*, what is grasped however is not the object itself, but rather imprints of the objects of that vision, residues, remnants bequeathed by the experience, threads lingering, yet markedly different from the thing itself. Images in this light are conceived of as indices or 'incomplete testimon[ies] to [...] past performance[s]', as well as 'invitation[s] to movements yet to come', our part, our participation with them, necessarily required.[39] For the trace exists as an inscription, needing an extant surface onto which it can leave its mark, a backdrop dissimilar to it so that its distinctiveness can be discerned, 'the photograph [...] always related to something other than itself, [s]ealing the traces of the past within its space-crossed image', movements across space and time, between now and then, far and near, entwined.[40] In this tarrying, traces leave tracks, they are the vestiges of movements once performed, 'pulling, dragging, or drawing'.[41] But '[b]eing past, being no more, is [nonetheless] passionately at work in things',[42] the task not simply to return, but rather to continue, following on, establishing new courses and connections in the journeying.

'[A]s an intermediary *between* two places',[43] the photograph as a medium 'entail[s] both separation and connection, or rather, connection across a certain separation'. Like the shuttle coursing across the loom, it enacts a 'separation that nonetheless binds, joins, not directly, but by means of a movement, a transmission, a transformation',[44] image worlds prospering amidst the exchange.

Place, it is said, emerges in every photograph from which image worlds emanate, the photograph bearing not only the hallmark of a past moment but also of its life yet to come.[45] It appears not as a single image, but only in the coming together of multiple exposures, 'intersection[s] of places [...] intruding, [...] revealing a place that holds itself in semi-transparency',[46] fragmentary in its illumination, the totality of its visibility animate though

74 *Image | Word*

somewhat concealed. And '[i]t is always we ourselves', it is said, who 'stand at the centre of these rare images',[47] moved by our own placedness together with the place of our being revealed, immured between the streets of the metropolis and white sands, moors and mountainsides of the Hebridean Isles, clothed in layers between the *Clò Mhór* and curtain wall, poised between photographic plates, traces and transferences enabling us to weave meaning, giving form to the immaterial and immemorial, enabling them to be sensually perceived, the result of a poetic thinking, a thinking that is still veiled.

Notes

1. To view performances of waulkings, see Bannal, *Bho Dhòrn gu Dòrn* (DVD and CD) (Portree, Isle of Skye: Macmeanmna, 2006); and *Eriskay: A Poem of Remote Lives*, dir. Werner Kissling, http://movingimage.nls.uk/film/1701. Accessed 18 March 2016.
2. See J. L. Campbell, ed., *Hebridean Folksongs: A Collection of Waulking Songs by Donald MacCormick in Kilphedir in South Uist in the Year 1863* (London: Oxford University Press, 1969), 7–8. '*Eibheal air gruaidh mnathan-luadhaidh is tàilleirean*' translates as: 'There are red cheeks before the tailor and the fulling women.'
3. Leatherbarrow notes that 'bale' is cognate with 'ball', of spherical form and profile, which, it would seem to suggest, is conceivable as a world, or indeed its very centre, an *omphalos* covered in a weave, a symbol of fecundity and emergence. See David Leatherbarrow, 'Levelling the Land: Or How Topography is the Horizon of Horizons', in *Topographical Stories: Studies in Landscape and Architecture* (Philadelphia, PA: University of Pennsylvania Press, 2004), 123–4.
4. This account is taken from Ada Goodrich Freer, *The Outer Isles*, quoted in Campbell, *Hebridean Folksongs*, 10–11.
5. It should be noted that not all waulkings were finished with a blessing, as Miss Annie Johnston of Barra commented, c. 1910: 'I never heard them have a blessing in Barra, though I asked many people about it, but one of the waulking women would say to the host, if the cloth were for him: "Enjoy and use it, pay the dance, and throw across the next cloth." If it were for a young man: "Enjoy and use it, tear and rend it, and marry before it wears out."' Miss Annie Johnston quoted in Francis Thompson, *Harris Tweed: Story of a Hebridean Industry* (Newton Abbot: David and Charles, 1969), 52.
6. Mary MacKellar, 'The Waulking Day', *Transactions of the Gaelic Society of Inverness* 13 (1886–7): 201.
7. For a discussion on 'the Orb' see Janet Hunter, *The Islanders and the Orb: The History of the Harris Tweed Industry 1835–1995* (Stornoway: Acair, 2001), 57–67. Thompson notes that 'the Orb' was derived from the Dunmore coat of arms in recognition of Lady Dunmore's activities, Thompson, *Harris Tweed*, 104. This, however, has proven not to be the case, with my thanks

to John B. Scott, second cousin of the current Earl of Dunmore, for alerting me to this fact, and providing me with a copy of the Dunmore coat of arms. John B. Scott, email correspondence with the author, 19 June 2010.

8 See Fiona Anderson, 'Spinning the Ephemeral with the Sublime: Modernity and Landscape in Men's Fashion Textiles 1860–1900', *Fashion Theory* 9, no. 3 (2005): 289.
9 See Hunter, *Islanders and the Orb*, 63–4, and Catherine Harper and Kirsty McDougall, 'The Very Recent Fall and Rise of Harris Tweed', *Textile: The Journal of Cloth and Culture* 10, no. 1 (2012): 82.
10 See 'Tweed: Trouble Looms', dir. Ian Denyer, *This is Scotland* (Glasgow: BBC 4, 8 September 2009).
11 See Anne Carson, *Economy of the Unlost (Reading Simonides of Keos with Paul Celan)* (Princeton, NJ: Princeton University Press, 1999), 12–13.
12 See Carson, *Economy of the Unlost*, 18–22.
13 Hans-Georg Gadamer, 'The Relevance of the Beautiful: Art as Play, Symbol and Festival', in *The Relevance of the Beautiful and Other Essays*, ed. Robert Bernasconi and trans. Nicholas Walker (Cambridge: Cambridge University Press, 1986), 31. Here Gadamer refers to the *symbolon* as a *tessera hospitalis*.
14 See Carson, *Economy of the Unlost*, 18.
15 Henri Focillon, 'In Praise of Hands', trans. S. L. Faison Jnr, in *The Life of Forms in Art* (New York: George Wittenborn Shultz, 1948), 78.
16 Aristotle, *Rhetoric* (1410b10–13), quoted in Anne Carson, 'Essay on What I Think about Most', in *Men in the Off Hours* (New York: Knopf, 2000), 30.
17 Aristotle, *Rhetoric* (3.2.1405a34), quoted in Anne Carson, *Eros the Bittersweet* (Champaign, MA: Dalkey Archive Press, 1998), 73.
18 *The Oxford English Dictionary* defines 'epiphora' as: 'A sudden afflux of humours; *esp.* "a superabundant flow of tears, or of an aqueous or serous humour from the eyes"'. *The Oxford English Dictionary*, www.oed.com/viewdictionaryentry/Entry /63456. Accessed 29 June 2011. The concept of the threshold, as such, could be said to be implicit within *epiphora*. Indeed, Benjamin, in German, termed the threshold as *Schwelle*, which, he claimed, shares a certain correspondence with our word 'sill'. As he was to note: 'The threshold must be carefully distinguished from the boundary. A *Schwelle* "threshold" is a zone. Transformation, passage, wave action are in the word *schwellen*, swell and etymology ought not to overlook these senses.' Walter Benjamin, *The Arcades Project*, trans. Howard Eiland and Kevin McLaughlin (Cambridge, MA: Belknap Press of Harvard University Press, 2004), [O2a,1]. But as Weber notes: '[t]he association made here by Benjamin [between *Schwelle* and *schwellen*] has no basis in etymology, even though he suggests that it does. [...] According to Duden's Etymological Dictionary (*Herkunftwörterbuch*), *Schwelle* is etymologically associated with the English, *sill*, whereas *schwellen* is derived from roots cognate with the English, *swell*.' Samuel Weber, '"Streets, Squares, Theatres": A City on the Move – Walter Benjamin's Paris', in *Benjamin's -abilities* (Cambridge, MA: Harvard University Press, 2008), 351, n. 7. Also refer to *The Arcades Project*, 991, n. 4.

76 Image | Word

19 Samuel Taylor Coleridge, *Collected Works of Samuel T. Coleridge*, quoted in W. J. T. Mitchell, *Picture Theory: Essays on Verbal and Visual Presentation* (Chicago: University of Chicago Press, 1994), 115, n. 9.
20 Gaston Bachelard, *The Poetics of Space*, trans. Maria Jolas (Boston, MA: Beacon Press, 1969), 75. Emphasis in Bachelard.
21 Viktor Shklovsky, 'The Structure of Fiction', in *Theory of Prose*, trans. Benjamin Sher (Normal, IL: Dalkey Archive Press, 1991), 62.
22 Anne Carson, *Eros the Bittersweet* (Champaign, MA: Dalkey Archive Press, 1998), 73. Emphasis added.
23 Marcel Proust, 'Within a Budding Grove', quoted in George Stambolian, *Marcel Proust and the Creative Endeavour* (Chicago: University of Chicago Press, 1972), 207. Here Stambolian substitutes 'image' for Moncrieff's 'picture'.
24 Georg Simmel, 'The Stranger', in *The Sociology of Georg Simmel*, ed. and trans. Kurt H. Wolff (Glencoe, IL: Free Press, 1950), 404.
25 Simmel, 'The Stranger', 402.
26 See Georg Simmel, 'Bridge and Door', *Lotus International* 47 (1985): 52–6.
27 Hannah Arendt, 'Introduction: Walter Benjamin: 1892–1940', in Walter Benjamin, *Illuminations: Essays and Reflections*, ed. Hannah Arendt and trans. Harry Zohn (New York, Schoken Books, 1969), 13.
28 Paul Valéry quoted in Peter Zumthor, 'Body and Image', in *Archipelago: Essays on Architecture for Juhani Pallasmaa*, ed. Peter MacKeith (Helsinki: Rakennustieto Oy, 2006), 201. As Arendt has noted: 'the sheer naming of things, the creation of words, is the human way of *appropriating* and, as it were, disalienating the world into which, after all, each of us is born as a newcomer and a stranger'. Hannah Arendt, *The Life of the Mind* (San Diego, CA: Harcourt, 1978), 100. Emphasis in Arendt.
29 Siegfried Kracauer, 'Photography', in *The Mass Ornament: Weimar Essays*, ed. and trans. Thomas Y. Levin (Cambridge, MA: Harvard University Press, 1995), 58.
30 See Georg Simmel, 'The Metropolis and Mental Life', in *The Sociology of Georg Simmel*, ed. and trans. Kurt H. Wolff (Glencoe, IL: Free Press, 1950), 410.
31 See Walter Benjamin, 'The Work of Art in the Age of Mechanical Reproduction', in *Illuminations: Essays and Reflections*, ed. Hannah Arendt and trans. Harry Zohn (New York: Schocken Books, 1969), 223.
32 Simmel, 'Metropolis and Mental Life', 414.
33 Walter Benjamin, Little History of Photography', trans. Edmund Jephcott and Kingsley Shorter, in *Selected Writings*, Volume 2, Part 2: *1931–1934*, ed. Michael W. Jennings, Howard Eiland and Gary Smith (Cambridge, MA: Belknap Press of Harvard University Press, 2005), 527.
34 See Benjamin, 'Little History of Photography', 510.
35 László Moholy-Nagy, 'Production-Reproduction', in *Photography in the Modern Era: European Documents and Critical Writings, 1913–1940*, ed. Christopher Phillips (New York: Aperture, 1989), 80. Emphasis in Moholy-Nagy.

36 Benjamin, 'Work of Art', 236. For a further discussion of the close-up, see, for example, Dawn Ades and Simon Barker, *Close-Up: Proximity and Defamiliarisation in Art, Film and Photography*, exhibition catalogue (Edinburgh: Fruitmarket Gallery, 2008).
37 Manfredo Tafuri and Francesco dal Co, *Modern Architecture*, vol. 2, trans. Robert Erich Wolf (New York: Rizzoli, 1986), 312.
38 Benjamin, *Arcades Project*, [M16a,4].
39 See David Leatherbarrow, 'The Image and its Setting: Or How Topography Traces Praxis', in *Topographical Stories: Studies in Landscape and Architecture* (Philadelphia, PA: University of Pennsylvania Press, 2004), 204.
40 See Eduardo Cadava, *Words of Light: Theses on the Photography of History* (Princeton, NJ: Princeton University Press, 1997), 63.
41 Leatherbarrow, 'Image and its Setting', 204.
42 Walter Benjamin, 'First Sketches', in *The Arcades Project*, trans. Howard Eiland and Kevin McLaughlin (Cambridge, MA: Belknap Press of Harvard University Press, 2004), [D°, 4].
43 Samuel Weber, 'Translatability II: Afterlife', in *Benjamin's -abilities* (Cambridge, MA: Harvard University Press, 2008), 81.
44 See Samuel Weber, 'Impart-ability: Language as Medium', in *Benjamin's -abilities* (Cambridge, MA: Harvard University Press, 2008), 34. Interestingly, the origins of the word 'shuttle' derive from the same origins as 'to shoot'. See *The Oxford English Dictionary*, www.oed.com/viewdictionaryentry/Entry/ 179072. Accessed 11 October 2011.
45 See Michael Jennings, 'Photography', in Walter Benjamin, *The Work of Art in the Age of its Technological Reproducibility, and other Writings on Media*, ed. Michael W. Jennings, Brigid Doherty and Thomas Y. Levin (Cambridge, MA: Belknap Press of Harvard University Press, 2008), 264.
46 Jeff Malpas, 'Repetitions', in *Repetitions*, exhibition catalogue (Hobart: Plimsoll Gallery, University of Tasmania, 2008), 7.
47 Walter Benjamin, 'Berlin Chronicle', trans. Edmund Jephcott, in *Selected Writings*, Volume 2, Part 2: *1931–1934*, ed. Michael W. Jennings, Howard Eiland and Gary Smith (Cambridge, MA: Belknap Press of Harvard University Press, 2005), 633.

Bibliography

Ades, Dawn and Simon Barker. *Close-Up: Proximity and Defamiliarisation in Art, Film and Photography*. Exhibition Catalogue. Edinburgh: Fruitmarket Gallery, 2008.
Anderson, Fiona. 'Spinning the Ephemeral with the Sublime: Modernity and Landscape in Men's Fashion Textiles 1860–1900', *Fashion Theory* 9, no. 3 (2005): 283–304.
Arendt, Hannah. 'Introduction: Walter Benjamin: 1892–1940'. In Walter Benjamin, *Illuminations: Essays and Reflections*. Edited by Hannah Arendt and translated by Harry Zohn, 1–55. New York: Schocken Books, 1969.
———. *The Life of the Mind*. San Diego, CA: Harcourt, 1978.

Bachelard, Gaston. *The Poetics of Space*. Translated by Maria Jolas. Boston, MA: Beacon Press, 1969.

Bannal. *Bho Dhòrn gu Dòrn*. (DVD and CD). Portree, Isle of Skye: Macmeanmna, 2006.

Benjamin, Walter. 'The Work of Art in the Age of Mechanical Reproduction'. In *Illuminations: Essays and Reflections*. Edited by Hannah Arendt and translated by Harry Zohn, 217–52. New York: Schocken Books, 1969.

———. *The Arcades Project*. Translated by Howard Eiland and Kevin McLaughlin. Cambridge, MA: Belknap Press of Harvard University Press, 2004.

———. 'Berlin Chronicle'. Translated by Edmund Jephcott. In *Selected Writings*, Volume 2, Part 2: *1931–1934*. Edited by Michael W. Jennings, Howard Eiland and Gary Smith, 595–637. Cambridge, MA: Belknap Press of Harvard University Press, 2005.

———. 'Little History of Photography'. Translated by Edmund Jephcott and Kingsley Shorter. In *Selected Writings*, Volume 2, Part 2: *1931–1934*. Edited by Michael W. Jennings, Howard Eiland and Gary Smith, 505–30. Cambridge, MA: Belknap Press of Harvard University Press, 2005.

Cadava, Eduardo. *Words of Light: Theses on the Photography of History*. Princeton, NJ: Princeton University Press, 1997.

Campbell, J. L., ed. *Hebridean Folksongs: A Collection of Waulking Songs by Donald MacCormick in Kilphedir in South Uist in the Year 1863*. London: Oxford University Press, 1969.

Carson, Anne. *Eros the Bittersweet*. Champaign, MA: Dalkey Archive Press, 1998.

———. *Economy of the Unlost (Reading Simonides of Keos with Paul Celan)*. Princeton, NJ: Princeton University Press, 1999.

———. 'Essay on What I Think about Most'. In *Men in the Off Hours*, 30–5. New York: Knopf, 2000.

Eriskay: A Poem of Remote Lives. Directed by Werner Kissling. http://movingimage.nls.uk/film/1701. Accessed 18 March 2016.

Focillon, Henri. 'In Praise of Hands'. Translated by S. L. Faison Jnr. In *The Life of Forms in Art*, 65–78. New York: George Wittenborn Schultz, 1948.

Gadamer, Hans-Georg. 'The Relevance of the Beautiful: Art as Play, Symbol and Festival'. In *The Relevance of the Beautiful and Other Essays*. Edited by Robert Bernasconi and translated by Nicholas Walker, 1–53. Cambridge: Cambridge University Press, 1986.

Harper, Catherine and McDougall, Kirsty. 'The Very Recent Fall and Rise of Harris Tweed', *Textile: The Journal of Cloth and Culture* 10, no. 1 (2012): 78–99.

Hunter, Janet. *The Islanders and the Orb: The History of the Harris Tweed Industry 1835–1995*. Stornoway: Acair, 2001.

Jennings, Michael. 'Photography'. In Walter Benjamin, *The Work of Art in the Age of its Technological Reproducibility, and other Writings on Media*. Edited by Michael W. Jennings, Brigid Doherty and Thomas Y. Levin, 263–9. Cambridge, MA: Belknap Press of Harvard University Press, 2008.

Kracauer, Siegfried. 'Photography'. In *The Mass Ornament: Weimar Essays*. Edited and translated by Thomas Y. Levin, 46–63. Cambridge, MA: Harvard University Press, 1995.

Leatherbarrow, David. 'The Image and its Setting: Or How Topography Traces Praxis'. In *Topographical Stories: Studies in Landscape and Architecture*, 200–34. Philadelphia, PA: University of Pennsylvania Press, 2004.

———. 'Levelling the Land: Or How Topography is the Horizon of Horizons'. In *Topographical Stories: Studies in Landscape and Architecture*, 114–30. Philadelphia, PA: University of Pennsylvania Press, 2004.

MacKellar, Mary. 'The Waulking Day', *Transactions of the Gaelic Society of Inverness* 13 (1886–7): 201–17.

Malpas, Jeff. 'Repetitions'. In *Repetitions*. Exhibition Catalogue, 6–20. Hobart: Plimsoll Gallery, University of Tasmania, 2008.

Mitchell, W. J. T. *Picture Theory: Essays on Verbal and Visual Presentation*. Chicago: University of Chicago Press, 1994.

Moholy-Nagy, László. 'Production–Reproduction'. In *Photography in the Modern Era: European Documents and Critical Writings, 1913–1940*. Edited by Christopher Phillips, 79–82. New York: Aperture, 1989.

Shklovsky, Viktor. 'The Structure of Fiction'. In *Theory of Prose*. Translated by Benjamin Sher, 52–71. Normal, IL: Dalkey Archive Press, 1991.

Simmel, Georg. 'The Metropolis and Mental Life'. In *The Sociology of Georg Simmel*. Edited and translated by Kurt H. Wolff, 409–24. Glencoe, IL: Free Press, 1950.

———. 'The Stranger'. In *The Sociology of Georg Simmel*. Edited and translated by Kurt H. Wolff, 402–8. Glencoe, IL: Free Press, 1950.

———. 'Bridge and Door', *Lotus International* 47 (1985): 52–6.

Stambolian, George. *Marcel Proust and the Creative Endeavour*. Chicago: University of Chicago Press, 1972.

Tafuri, Manfredo and Francesco Dal Co. *Modern Architecture*, vol. 2. Translated by Robert Erich Wolf. New York: Rizzoli, 1986.

Thompson, Francis. *Harris Tweed: The Story of a Hebridean Industry*. Newton Abbot: David and Charles, 1969.

'Tweed: Trouble Looms'. Directed by Ian Denyer. *This is Scotland*. Glasgow: BBC 4, 8 September 2009.

Weber, Samuel. 'Impart-ability: Language as Medium'. In *Benjamin's -abilities*, 31–52. Cambridge, MA: Harvard University Press, 2008.

———. '"Streets, Squares, Theatres": A City on the Move – Walter Benjamin's Paris'. In *Benjamin's -abilities*, 227–39. Cambridge, MA: Harvard University Press, 2008.

———. 'Translatability II: Afterlife'. In *Benjamin's -abilities*, 79–94. Cambridge, MA: Harvard University Press, 2008.

Zumthor, Peter. 'Body and Image'. In *Archipelago: Essays on Architecture for Juhani Pallasmaa*. Edited by Peter MacKeith, 200–11. Helsinki: Rakennustieto Oy, 2006.

Surface

Figure 5.1 S. Albany Newall, *Men Stretching and Rolling Up a Length of Harris Tweed*, c. 1920.

Pattern

Figure 5.2 Gisela Vogler, *Marion Campbell, Hanging Tweeds Out to Dry*, n.d.

The world was stripped of its surface, of its skin, and the skin was spread flat on the flatness of the picture plane.

Clement Greenberg

Life is to be recreated so that it will of necessity express itself as a pattern.
Friedrich Nietzsche

84 *Surface | Pattern*

An ancient myth of origin tells us that a cloth was once woven, its surface depicting the earth with its continents and seas, and was then presented as a nuptial gift, a means of salutation, such attire when worn thus enabling the world to appear. No longer formless and emergent, it took shape and was distinguished from the chaos and darkness that preceded it. Transformational, this vestment wedded the heights with the depths, while simultaneously dividing all that lay above from that which lay below, a horizon hence established, planarity necessary for its reading.[1] A seam and distant border joining once separated planes, the horizon enables the unity and flow of life to be experienced, not as a fixed and rigid boundary, but as something that moves with us, calling us to advance. Marking the limits of the range of vision, the horizon locates all that falls into view, visible from a particular perspective, establishing a certain stand point. Place, it is said, in one of its formulations, is understood as flat, *plateia*, suggestive of an open space, a broad way,[2] necessarily delimited within a field of vision, fleeting or otherwise fixed, severed from the unity of nature, partial to a larger fabric, even so.

So close, so familiar, however, is the ground, the horizontal plane on which we stand, that our eyes rarely rest upon it to ponder.[3] This has not always been the case though: in the nineteenth century the woven surface of the carpet was very much in focus.[4]

Semper conceived 'the absolute concept of a horizontal surface in terms of a smooth carpet spread out on the floor',[5] a plane differentiated from its surrounds, mats and rugs establishing the terrain, hung upright, guarding against the inclemency of the weather, setting apart one's property, partitioning the spaces within and containing them.[6] On a grander scale, carpets once contributed to the festival spirit, laid out to mark the *dromos*, the course which a pageant would follow, a carpet thus unfurled recalling a surface once designated for deities alone, the *pegmata*, perpendicular to it, a figural backdrop displayed.[7]

Flatness was tantamount to the design of the carpet's surface, its delineation, whether drawn from nature or otherwise, was to display no shading or any other indication of depth liable to challenge the seamless figure–ground relationship; its design, in accordance, capable of being composed of simple shapes,[8] a geometry amenable to the loom. 'Naturalistic subjects', and their rendering as such, were said to 'violate decorative principles' lying in contradiction to the very planarity of the surface.[9] For '*surface ornamentation* arises from the basic idea of the *surface* as such and accordingly reaffirms it'. The design of a carpet, in keeping with this tenet, was subject to an '"all-over" treatment', the movement between the edge of the carpet and its centre to be captured and conveyed in a 'concentric or radial arrangement, or a mixture of the two', its polychrome patterning in agreement with the principles of 'regular distribution' or 'subordination and hierarchy', the former despite luxuriousness generating monotony, the latter through variation in intensification, highlighting dominant elements, a 'unity in diversity' created through the combination of contesting forces artfully woven. Edging and borders were symbolic of the frame, mediating between ideal centre and perimeter, 'enclos[ing] and encircl[ing] the carpet' when completed, further delineating its limits, its beginning or its end in encountering the room. The finishing of a carpet, its fringes, were deemed significant, 'extend[ing] beyond the fabric [...] twisted together and knotted to prevent unravelling',[10] a device established through which the horizon is recalled.[11]

Reoriented and alternatively composed, 'hanging carpets', colourful and woven, were said to be 'the true walls, the visible boundaries of space',[12] place constructed and enclosed, the movement captured in the design, no longer radial or 'all-over', but 'up and down', serving further to emphasise the vertical orientation, this turning from a prone to an upright position conceivably hinged. While upright surfaces, rigid and load-bearing, and those that were hung were by and large similar, their termination was to be expressed differently, the rigid form countering gravity, its upper border embellished at its head, the draping fabric in agreement, ornamented at its lower end.[13]

The basis of all representations of the cosmos, the carpet, we are told, was to play a central role in the history of art.[14]

> Yet it is both logical and appropriate that paintings were associated with true embroidered carpets in such a way that each could, to a certain extent, be identified with the other. And why should parts of the *pegmata* – namely, the frames stretched with canvas – not also have been called *tabulae*, or even, in Greek, *pinakes*, as these expressions, at least in their later, improper usage, refer only to the formal concept of a surface suited to painting or sculpture and no longer to the material. In modern languages the words *Schilderei*, *Tafel*, *toile*, *quadre*, *fraim*, and tablet are abstractions; no thought at all is given to the three-dimensional object but only to the image presented – the paint on the framed surface. The concept of *Täfelung* is not only similar to what ancient writers meant by the words *tabula*, *pinax*, *abacus*, and *crusta* but also very close to the more general art-technical expressions picture and *graphe*. And it has grown closer to the aesthetic concept of painting than modern surface decoration has, to the extent that ancient paint was part of wall decoration and its style was and remained panel painting.[15]

While *tableau* was understood as a painting, in architecture it was also to refer to 'elevations, doorways, windows and casements', surfaces replete with openings, in which two aspects of the same word are contained, bounded by the concept of the frame.[16] For, without a frame, it is said, nothing can be woven, the loom establishing a spatial limit from which the surface and its decorative designs can emerge.[17]

Michel-Eugène Chevreul (1786–1889), Director of Dyes at the Gobelins Tapestry Works, was concerned with the design of hanging carpets, tapestries,[18] the nature of colour central to his investigations. His treatise, *The Principles of Harmony and Contrast of Colours and their Application to the Arts* (1839), was published the year the invention of photography was announced and, according to one report, the self-same year in which Harris Tweed was originally commissioned.[19] The result of an extensive series of experiments which he was exhorted to formulate, the outcomes of his research were to exert considerable influence upon painting, as well as the mechanical or industrial arts, the design of the interior of the Crystal Palace an early exemplar of its application.[20] His fundamental premise, founded upon the interaction of colours when juxtaposed, was encapsulated thus:

> I beg the reader never forget when it is asserted of the phenomena of simultaneous contrast, that one colour placed beside another receives such modifications from it, that this manner of speaking does not mean that the two colours, or rather the two material objects that present them to us, have a mutual action, either physical or chemical; it is really only applied to the modification that takes place before us when we perceive the simultaneous impression of these two colours.[21]

The weavers of the Hebridean Isles know this principle well, knowledge innate, handed down, and drawn from the crucible of experience, colours combined, patterns devised, the tried and true result of experiment.[22] Columns of warp threads colour varying are crossed with spandrels of weft also diverse, in the weaving a test-screen of sorts emerging.[23] From the early twentieth century pattern books were arranged gridded with samples of Harris Tweed, all variation and combination, subtlety and contrast apparent in the patternings, page upon page, gridded with fabric samples and their codes.[24] Four weaves, in general, predominate, one in which the warp and weft are of the same colour; the 'two-by-two' weave, in which 'two threads of one colour are followed by two threads in a different colour in the warp', the 'herringbone' weave in which one colour in the warp is contrasted with another in the weft; the loom set up to accommodate a variation on the 'herringbone', the 'diamond' or 'Bird's Eye' pattern; though others such as tartans and variable checks are often worked, the skill of the weaver, inventiveness, evidenced in the web.[25]

A survey of curtain walls similarly composed was published in a special issue of *Architectural Review* entitled 'Machine Made America' (1957), the façades within categorised and catalogued according to their surface articulation, the emphasis on appearance.[26] This review too was founded upon a fascination with pattern, with the facture of the surface featuring, its means of classification premised upon the interplay between structure and skin. Four types were registered, reminiscent of weaves: 'sheath' walls, in which no structural elements were indicated on the exterior skin; 'grid' walls, in which horizontal and vertical framing elements were expressed with equal weighting; 'mullion' walls, with the emphasis on vertical elements stressed; and 'spandrel' walls, in which horizontal elements predominated.[27]

Presented as a series of diagrammatic surfaces, all dimensionality was mitigated, displaying a 'fetish for flatness',[28] the superficial interaction between the profiles of mullions and columns amidst the sheathing catalogued, the variance in their projection merely indexed in the fall of the barest of shadows, in the unavoidably perspectival rendering of the camera. Like a series of portraits, the purpose of the photographic survey sought to emphasise traits, conveying rhythms and their modulations in the articulation of built surfaces. Colour did not feature, though materiality was engaged with, the focus by and large on the structure of the weave, the surface effect of warp and weft, and its enveloping of a range of typologies, a homogenising vernacular.

Weaving, it has been observed, 'consists of the interlacing *at right angles* by one series of filaments or threads, known as the weft [...] of another series, known as the warp, both being in the same plane',[29] the grid a natural consequence of its making. Emblematic of modernity, the grid in modern art, with particular reference to painting, was said to be 'autonomous and autotelic',[30] an end in itself, self-referential, its formalist drive enlarging and reframing the very structure of its substrate. Conceivably cut from a larger fabric or alternatively introjecting its very framing onto itself, a patterned surface emerged, its referent obscured, colour liminally applied, adorning the canvas as it concealed it.[31]

> For the grid follows the canvas surface, doubles it. It is a representation of the surface, mapped, it is true, onto the same surface it represents, but even so, the grid remains a figure, picturing various aspects of the 'originary' object: through its mesh it creates an image of the woven infrastructure of the canvas; through its network of coordinates it organises a metaphor for the plane geometry of the field; through its repetition it configures the spread of lateral continuity. The grid thus does not reveal the surface, laying it bare at last; rather it veils it through a repetition.[32]

88 *Surface | Pattern*

A valorisation of flatness, the gridded surface, as such, was conceived of as the apotheosis of ornament's erasure, or conversely as the very transformation of works of art into ornament absolute,[33] the surface becoming 'the basis of composition, [...] the human eye aw[akening] to the spectacle of form, line, and colour',[34] the whole grammar of design engaged. Stretched and tautened, the repeat of the motif was not limited to the surface of the canvas alone, for the work of art was merely one surface among the many.

Unfolding the adjacent surfaces of an interior, flattening them out on the same plane, De Stijl artists and architects[35] developed the surface,[36] 'new design' as it was termed, embracing the potential of the surface's make-up. Primary colours, red, blue and yellow, perceived as objective, were perpendicularly applied, the surface then enfolded, the spatial consequences of its enveloping divulged through its surface emanations. Fluctuating between cartographic and orthographic modes, the hierarchy between painting and architecture was thus allayed, the gridded surface becoming vitalised, enlivened and lived, the wall dematerialising,[37] via the placement of 'man *within* the painting', rather than 'in front of it'.[38] For ultimately, it was thought that it is '*only the [...] surface which defines architecture*, since man does not live within the construction, but within an *atmosphere* that has been established by the [...] surface',[39] scenes of daily life performed in and amidst a series of changing *tableaux vivants*.

Between the late 1930s and 1950s, a move towards a 'synthesis between painting and architecture' was foregrounded,[40] the mural playing a central role, its polychrome patterning dematerialising the structure and solidity of the wall, while at the same time subverting the nature of decoration, understood, then, as recidivist.[41] For the skin, as the laminar surface of the mural might be conceived, was not merely a painterly envelope, but rather a 'quivering [surface] under the thrust of internal reliefs which [sought] to come up into space and revel in the light, [...] the evidence of a mass convulsed' by secreted movements, to its very depths.[42]

Traversing between canvas, mural and polychrome wall, the architect and painter Le Corbusier (1887–1965) drew from the writings of Semper appropriating them for *l'esprit nouveau*, polychromy presented as a feature necessary for modern life. Colour in its conquest of the wall, differing in hue between them, was seen to reallocate their partitioning, the ordering of their positioning affecting the plan as much as the elevation, multicoloured murals exploding the wall instead, its fragments of colour dispersed,[43] the rendering of the detail of the mural and the scale of polychrome architecture conceivably a matter of degree. In his encounters with tapestry, however, this distinction between the colourful wall and the mural, so often made, was overturned, the focus no longer on the play between surfaces but concentrated within one, the multicoloured weave of the tapestry synoptic, 'join[ing] the polychrome scheme in making space "palpitate," becoming "integral to the architecture" it might merely decorate'.[44]

Separable and transportable, portable domestic furnishings, we are told, were the antecedents to the monumental building,[45] a transference conveyed in the French terms for furniture and building, *meuble* (literally movable), *immeuble* (literally immovable), respectively.[46] While the mural was seen to mobilise the wall, the wall regardless remaining fixed in place, the mobility of tapestry displaced the need for a permanent frame, its surface itinerant and liberated, in establishing its own limits. The mobility of the surface was thus extolled, the tapestry, or *Muralnomad*, as Le Corbusier would refer to it, accommodating the increasingly nomadic character of modern life.

> Our nomad moves because his family increases in number, or, on the contrary, because his children have married. Tapestry gives him the opportunity to possess a 'mural', that is, a large painting of architectural potential. He unrolls the tapestry and spreads it on the wall such that it touches the ground. Is he moving? He will roll up his mural, tuck it under his arm and go down the stairs to install it in his [new] shelter.[47]

Modern man was thus seen to journey with his hanging carpets and wares, 'wrapping himself in colour',[48] such trekking enfolded recalling the *feileadh mhor*, the ancient garb of the Hebrideans and that of their Highland *confrères*. In correspondence, co-ordinating with the landscape, this large wrap, a belted plaid, was first spread out on the ground, a belt placed beneath it, the swathe of cloth then pleated along its length, its wearer lying atop it arranging its folds, securing the belt about his waist in advance of standing. Erect a pleated skirt was thence arrayed, the mantle above the belt variously arranged, shrouding the upper body or otherwise draped 'allow[ing] the arms complete freedom of movement' during the course of activities.[49] At day's end the belt was released, one's diurnal attire becoming a nocturnal sheath, a blanketing safeguard from the elements.

'Place', it is said, 'is thought to be some surface and like a vessel and surrounder';[50] and in one of its manifestations *chōra* is translated as a room. Its aspects, though seemingly diminutive, are experienced through roaming, *chōrein*, understood in this sense, meaning 'to go'.[51] The Greeks, we are told, on leaving their homeland to colonise and settle, were farewelled with the famous phrase: 'Wherever you go, you will be a *polis*,'[52] no longer enclosed by their city, wrapped within its walls, they nonetheless 'moved "in context"', as it were, within a nexus of kinships and social patterns for which the physical fabric of [the *polis*] was a metaphor'. As such, it was not so much a sense of being 'anchored in a specific place, but also [of] having a life within it', activity inextricable from being so.[53]

Establishing a sense of place, man, it is said, projects himself onto the wall,[54] the floor capturing his shadow in the casting, a small room sometimes appended in the form of a camera, its interior containing facets of light inscribed and captured in the journeying. In confronting a well-written room composed of carpets, whether literally or conceptually arrayed, the import of one's of surroundings, regardless, must be grasped instinctively, moved by the detail of the patterning and engaged. For:

> In looking at a carpet, by following one colour a certain pattern is suggested, by following another colour, another: so in life the seer should watch that pattern among general things which his idiosyncrasy moves him to observe.[55]

Notes

1. This is the wedding story of Zas and Cthonie told by the Pre-Socratic historian Pherekydes of Syros (c. 600–c. 550 B.C.). See John Scheid and Jesper Svenbro, *The Craft of Zeus: Myths of Weaving and Fabric*, trans. Carol Volk (Cambridge, MA: Harvard University Press, 1996), 63–6.
2. See J. E. Malpas, *Place and Experience: A Philosophical Topography* (Cambridge: Cambridge University Press, 1999), 22.
3. See for example, Hagi Kenaan, 'The Ground's Hidden Surface', *Wolkenkuckucksheim: International Journal of Architectural Theory* 12, no. 1 (2007) www.cloud-cuckoo.net/openarchive/wolke/eng/Subjects/071/Kenaan/kenaan.htm. Accessed 23 March 2016.
4. See, for example, Joseph Masheck, 'The Carpet Paradigm: Critical Prolegomena to a Theory of Flatness', *Arts Magazine* 51 (1976): 82–109; and Margaret Olin, 'Self-Representation: Resemblance and Convention in Two Nineteenth-Century Theories of Architecture and the Decorative Arts', *Zeitschrift für Kunstgeschichte* 49, no. 3 (1986): 376–97.
5. Gottfried Semper, *Style in the Technical and Tectonic Arts: or, Practical Aesthetics*, trans. Harry Francis Mallgrave and Michael Robinson (Los Angeles: Getty Research Institute, 2004), 131.
6. Gottfried Semper, 'The Four Elements of Architecture: A Contribution to the Comparative Study of Architecture', in *The Four Elements of Architecture and Other Writings*, trans. Harry Francis Mallgrave and Wolfgang Herrmann (Cambridge: Cambridge University Press, 1989), 103.
7. See Semper, *Style*, 283–4.
8. See Olin, 'Self-Representation', 380.
9. Semper quoting from Richard Redgrave, 'Supplementary Report on Design', cited in Olin, 'Self-Representation', 379.
10. Semper, *Style*, 126–40. Emphasis in Semper.

11 See Hans-Georg Gadamer, *Truth and Method*, 2nd ed. rev., trans. Joel Weinsheimer and Donald G. Marshall (London: Continuum, 2004), 245. As Gadamer notes, Husserl's concept of the horizon springs from a textile motif, William James's discussion of 'fringes'. See 245–6, n. 148.
12 Semper, 'Four Elements of Architecture', 104.
13 See Semper, *Style*, 126–31.
14 See Semper, 'Four Elements of Architecture', 103. Semper, perhaps with a sense of false modesty, was to claim that this proposition was put forth 'without the support of a single authority'.
15 Semper, *Style*, 286.
16 See *Dictionnaire des Arts et des Sciences par M. D. C. de l'Académie Française*, vol. 3 (Paris, 1694), s.v. 'Tableau', quoted in Victor I. Stoichita, *The Self-Aware Image: An Insight into Early Modern Meta-Painting*, trans. Anne-Marie Glasheen (Cambridge: Cambridge University Press, 1997), xiii.
17 See Semper, *Style*, 286.
18 It should be noted that the production of tapestries is distinct from woven cloth, such as Harris Tweed, one of the main differences being that the weft does not travel from edge to edge in one pass. For a further discussion, see 'Tapestry'. In *Oxford Art Online*, www.oxfordartonline.com:80/subscriber/article/ grove/art/T083308. Accessed 30 December 2011.
19 1839 was the year that the invention of photography was announced by Louis-Jacques-Mandé Daguerre to the public at the Academie des Sciences (7 January 1839), and Harris Tweed, in one instance, was reportedly to receive its first commission. See Michel-Eugène Chevreul, *The Principles of Harmony and Contrast of Colours and their Application to the Arts* (New York: Van Nostrand Reinhold, 1981); Geoffrey Batchen, *Burning with Desire: The Conception of Photography* (Cambridge, MA: MIT Press, 1999), 25; and Janet Hunter, *The Islanders and the Orb: The History of the Harris Tweed Industry 1835–1995* (Stornoway: Acair, 2001), 42.
20 See Carol A. Hrvol Flores, *Owen Jones: Design, Ornament, Architecture, and Theory in the Age of Transition* (New York: Rizzoli, 2006), 245.
21 Michel-Eugène Chevreul, *The Principles of Harmony and Contrast of Colours and Applications to the Arts*, quoted in William W. Braham, 'Solidity of the Mask: Colour Contrasts in Modern Architecture', *Res: Journal of Anthropology and Aesthetics* 39 (2001): 194. Semper discusses and briefly elaborates on this effect, having read Chevreul, in *Style*, 163–4, n. 12.
22 Weavers sometimes experimented with odd bobbins of colour at the end of the web. See Gisela Vogler, *A Harris Way of Life: Marion Campbell (1909–1996)* (West Tarbert: Harris Voluntary Service, 2002), 31.
23 As part of a tour of the Harris Tweed Hebrides mill in Shawbost, I was fortunate to see some of these test weaves, which were reminiscent of television test patterns from the 1970s. My thanks to Kelly Kennedy for generously showing me around the mill and for sharing with me her insightful knowledge of contemporary Harris Tweed production.
24 My thanks to Ronnie MacKenzie, custodian of the Lewis Loom Centre, Stornoway, who generously allowed me to view these books.

92 *Surface | Pattern*

25 See Vogler, *A Harris Way of Life*, 31.
26 '[T]he first classification of curtain walls should be based on appearance.' 'Syntax: Contributions of the Curtain Wall to a New Vernacular', quoted in Reinhold Martin, *The Organizational Complex: Architecture, Media and Corporate Space* (Cambridge, MA: MIT Press, 2003), 99.
27 See Martin, *Organizational Complex*, 99.
28 'Syntax: The Contribution of the Curtain Wall to a New Vernacular', quoted in Martin, *Organizational Complex*, 102. As Martin notes, Mies van der Rohe's 'Lake Shore Drive Apartments' (1948), and his later buildings, by extension, were an exception to this rule.
29 H. Ling Roth, 'Studies in Primitive Looms', quoted in Indra Kagis McEwen, *Socrates' Ancestor: An Essay in Architectural Beginnings* (Cambridge, MA: MIT Press, 1993), 83. Emphasis in McEwen.
30 Krauss, 'Grids', 52.
31 See Krauss, 'Grids', 60–1. This sense of opening out, but also in, recalls the very nature of place. As Malpas observes: 'Every place opens up, not merely outward to other places, but also inwards, to the places that are found within it.' Jeff Malpas, 'Repetitions', in *Repetitions*, exhibition catalogue (Hobart: Plimsoll Gallery, University of Tasmania, 2008), 15.
32 Rosalind Krauss, 'The Originality of the Avant-Garde: A Postmodernist Repetition', *October* 18 (1981): 57.
33 See Mark C. Taylor, *Hiding* (Chicago: University of Chicago Press, 1997), 107.
34 Sigfried Giedion, *Space, Time and Architecture: The Growth of a New Tradition*, quoted in Janet Ward, *Weimar Surfaces: Urban Visual Culture in 1920's Germany* (Berkeley, CA: University of California Press, 2001), 55.
35 It is said that the De Stijl artists took their name from Semper's *Der Stil*, or *Style*, as it is referred to in English. See Masheck, 'Carpet Paradigm', 99.
36 This kind of drawing is referred to as a 'developed surface interior'. As Evans observes: 'In descriptive geometry, folding out the adjacent surfaces of a three-dimensional body so that all its faces can be shown on a sheet of paper is called developing a surface, so we will call [this] kind of drawing [...] the *developed surface interior*.' Robin Evans, 'The Developed Surface: An Enquiry into the Brief Life of an Eighteenth-Century Drawing Technique', in *Translations from Drawing to Building and Other Essays* (London: Architectural Association, 1997), 202. Emphasis in Evans.
37 See Romy Golan, 'From Monument to *Muralnomad*: The Mural in Modern European Architecture', in *The Built Surface: Architecture and the Pictorial Arts from Romanticism to the Twenty-First Century*, vol. 2, ed. Karen Koehler (Aldershot: Ashgate, 2002), 187.
38 Theo van Doesburg, 'Space, Time and Colour', quoted in Fritz Neumeyer, 'Head First through the Wall: An Approach to the Non-Word "Façade"', *Journal of Architecture* 4 (1999): 252. Emphasis in Neumeyer. As Pollock was to note of his production of paintings on the floor instead of vertically, on an easel or wall: 'On the floor I am more at ease. I feel nearer, more a part of the painting, since this way I can walk around it, work from the four

Surface | Pattern 93

sides and literally be in the painting.' Jackson Pollock, 'Statement – 1947'. In Herschel Browning Chipp, *Theories of Modern Art: A Source Book by Artists and Critics* (Berkeley, CA: University of California Press, 1968), 546.

39 Theo van Doesburg, 'Space, Time and Colour', in *Colour: Documents of Contemporary Art*, ed. David Batchelor (London: Whitechapel and Cambridge, Massachusetts: MIT Press, 2008), 88. Emphasis in van Doesburg. As Wigley notes, for van Doesburg, this concept of the surface was to extend to people's 'features, posture, gait, [and] clothing', and featured in another article in which similar sentiments regarding the surface are expressed. See Theo van Doesburg, 'Stuttgart-Wiessenhof 1927: *Die Wohnung*', quoted in Mark Wigley, *White Walls, Designer Dresses: The Fashioning of Modern Architecture* (Cambridge, MA: MIT Press, 2001), 348.

40 Golan, 'From Monument to *Muralnomad*', 196.

41 See Golan, 'From Monument to *Muralnomad*', 186–7. Golan here refers to Adolf Loos's essay 'Ornament and Crime'.

42 See Henri Focillon, *The Life of Forms in Art*, trans. Charles Becher Hogan and George Kubler (New York: George Wittenborn Schultz, 1948), 25. Focillon here discusses the relationship of the fluid interplay between statues and the space in which they inhabit, describing this as the 'baroque state of all styles'.

43 Le Corbusier, 'Peinture, Sculpture et Architecture Rationale', quoted in Golan, 'From Monument to *Muralnomad*', 194.

44 See Wigley, *White Walls, Designer Dresses*, 252.

45 See Semper, *Style*, 623–4.

46 See Sigfried Giedion, *Mechanisation Takes Command: A Contribution to an Anonymous History*, quoted in Golan, 'From Monument to *Muralnomad*', 202. Benjamin, with reference to the art historian Adolf Behne (1885–1948), also commented on this phenomenon, inversing, however, the order of precedence: 'Movables (furniture) quite clearly developed out of immovables (real estate).' Adolf Behne, *Neues Wohnen – Neues Bauen*, quoted in Walter Benjamin, *The Arcades Project*, trans. Howard Eiland and Kevin McLaughlin (Cambridge, MA: Belknap Press of Harvard University Press, 2004), [I,2].

47 Le Corbusier, 'À Propos de la Tapisserie', quoted in Wigley, *White Walls, Designer Dresses*, 251. As Wigley notes: 'The Semperian sense of space produced by polychrome fabrics became completely literalised in the tapestries that Le Corbusier produced from 1936 onward', 250.

48 Wigley, *White Walls, Designer Dresses*, 251. The philosopher of technology Ernst Kapp (1808–96), who was apparently unaware of Semper's work, proposed that *Bekleidung* be understood as 'a portable habitation'. See Alina Payne, *From Ornament to Object: Genealogies of Architectural Modernism* (New Haven, CT: Yale University Press, 2012), 80.

49 For a further discussion of the *feileadh mhor*, see H. F. McClintock, *Old Highland Dress and Tartans* (Dundalk: W. Tempest Dundalgan Press, 1949), 18–35. Women did not wear the *feileadh mhor* but were instead enshrouded in a large shawl known as the *arisaid*. See George F. Collie, *Highland Dress* (London: Penguin, 1948), 25. Interestingly, Le Corbusier was said to have

94   *Surface | Pattern*

   travelled around the East with a carpet which he often used when sleeping under the stars. See Wigley, *White Walls, Designer Dresses*, 251.
50 Aristotle, *Physics*, quoted in Edward S. Casey, *The Fate of Place: A Philosophical History* (Berkeley, CA: University of California Press, 1997), 53.
51 See Casey, *Fate of Place*, 83.
52 Hannah Arendt, *The Human Condition* (Chicago: University of Chicago Press, 1958), 198.
53 See Rykwert's discussion of Amerindians farmers who moved once the earth they were exploiting was exhausted, taking their culture, its structure and means with them. In the instance of the Greeks, this wholesale migration bears well, it would seem, in light of the body of historical evidence that describes their numerous colonisations and settlements. Joseph Rykwert, 'Topo-philia and -phobia', in *Topophilia and Topophobia: Reflections on Twentieth-Century Human Habitat*, ed. Xing Ruan and Paul Hogben (London: Routledge, 2007), 16–17.
54 See Oskar Bie, *Die Wand und ihre künstlerische Behandlung*, quoted in Neumeyer, 'Head First through the Wall', 250–1. As Breitschmid notes, Bie's essay, translated as 'The Wall and its Artistic Treatment', 'analyses the transformation from the wall of antiquity, to the wall of the Renaissance, forward to the modern wall [...] the fundamental aspect of all wall design [lying in] the overcoming of the wall itself. [...] [Its] dematerialisation [...] is not to be understood [however] as the doing away with material altogether as some modern architects have suggested, [...] instead, it is the dematerialisation in the sense that the wall is not foremost a material expression of the matter but an expression of man's, [...] "desires and dreams".' Markus Breitschmid, *Can Architectural Art-Form Be Designed out of Construction? Carl Boetticher, Gottfried Semper, and Heinrich Woelfflin: A Sketch of Various Investigations on the Nature of 'Tectonic' in Nineteenth-Century Architectural Theory* (Blacksburg, VA: Architecture Edition, 2004), 45.
55 Thomas Hardy, *The Life and Work of Thomas Hardy*, ed. Michael Millgate (London: Macmillan, 1984), 158. Hardy, we might also recall, was an erstwhile architect.

Bibliography

Arendt, Hannah. *The Human Condition*. Chicago: University of Chicago Press, 1958.
Batchen, Geoffrey. *Burning with Desire: The Conception of Photography*. Cambridge, MA: MIT Press, 1999.
Benjamin, Walter. *The Arcades Project*. Translated by Howard Eiland and Kevin McLaughlin. Cambridge, MA: Belknap Press of Harvard University Press, 2004.
Braham, William W. 'Solidity of the Mask: Colour Contrasts in Modern Architecture', *Res: Journal of Anthropology and Aesthetics* 39 (2001): 192–214.

Breitschmid, Markus. *Can Architectural Art-Form Be Designed out of Construction? Carl Boetticher, Gottfried Semper, and Heinrich Woelfflin: A Sketch of Various Investigations on the Nature of 'Tectonic' in Nineteenth-Century Architectural Theory*. Blacksburg, VA: Architecture Edition, 2004.

Casey, Edward S. *The Fate of Place: A Philosophical History*. Berkeley: University of California Press, 1997.

Chevreul, Michel-Eugène. *The Principles of Harmony and Contrast of Colours and their Application to the Arts*. New York: Van Nostrand Reinhold, 1981.

Collie, George F. *Highland Dress*. London: Penguin, 1948.

Dunbar, John Telfer. *History of Highland Dress*. London: B. T. Batsford, 1979.

Evans, Robin. 'The Developed Surface: An Enquiry into the Brief Life of an Eighteenth-Century Drawing Technique'. In *Translations from Drawing to Building and Other Essays*, 195–231. London: Architectural Association, 1997.

Flores, Carol A. Hrvol. *Owen Jones: Design, Ornament, Architecture, and Theory in the Age of Transition*. New York: Rizzoli, 2006.

Focillon, Henri. *The Life of Forms in Art*. Translated by Charles Becher Hogan and George Kubler. New York: George Wittenborn Schultz, 1948.

Gadamer, Hans-Georg. *Truth and Method*, 2nd ed. rev. Translated by Joel Weinsheimer and Donald G. Marshall. London: Continuum, 1989.

Giedion, Sigfried. *Mechanization Takes Command: A Contribution to an Anonymous History*. New York: W. W. Norton, 1948.

Golan, Romy, 'From Monument to *Muralnomad*: The Mural in Modern European Architecture'. In *The Built Surface: Architecture and the Pictorial Arts from Romanticism to the Twenty-First Century*, vol. 2. Edited by Karen Koehler, 186–208. Aldershot: Ashgate, 2002.

Hardy, Thomas. *The Life and Work of Thomas Hardy*. Edited by Michael Millgate. London: Macmillan, 1984.

Hunter, Janet. *The Islanders and the Orb: The History of the Harris Tweed Industry 1835–1995*. Stornoway: Acair, 2001.

Kenaan, Hagi. 'The Ground's Hidden Surface', *Wolkenkuckucksheim: International Journal of Architectural Theory* 12, no. 1 (2007) www.cloud-cuckoo.net/openarchive/wolke/eng/Subjects/071/Kenaan/kenaan.htm. Accessed 23 March 2016.

Krauss, Rosalind. 'Grids', *October* 9 (1979): 50–64.

———. 'The Originality of the Avant-Garde: A Postmodernist Repetition', *October* 18 (1981): 47–66.

McClintock, H. F. *Old Highland Dress and Tartans*. Dundalk: W. Tempest Dundalgan Press, 1949.

McEwen, Indra Kagis. *Socrates' Ancestor: An Essay in Architectural Beginnings*. Cambridge, MA: MIT Press, 1993.

Malpas, J. E. *Place and Experience: A Philosophical Topography*. Cambridge: Cambridge University Press, 1999.

———. 'Repetitions'. In *Repetitions*. Exhibition Catalogue, 6–20. Hobart: Plimsoll Gallery, University of Tasmania, 2008.

Martin, Reinhold. *The Organizational Complex: Architecture, Media and Corporate Space*. Cambridge, MA: MIT Press, 2003.

Masheck, Joseph. 'The Carpet Paradigm: Critical Prolegomena to a Theory of Flatness', *Arts Magazine* 51 (1976): 82–109.

Neumeyer, Fritz. 'Head First through the Wall: An Approach to the Non-Word "Façade"', *Journal of Architecture* 4 (1999): 245–59.

Olin, Margaret. 'Self-Representation: Resemblance and Convention in Two Nineteenth-Century Theories of Architecture and the Decorative Arts', *Zeitschrift für Kunstgeschichte* 49, no. 3 (1986): 376–97.

Payne, Alina. *From Ornament to Object: Genealogies of Architectural Modernism*. New Haven, CT: Yale University Press, 2012.

Pollock, Jackson. 'Statement – 1947'. In *Theories of Modern Art: A Source Book by Artists and Critics*. Edited by Herschel B. Chipp, 546–8. Berkeley, CA: University of California Press, 1968.

Rykwert, Joseph. 'Topo-philia and -phobia'. In *Topophilia and Topophobia: Reflections on Twentieth-Century Human Habitat*. Edited by Xing Ruan and Paul Hogben, 12–22. London: Routledge, 2007.

Scheid, John and Jesper Svenbro. *The Craft of Zeus: Myths of Weaving and Fabric*. Translated by Carol Volk. Cambridge, MA: Harvard University Press, 1996.

Semper, Gottfried. 'The Four Elements of Architecture: A Contribution to the Comparative Study of Architecture'. In *The Four Elements of Architecture and Other Writings*. Translated by Harry Francis Mallgrave and Wolfgang Herrmann, 74–129. Cambridge: Cambridge University Press, 1989.

———. *Style in the Technical and Tectonic Arts: or, Practical Aesthetics*. Translated by Harry Francis Mallgrave and Michael Robinson. Los Angeles: Getty Research Institute, 2004.

Stoichita, Victor I. *The Self-Aware Image: An Insight into Early Modern Meta-Painting*. Translated by Anne-Marie Glasheen. Cambridge: Cambridge University Press, 1997.

Taylor, Mark C. *Hiding*. Chicago: University of Chicago Press, 1997.

van Doesburg, Theo. 'Space, Time and Colour'. In *Colour: Documents of Contemporary Art*. Edited by David Batchelor, 84–8. London: Whitechapel and Cambridge, MA: MIT Press, 2008.

Vogler, Gisela. *A Harris Way of Life: Marion Campbell (1909–1996)*. West Tarbert: Harris Voluntary Service, 2002.

Ward, Janet. *Weimar Surfaces: Urban Visual Culture in 1920's Germany*. Berkeley, CA: University of California Press, 2001.

Wigley, Mark. *White Walls, Designer Dresses: The Fashioning of Modern Architecture*. Cambridge, MA: MIT Press, 2001.

Place

Figure 6.1 Edward Burt, *Men Attired in the Feileadh Mhor*, c. 1720.

Dressing

Figure 6.2 Eadweard Muybridge, *Animal Locomotion*, 1887, Plate 428, Detail.

Beings surround themselves with the places where they find themselves, the way one wraps oneself up in a garment.

Georges Poulet

Everything that 'adorns' man can be ordered along a scale in terms of its closeness to the physical body. The 'closest' adornment is typical of nature peoples: tattooing. The opposite extreme is represented by metal and stone adornments, which are entirely unindividual and can be put on everybody.

Georg Simmel

102 *Place | Dressing*

An ancient scribe tells us that the Attic chiton (χιτών) was originally designed by Aeschylus (c. 525–456 B.C.) as a linen or woollen costume to be worn on the stage. This swathe of cloth, elegantly draped, was later to be adopted by priests and torch-bearers, finding itself as an ornament to festivities, thereafter being worn by the populace at large;[1] the prefacing figure, χ (*chi*), reminiscent of a rudimentary signature and a designation of place, the mark of a destination, an address inscribed on a map. Such drapery too, it is said, formed the mainstay of Highland wear, the *feileadh mhor* or large wrap,[2] hitched higher and belted to the body, the tweed's malleable form providing protection from the elements, whilst also operating as a minimal shelter, shrouding the body as a makeshift domicile in the midst of the landscape; the big cloth, Harris Tweed, and the large wrap, one in the same cloth and familiarly interchangeable.

In the waulking song 'This Morning I Have Risen Early' there is a line, '[a]nd in my tartan plaid I fold her',[3] that speaks not only of the tender intimacies of courtship but perhaps even more profoundly of Harris Tweed's authenticity and its inextricable connectedness to place and to the people who inhabit its Isles. The fabric's very situatedness is constitutive of its unique existence, further embodied in its rich history,[4] the customs of which are held fast in oral form, though captured not readily enough through more contemporary means, the tradition regardless continuing to be passed on, and is to this day very much lived.

Traditionally, before the introduction of commercial dyes and the milled carding and spinning of the wool, fleeces were sourced from the Blackface and the Cheviot sheep[5] that wandered the Islands' machair and mountainsides, the fibres further coloured by that land, the tweed's variegated web infused by plants indigenous to it; the mixture of specimens and mordents, recipes closely guarded, passing from one generation to the next, from mother to daughter.[6]

In the Hebrides, the ling heather or *fraoch*, we are told, bequeathed a deep green, stone parmelia or *crotal* lending red, cudbear, *corcar* bestowing purple, woad, *glas-lus* or *guirmean* instilling blue and an intense yellow received from dyer's rocket or *lus-bhuidhe mor*, to name only a handful; the flora staining the wool, the dying undertaken in a large cast iron vat prepared over a fire, amidst the elements, in the open.[7] The different coloured wools were then carded together and spun, additional combinations in hue and tone ensured in the weaving of warp and weft, the scent of the weaver's peat fire further imbuing it; the web itself an iridescent and shifting landscape, sensorial and concinnous, incanted over during the waulking, its surface redolent with histories and local lore. The lovers in the midst of the terrain, enfolded in the *feileadh mhor*, camouflaged and flattened, indistinguishable and blending with it,[8] were one with the land as they were with each other, the cloth, the large wrap, lending visibility through its fine craftsmanship, but drawn from the land, re-immersed in it, now unified. The visible surface, *epiphaneia*, we might recall, is 'coming-to-light', the bearer of 'prominence and impressiveness', qualities conferred upon it by the skilfulness of its weave, its association with conspicuousness, however, of little consequence.[9]

In ancient Greece, *kosmos* in its Homeric form was generally understood as a 'rhythm or an order [...] rediscovered with each new tracing of the figure', as is the case with Harris Tweed, with its endless permutations of patternation and colouration, but the term *kosmēse* was also to signify arranging, ordering and adorning.[10] Manifest in the acts of building and making, the crafted surface, its very appearing, was an acknowledgement of existence.[11] So when a woman adorned herself, *kosmēse*, wrapping her skin, *chrōs* (skin or colour), in yet another skin, she lent body, 'bring[ing] living surface-body so clothed to light; [...] mak[ing] it appear'.[12] Our word 'cosmetics' takes its leave from such enhancement and recalls Baudelaire's advocation, that: '[m]aquillage has no need to hide itself or to shrink from being suspected; on the contrary, let it display itself, at least if it does so with frankness and honesty'.[13] As 'a continuous coloured surface, a fabric',[14] adornment was not simply understood as mere appliqué, a discerningly piecemeal embellishment, but rather as an enveloping, a swathing or draping, a dressing binding, yet abounding in its entirety; the adorned memorialising adornment.[15]

Greek architecture was so conceived, 'the art form and decoration [...] profoundly and intimately bound and influenced by [the] principle of surface dressing, [so much so] that it [was] impossible to consider them separately',[16] a conception which was to inform both architecture and vestiary arts from that time onward.[17] According to Vitruvius, the woven cloth facilitated not only the covering and protecting of the body, but also enabled a certain adornment so that the fabric might enhance the body's honour, enabling visibility and allowing the wearer to assume one's place in the world.[18] The Latin term *honestas*, we are told, did not only confer honour, but was also a bestowal of reputation, character, respectability, virtue, integrity, dignity: rightful Roman qualities, and hence necessarily public.[19] For Ruskin, adornment was conceived of as a form of ornament attendant to an *existing* structure, with architecture being proposed as 'an art that "adorns the edifice raised by man for whatsoever use"',[20] such embellishment understood as separate, lying in contradistinction to the very surface to which it was applied.[21] Semper conceived of adornment similarly, but understood it as a cosmic imperative, experienced as 'a manifestation of the universal world order within the phenomenal world'.[22] Premised upon his theory of formal beauty, and its principal axes of symmetry, proportionality, along with directionality, such embellishment was co-extensive with his concept of dressing, conceivable as an all-encompassing ensemble; a *Gesamtkunstwerk*, a 'synthesis of the arts'.[23] In adornment, as in dressing, '[c]entripetal and centrifugal tendencies [were understood as] fused',[24] individual elements orchestrated through their very participation.

A legacy of his long-held interest in textiles, Semper's preoccupation with the woven cloth, it has been suggested, marks the culmination of his interests in polychromy,[25] 'light and colour [...] treated as one [...] heightened by the juxtaposition of fragments of pure hues', reminiscent of the Luminists' portrayal of the landscape and their concern with atmospherics.[26] For Semper, such chromo-luminarism conceivably registered as a vestige of the ancient technique of toreutics, the weaving together of a diversity of stuffs, manifest now as colour, 'the subtlest and most incorporeal dressing',[27] a symbolic, indexical homage to the crafted, iridescent surface.[28] Painted and applied, colour was understood as 'fluid, the medium of all changes',[29] binding disparate elements of a building together and, further, to their environment and surrounds, the play of light upon these surfaces said to epitomise Divinity.

The interplay between the liminal materiality of colour with the varying intensity of light was to find its apotheosis in his theory of dressing or *Bekleidung* as he was to term it, a principle which enabled him to 'posit a unitary origin for all the arts',[30] its 'motives borrowed from the realm of costume and finery',[31] though evident earlier in his conception of the architectural enclosure.[32] For 'delight in colour', it is said, 'is fundamental to our being, residing in our instinct for play and adornment'.[33]

Bekleidung, we are told, is derived from the German *kleiden*, and is generally understood as 'to clothe' or 'to dress', finding its origins in *Kleit* or cloth, which upon further derivation is revealed in the mixture applied to the cloth, *Klei*, a clay or loam,[34] in order that it be fulled and waulked, the preparation and finishing of the cloth undertaken between loom and body, and, by extension, the workmanship enacted upon stone between quarry and wall, enabling both cloth and stone to become wearable and, hence, inhabitable.

For Semper, speech, the spoken word, further supported his concept of dressing; words were not simply 'linguistic symbols applied to building at a later stage but clear indications of the textile origin[s]' of architecture. Homonymous word-plays in German, his native tongue, were said to have revealed associations, analogies that informed the symbolic and unitary origins of the formal language of the arts as a whole. Correspondences between *Wand* and *Gewand*, wall and garment, associations between *Zaun*, a hedge or fence, and *Saum*, hem or fillet, further exemplified in the double meaning of *Decke* as both ceiling and cover, manifested as the '*pre*architectural conditions' of 'dwelling [which were to] assume monumental form'.[35]

His founding of structural–symbolic ornamental motifs on the technical arts sought to expose, it is said, 'universal principles that always retained a certain stylistic necessity', revealed, for example, in the correspondence between the triglyphs of the Doric temple and the fringed and decorative borders of fabrics, both seams of sorts, one, however, not informing the other, but rather, both the result of necessity, the virtuous termination and resolution of an edge condition.[36] In these shifts between media and modes, a transfiguration occurs, movements reverberating between body and building, between the intimate and the architectural, regardless of scale, dressing. For:

> In principle what the human body is to its coverings (cloth, cosmetic paint, or jewellery), load-bearing materials are to finishing materials. The analogy rests on equivalent 'experiences' of sheltering, modesty and decoration. In neither case was nakedness evident, not for stone nor flesh; in both cases there was something unseen and supporting, and something visible and supported.[37]

Semper's concept of dressing draws, it is said, from an understanding of the festive nature of the theatre, 'the haze of carnival candles [being] the true atmosphere of art',[38] replete with its religious nuances, which were given form, not only in the 'stone dramas by Phidias',[39] but also on the festival stage, its joyous and temporary bedecking informing his conception of monumental architecture, the anchoring of ritual in place and its rendering as tangible.[40]

> The festival apparatus – the improvised scaffold with all its splendour and frills that specifically marks the occasion for celebrating, enhances, decorates, and adorns the glorification of the feast, and is hung with tapestries, dressed with festoons and garlands, and decorated with fluttering bands and trophies – is the motive for the permanent monument, which is intended to proclaim to future generations the solemn act or event celebrated.[41]

For Semper, 'dressing and the mask [were] as old as human civilisation',[42] the 'masking of reality'[43] recalling the role of the mask in ancient Greece, those worn by the gods in particular, which served 'to express tensions between contrary terms',[44] manifest in the contest between that which is supported and that which is covered, a veiling, a veritable 'dissimulating fabric' inextricably woven into the 'fabrication of architecture'.[45] For the structure beneath the textile surface or mask operates as nothing more than a prop, it is 'merely a supporting player, playing the role of support, supporting precisely because it does not play'.[46] The

106 *Place | Dressing*

outer surface is necessarily performative and is rendered so only in and through its dressing, differentiating itself from its fixed and voiceless scaffold, such 'adornment implicit [in] the dialectics of concealment and illumination'.[47]

Semper's interest in the performing arts, however, was not limited to theatre alone, but was also informed by dance and music; those 'cosmic arts'[48] inspired by Mnemosyne and her sorory, *mimesis*, the 'forming of images'[49] as opposed to mere copies, it is said, 'deriv[ing] from the star-dance of the heavens'.[50] In ancient Greece, *choros*, earthbound, was understood not only as the dance floor or the dance place, but the very dance itself,[51] place appearing with the dance, those sets of steps and turns figured and repeated, place dissolving when the dance was completed,[52] tethered in memory, lived, nonetheless.[53]

The German words for wall and for garment, *Wand* and *Gewand* respectively, find their origins in '*wenden*, to turn, and *winden* to wind or to twist',[54] a surface enclosing, well-crafted, appearing. In the Hebrides, the cloth was waulked in a sunrise direction, turning round the table, as the cloth had previously been wound around its beam in the weaving, the cloth then tailored encircling the body, as the walls enclosed the room in which the dressing took place, the wearer's journeying through the city, mirroring, more or less, the ancients' cycling movements about the *polos*, symbolic of the *polis* and the very appearance of the place.[55]

The word itself, *polis*, it is said, is suggestive of a ring-wall, its Latin derivation, *urbs*, containing within it the figure of a circle, derived as it was from the same root as *orbis*, from which we get orbit. Our word 'town' comes to us through German and originated in the word *Zaun*, a surrounding hedge or fence,[56] which also, as we have seen, bears comparison to *Saum*, or hem.[57] Semper posited 'the surrounding wall' (*Einfassungsmauer*) as the 'first element of antique architecture' as well as the 'primordial seed' (*Urkeim*); germane to the dwelling, the wall unfurling further to encompass both temple and city,[58] drawing closer, conceivably clothing the body.

The curtain wall, as we are aware, takes its name from its enclosing and fortification of ancient citadels. Office towers, now thus attired, form a sentinel and silent chorus, lining the streets of the city further enshrouding us as a backdrop. Through the dilated lens of a camera, a landscape is revealed, refocused disclosing a room; stopping down further architecture's textile foundations are illumined. The city's architecture, we are told, can be 'appropriated in a twofold manner: by use and by perception – or rather, by touch and sight',[59] though the other senses necessarily come into play. Engagement with built form cannot simply be grasped in its entirety through studied contemplation alone; habitual use too informs our understanding of it, and to a large extent even how we view it, its familiarity rendering it both preponderant and peripheral, its features registering only intermittently, in a distracted, non-concerted way. For:

> Lasting impressions, impressions which differ only slightly from one another, impressions which take a regular and habitual course and show regular and habitual contrasts – all these use up, so to speak, less consciousness than does the rapid crowding of changing images, the sharp discontinuity in the grasp of a single glance.[60]

The mind, it has been suggested, is composed of two layers,[61] like the double face of a wall, or a costume well-lined, with an inner receptive surface and an outer protective shield, and the concept of habit can be likewise conceived, as a surface, separating the inner life from that which lies beyond.[62] Habit, it is said, springs from the Latin *habitus*, a noun conveying activity, which is derived from *habere*, to have or to hold, and is understood as the possession of interior qualities, a mode of being, the cultivation of mental and moral traits, which result in a constitution that confers a 'power of use and enjoyment'.[63] But habit, similarly derived, also extends to exterior features and outward appearance; to modes of apparel, to fashion and dressing, but also through *in*-habitation to the place of abode, an *ad*-dress. 'To dwell', we are told, is:

> a transitive verb – as in the notion of 'indwelt space': herewith an indication of the frenetic topicality concealed in habitual behaviour. It has to do with fashioning a shell for ourselves.[64]

Habit, too, takes on a performative role, through use and usage, customarily repeated, to the point where such action is performed unconsciously, eliciting a 'mechanical' reaction, an automatic response, the result of repetition.[65] In our coursing through the city, on our daily journeys, liminal layers are acquired through our re-experiencing of the streets and the architecture that defines them, threads are slowly woven through quotidian re-enactment, until a garment is gradually borne, lined with memories of other places, impressed upon us by the flurry of images, unconsciously clothing our existence. Inhabiting the city, we become increasingly attired in place, already enclothed ourselves. For:

> [w]hen the scope of surface tactilism is extended, clothes, architecture, interior design, cosmetics, and the moving image appear as coterminous spaces of inhabitation. As the mutable skin of a social body, they are all part of a shared interactive experience. In defining our way of living space, they tailor our own contours. They shape

our passage as moving surfaces in space and mark the traces we make along the way, for 'to live is to leave traces'.[66]

'Erase the traces!',[67] however, was an insistent refrain that echoed throughout the first decades of the twentieth century, a period heady with Modernist zeal which sought to dissociate itself from precedence, to disencumber itself of the weight of history, progress seemingly taking one form in the office building, which emerged as a new type, a 'house of work, of organisation, of clarity, of economy',[68] a reductive construction unadorned and ossified, largely colourless and indifferent, 'by nature, skeletal'.[69] New materials, concrete, iron and glass, were lauded, 'Scheerbart with his glass and the Bauhaus with its steel [...] opened up the way: [...] creat[ing] spaces in which it [was] difficult to leave traces',[70] resistance internalised, offered only by the plush nap of upholstery and its textiles.[71] A furtive and fugitive existence was proposed, life, its vitality diminished and depreciated, devoid of existential vestiges. Uncovered and exposed, '[r]educed to skin and bones', the office building was inexorably rendered as 'a jejune thing',[72] divested and revealed as inconspicuous, lack-lustred, another one among the many. And while the comportment of its surfaces was acknowledged,[73] the metaphoric potential of the weave was ignored, by and large; it was read, if at all, as 'speculative cubage wrapped in exterior wallpaper',[74] an indiscriminate and undistinguished substitute for the woven tapestries, the grid repeating, *ad infinitum*, self-reflexive, a *mise en abyme*, a 'naked and determined materialism',[75] its formalist drive eschewing or ignorant of its textile origins, a mass-reproduced surface, 'detache[d] from the domain of tradition'.[76]

It is said that '[i]f the place enriches the being who is found there, the being confers on the place where it is found something of its own individuality'.[77] Or perhaps to put it another way, we are coloured by place, dyed in the wool so to speak, but so too do we cast upon it our own hues and enliven it, as we (the very threads of our being) interweave in between the one and the other, between here and there enclosed in place, moving in between and in certain lights, igniting. For colour that imbues the woven cloth, like place, is by nature reflexive, 'encompass[ing] that on which it reflects [...] but never fully illuminat[ing] that which it encompasses'.[78] Place and colour are both inextricably linked and revealed in the shifting, animate and dynamic nature of the surface, whether woven, painted, knitted or built, chiasmatic in their tidal unfurlings and enfoldings, from the intimate to the architectural, place and cloth dressing, binding the body to its environment, to the landscapes and its surrounds, to the city and the buildings which compose it, establishing contexts immediately apparent, while spanning across divides, latent memories concealed within the folds, revealed and complemented in their afterimages.

Notes

1 See Harry Francis Mallgrave, *Gottfried Semper: Architect of the Nineteenth Century* (New Haven, CT: Yale University Press, 1996), 296. A similar version of this essay was published in *Craft + Design Enquiry* 7 (2015): 69–80, available online at: http://press.anu.edu.au/apps/bookworm/view/craft+%2B+design+enquiry%3A+issue+7%2C+2015/11901/ch05.xhtml. Accessed 21 March 2016.

2 For a discussion of the *feileadh mhor* see, for example, H. F. McClintock, *Old Highland Dress and Tartans* (Dundalk: W. Tempest Dundalgan Press, 1949), 18–35.

3 'S Moch An Diu A Rinn Mi Éirigh' otherwise known as 'This Morning I Have Risen Early' in J. L. Campbell, ed., *Hebridean Folksongs: A Collection of Waulking Songs by Donald MacCormick in Kilphedir in South Uist in the Year 1863* (London: Oxford University Press, 1969), 134–5.

4 See Walter Benjamin, 'The Work of Art in the Age of Mechanical Reproduction', in *Illuminations: Essays and Reflections*, ed. Hannah Arendt and trans. Harry Zohn (New York: Schocken Books, 1969), 223.

5 Francis Thompson, *Harris Tweed: Story of a Hebridean Industry* (Newton Abbot: David and Charles, 1969), 31–2.

6 Thompson, *Harris Tweed*, 34. For a discussion of dyeing in Semper, see *Style in the Technical and Tectonic Arts: or, Practical Aesthetics*, trans. Harry Francis Mallgrave and Michael Robinson (Los Angeles: Getty Research Institute, 2004), 198 and 232–6.

7 The italicised words are the Gaelic names of the plants. See Thompson, *Harris Tweed*, 32–9.

8 '[W]hen they lie amongst the hadder [heather] the bright colour of their plaids shall not betray them …' A 1582 account of Harris Tweed cited in Thompson, *Harris Tweed*, 21. The quote comes from the Scottish historian and scholar George Buchanan (1506–82) and his *Rerum Scoticarum Historia* (1582). See Iain Zaczek and Charles Phillips, *The Complete Book of Tartan: A Heritage Encyclopedia of over 400 Tartans and the Stories that Shaped Scottish History* (London: Hermes House, 2004), 13.

9 Indra Kagis McEwen, *Socrates' Ancestor: An Essay in Architectural Beginnings* (Cambridge, MA: MIT Press, 1993), 87–8.

10 McEwen, *Socrates' Ancestor*, 42–3. Prior to Anaximander's instigation of his cosmology in prephilosophical times, *kosmos* was understood as order of any kind. See McEwen, *Socrates' Ancestor*, 136, n. 13.

11 McEwen, *Socrates' Ancestor*, 43. Papapetros notes that Semper's understanding of *kosmos* was derived from its Greek foundations, and came to 'signify three distinct worlds or parallel cosmic faculties, [philology, the natural sciences and the ethnographic sciences] which would ultimately converge into one epistemological system'. See Spyros Papapetros, 'World Ornament: The Legacy of Gottfried Semper's 1856 Lecture on Adornment', *Res: Journal of Anthropology and Aesthetics* 57/58 (2010): 311–12. Asman also proposes that Semper restored the concept of *kosmos* to its tripartite meaning: '1. ornament; 2. world or world order; and 3. moral order or

decorum', the individual inhabiting the space the fourth element. See Carrie Asman, 'Ornament and Motion: Science and Art in Gottfried Semper's Theory of Adornment', in *Herzog and De Meuron: Natural History*, ed. Philip Ursprung (Montreal: Canadian Centre for Architecture and Baden: Lars Müller Publishers, 2002), 391.

12 See McEwen, *Socrates' Ancestor*, 43–4. As Semper observed, 'Chevreul, in his little book on colour harmony, gives useful hints as to this and other points of the art of the toilette.' Gottfried Semper, 'From "Concerning the Formal Principles of Ornament and Its Significance as Artistic Symbol"', in *The Theory of Decorative Art: An Anthology of European and American Writings, 1740–1940*, ed. Isabelle Frank and trans. David Britt (New Haven, CT: Yale University Press, 2000), 98.

13 Charles Baudelaire, 'The Painter of Modern Life', in *The Painter of Modern Life and Other Essays*, ed. and trans. Jonathan Mayne (London: Phaidon Press, 1964), 34.

14 Mark Wigley, *White Walls, Designer Dresses: The Fashioning of Modern Architecture* (Cambridge, MA: MIT Press, 2001), 250.

15 See Semper, *Style*, 93.

16 Semper, *Style*, 246. Emphasis in Semper.

17 In the nineteenth century the philosopher and essayist Thomas Carlyle (1795–1891), for example, was to note: 'In all his Modes, and habilatory endeavours, an Architectural Idea will be found lurking; his Body and Cloth are the site and materials whereon and whereby his beautiful edifice, of a Person, is to be built.' Thomas Carlyle, *Sartor Resartus* (Oxford: Oxford University Press, 1999), 28.

18 Indra Kagis McEwen, 'Instrumentality and the Organic Assistance of Looms', in *Chora 1: Intervals in the Philosophy of Architecture*, ed. Alberto Pérez-Gómez and Stephen Parcell (Montreal: McGill University Press, 1994), 134.

19 McEwen, 'Instrumentality', 138.

20 John Ruskin, *The Seven Lamps of Architecture*, quoted in Andrew Benjamin, 'Surface Effects: Borromini, Semper, Loos', *Journal of Architecture* 11, no. 1 (2006): 16.

21 See Benjamin, 'Surface Effects', 16. For a further discussion of Ruskin and his interest in the surface, see Anuradha Chatterjee, *John Ruskin and the Fabric of Architecture* (Abingdon: Routledge, 2018).

22 Semper, 'From "Concerning the Formal Principles of Ornament"', 91.

23 In the 1840s, Semper and the composer Richard Wagner (1813–83) developed together the concept of the *Gesamtkunstwerk*. See Harry Francis Mallgrave, introduction to *Style in the Technical and Tectonic Arts: or, Practical Aesthetics* (Los Angeles: Getty Research Institute, 2004), 51. For a further discussion of the concept of *Gesamtkunstwerk* in relationship to Semper see, for example, Mari Hvattum, *Gottfried Semper and the Problem of Historicism* (Cambridge: Cambridge University Press, 2004), 160–73.

24 Georg Simmel, 'Adornment', in *The Sociology of Georg Simmel*, ed. and trans. Kurt H. Wolff (Glencoe, IL: Free Press, 1950), 343.

25 Mallgrave, *Gottfried Semper*, 290.

26 See David van Zanten, *The Architectural Polychromy of the 1830's* (New York: Garland Publishing, 1977), 63, and for a discussion of Semper and his understanding of light and colour in relationship to Luminism, see 63–71.
27 Semper, *Style*, 379.
28 With reference to Indian architecture, Semper was to comment that following on from the dressing of walls with mosaics, painting stucco then developed, with the simple painting of stone ensuing, all these techniques 'conceptually the same, [but] differing only in thickness'. Semper, *Style in the Technical and Tectonic Arts*, 269.
29 Walter Benjamin, 'A Child's View of Colour', trans. Rodney Livingstone, in *Selected Writings*, Volume 1: *1913–1926*, ed. Marcus Bullock and Michael W. Jennings (Cambridge, MA: Belknap Press of Harvard University Press, 1996), 50.
30 Joseph Rykwert, 'Gottfried Semper and the Conception of Style', in *Gottfried Semper und die Mitte des 19.Jahrhunderts*. Conference Proceedings (Basel: Birkhäuser, 1976), 78.
31 Mallgrave, *Gottfried Semper*, 293.
32 See Harry Francis Mallgrave, introduction to *The Four Elements of Architecture and Other Writings*, by Gottfried Semper (Cambridge: Cambridge University Press, 1989), 24. It has also been suggested that 'Schelling [...] open[ed] the door to the metaphor of *Bekleidung* by noting the architectonic nature of "drapery and cladding [*Bekleidung*]" in the context of architecture'. See Margaret Olin, 'Self-Representation: Resemblance and Convention in Two Nineteenth-Century Theories of Architecture and the Decorative Arts', *Zeitschrift für Kunstgeschichte* 49, no. 3 (1986): 385, n. 35.
33 Mallgrave, introduction to *The Four Elements of Architecture*, 14.
34 Elizabeth Rowe Spelman, *Gottfried Semper and the Profound Surface of Architecture* (Master's Thesis: Rice University, 1997), 48.
35 See Semper, *Style*, 248. Emphasis in Semper. Semper's understanding of comparative linguistics was informed by the writings of Albert Höfer, a disciple of Wilhelm von Humboldt. See Joseph Rykwert, 'Architecture Is All on the Surface: Semper and *Bekleidung*', *Rassegna* 73 (1998): 22.
36 Mallgrave, introduction to *Style in the Technical and Tectonic Arts*, 32.
37 David Leatherbarrow, *The Roots of Architectural Invention: Site, Enclosure, Materials* (New York: Cambridge University Press, 1993), 202–3. For a discussion of the nude and its differentiation from nakedness, see Mary McLeod, 'Undressing Architecture: Fashion, Gender and Modernity', in *Architecture: In Fashion*, eds. Deborah Fausch, Paulette Singley, Rodolphe El-Khoury and Zvi Efrat (New York: Princeton Architectural Press, 1994), 99, n. 22.
38 Semper, *Style*, 439, n. 85.
39 Semper, *Style*, 439, n. 85.
40 See Hvattum, *Gottfried Semper*, 67.
41 Semper, *Style*, 249. Emphasis in Semper.
42 Semper, *Style*, 438–9, n. 85.

112 *Place | Dressing*

43 Described by philosopher Friedrich Nietzsche (1844–1900) as 'the most significant living architect', Semper's writings on 'the masking of reality' are said to have informed his 1872 publication, *The Birth of Tragedy*. See Mallgrave, introduction to *Style*, 43 and 51.
44 Jean-Pierre Vernant and Françoise Frontisi-Ducroux, 'Features of the Mask in Ancient Greece', in *Myth and Tragedy in Ancient Greece*, ed. Jean-Pierre Vernant and Pierre Vidal-Naquet and trans. Janet Lloyd (New York: Zone Books, 1990), 206.
45 Mark Wigley, 'Untitled: The Housing of Gender', quoted in Mallgrave, *Gottfried Semper*, 300.
46 Mark Wigley, *White Walls, Designer Dresses: The Fashioning of Modern Architecture* (Cambridge, MA: MIT Press, 2001), 12.
47 Spyros Papapetros, 'World Ornament: The Legacy of Gottfried Semper's 1856 Lecture on Adornment', *Res: Journal of Anthropology and Aesthetics* 57/58 (2010): 309.
48 See Mallgrave, introduction to *The Four Elements of Architecture*, 33.
49 Leatherbarrow, *Roots of Architectural Invention*, 87.
50 Hans-Georg Gadamer, 'The Relevance of the Beautiful: Art as Play, Symbol and Festival', in *The Relevance of the Beautiful and Other Essays*, ed. Robert Bernasconi and trans. Nicholas Walker (Cambridge: Cambridge University Press, 1986), 36.
51 McEwen, *Socrates' Ancestor*, 58.
52 McEwen, *Socrates' Ancestor*, 63.
53 As Aristotle was to note: 'For place does not perish when the things in it cease to be' (Aristotle, *Physics* IV, i, 209a1). From Aristotle, *Physics: Books III and IV*, trans. Edmund Hussey (Oxford: Clarendon Press, 1993), 21.
54 Spelman, *Gottfried Semper*, 51. Frampton suggests that *winden* also means 'to embroider'. See Kenneth Frampton, '*Rappel à l'Ordre*, the Case for the Tectonic', in *Theorizing a New Agenda for Architecture: An Anthology of Architectural Theory 1965–1995*, ed. Kate Nesbitt (New York: Princeton Architectural Press, 1996), 524.
55 See Martin Heidegger, *Parmenides*, quoted in Jeff Malpas, 'Heidegger in Benjamin's City', *Journal of Architecture* 12, no. 5 (2007): 494.
56 See Hannah Arendt, *The Human Condition* (Chicago: University of Chicago Press, 1958), 64, n. 64.
57 Semper, *Style*, 248.
58 With reference to a lecture by Semper in 1848 or 1849, see Mallgrave, introduction to *The Four Elements of Architecture*, 23.
59 Benjamin, 'Work of Art', 240. Schwartz comments that Benjamin's propositions regarding the experience of architecture by touch and through sight were informed by his correspondence with the architect Carl Linfert. For Linfert, '[a]rchitectural space requires more than an eye to be grasped in its *totality*'. He notes, '[i]nstead of *seeing*, the eye must *feel its way through* [*durchspüren*] structures'. Carl Linfert quoted in Frederic J. Schwartz, *Blind Spots: Critical Theory and the History of Art in Twentieth-Century Germany* (New Haven, CT: Yale University Press, 2005), 65.

60 Georg Simmel, 'The Metropolis and Mental Life', in *The Sociology of Georg Simmel*, ed. and trans. Kurt Wolff (Glencoe, IL: Free Press, 1950), 410.
61 See Sigmund Freud, 'A Note on the Mystic Writing-Pad', in *The Archive: Documents of Contemporary Art*, ed. Charles Merewether (London: Whitechapel and Cambridge, MA: MIT Press, 2006), 22.
62 For a discussion of the concept of 'facing' in architecture, see David Leatherbarrow, 'Facing and Spacing', in *Paradoxes of Appearing: Essays on Art, Architecture and Philosophy*, ed. Michael Asgaard Andersen and Henrik Oxvig (Baden: Lars Müller, 2009), 185–207.
63 Henri Lefebvre, *The Production of Space*, quoted in Giuliana Bruno, *Atlas of Emotion: Journeys into Art, Architecture, and Film* (New York: Verso, 2002), 322.
64 Walter Benjamin, *The Arcades Project*, trans. Howard Eiland and Kevin McLaughlin (Cambridge, MA: Belknap Press of Harvard University Press, 2004), [I4, 5].
65 Refer to *The Oxford English Dictionary* for an elucidation of the complexities contained within the term 'habit'. www.oed.com/view/Entry/82978. Accessed 13 October 2007.
66 Bruno, *Atlas of Emotion*, 322.
67 'Erase the traces!' is the refrain in the first poem of Bertolt Brecht's (1898–1956) *Lesebuch für Städtebewohner* or 'Reader for City-Dwellers', cited in Walter Benjamin, 'Experience and Poverty', trans. Rodney Livingstone, in *Selected Writings, Volume 2: 1927–1934*, ed. Michael W. Jennings, Howard Eiland and Gary Smith (Cambridge, MA: Belknap Press of Harvard University Press, 1999), 734.
68 Ludwig Mies van der Rohe, 'Working Theses', quoted in Joseph Rykwert, *The Dancing Column: On Order in Architecture* (Cambridge, MA: MIT Press, 1996), 382.
69 Ludwig Mies van der Rohe, 'Working Theses', in *Programs and Manifestos on 20th-Century Architecture*, ed. Ulrich Conrads (Cambridge, MA: MIT Press, 1971), 74. Colomina discusses the 'skinless' quality of modern architecture, which she correlates with the development of the x-ray. See Beatriz Colomina, 'Skinless Architecture', *Thesis: Wissenschaftliche Zeitschrift der Bauhaus-Universität Weimar* 3 (2003): 122–4.
70 Benjamin, 'Experience and Poverty', 734.
71 See Benjamin, *Arcades Project*, [I3,1] and [I5,2].
72 See Rykwert, *Dancing Column*, 382.
73 The curtain wall was categorised according to its surface condition, which alluded to its weave, in the 1957 'Machine Made America' special issue of *Architectural Review*. See Reinhold Martin, 'Atrocities: Or, Curtain Wall as Mass Medium', *Perspecta* 32 (2001): 67.
74 Peter Blake, 'Slaughter on 6th Avenue', quoted in Martin, 'Atrocities', 68.
75 Rosalind Krauss, 'Grids', *October* 9 (1979): 52.
76 Benjamin, 'Work of Art', 221.
77 Georges Poulet, *Proustian Space*, trans. Elliott Coleman (Baltimore, MD: Johns Hopkins University Press, 1977), 28.

78 Jeff Malpas, 'Repetitions', in *Repetitions*, exhibition catalogue (Hobart: Plimsoll Gallery, University of Tasmania, 2008), 10.

Bibliography

Arendt, Hannah. *The Human Condition*. Chicago: University of Chicago Press, 1958.

Aristotle. *Physics: Books III and IV*. Translated and introduced by Edward Hussey. Oxford: Clarendon Press, 1993.

Asman, Carrie. 'Ornament and Motion: Science and Art in Gottfried Semper's Theory of Adornment'. In *Herzog and De Meuron: Natural History*. Edited by Philip Ursprung, 385–97. Montreal: Canadian Centre for Architecture and Baden: Lars Müller Publishers, 2002.

Baudelaire, Charles. 'The Painter of Modern Life'. In *The Painter of Modern Life and Other Essays*. Edited and translated by Jonathan Mayne, 1–40. London: Phaidon Press, 1964.

Benjamin, Walter. 'The Work of Art in the Age of Mechanical Reproduction'. In *Illuminations: Essays and Reflections*. Edited by Hannah Arendt and translated by Harry Zohn, 217–52. New York: Schocken Books, 1969.

———. 'A Child's View of Colour'. Translated by Rodney Livingstone. In *Selected Writings*, Volume 1: *1913–1926*. Edited by Marcus Bullock and Michael W. Jennings, 50–1. Cambridge, MA: Belknap Press of Harvard University Press, 1996.

———. 'Experience and Poverty'. Translated by Rodney Livingstone, in *Selected Writings*, Volume 2: *1927–1934*. Edited by Michael W. Jennings, Howard Eiland and Gary Smith, 731–6. Cambridge, MA: Belknap Press of Harvard University Press, 1999.

———. *The Arcades Project*. Translated by Howard Eiland and Kevin McLaughlin. Cambridge, MA: Belknap Press of Harvard University Press, 2004.

Bruno, Giuliana. *Atlas of Emotion: Journeys into Art, Architecture, and Film*. New York: Verso, 2002.

Campbell, J. L., ed. *Hebridean Folksongs: A Collection of Waulking Songs by Donald MacCormick in Kilphedir in South Uist in the Year 1863*. London: Oxford University Press, 1969.

Carlyle, Thomas. *Sartor Resartus*. Oxford: Oxford University Press, 1999.

Chatterjee, Anuradha. *John Ruskin and the Fabric of Architecture*. Abingdon: Routledge, 2018.

Colomina, Beatriz. 'Skinless Architecture', *Thesis: Wissenschaftliche Zeitschrift der Bauhaus-Universität Weimar* 3 (2003): 122–4.

Frampton, Kenneth. '*Rappel à l'Ordre*, the Case for the Tectonic'. In *Theorizing a New Agenda for Architecture: An Anthology of Architectural Theory 1965–1995*. Edited by Kate Nesbitt, 516–28. New York: Princeton Architectural Press, 1996.

Freud, Sigmund. 'A Note on the Mystic Writing-Pad'. In *The Archive: Documents of Contemporary Art*. Edited by Charles Merewether, 20–4. London: Whitechapel and Cambridge, MA: MIT Press, 2006.

Gadamer, Hans-Georg. 'The Relevance of the Beautiful: Art as Play, Symbol and Festival'. In *The Relevance of the Beautiful and Other Essays*. Edited by Robert Bernasconi and translated by Nicholas Walker, 1–53. Cambridge: Cambridge University Press, 1986.

Hvattum, Mari. *Gottfried Semper and the Problem of Historicism*. Cambridge: Cambridge University Press, 2004.

Krauss, Rosalind. 'Grids', *October* 9 (1979): 50–64.

Leatherbarrow, David. *The Roots of Architectural Invention: Site, Enclosure, Materials*. New York: Cambridge University Press, 1993.

———. 'Facing and Spacing'. In *Paradoxes of Appearing: Essays on Art, Architecture and Philosophy*. Edited by Michael Asgaard Andersen and Henrik Oxvig, 185–207. Baden: Lars Müller, 2009.

McClintock, H. F. *Old Highland Dress and Tartans*. Dundalk: W. Tempest Dundalgan Press, 1949.

McEwen, Indra Kagis. *Socrates' Ancestor: An Essay in Architectural Beginnings*. Cambridge, MA: MIT Press, 1993.

McLeod, Mary. 'Undressing Architecture: Fashion, Gender and Modernity'. In *Architecture: In Fashion*. Edited by Deborah Fausch, Paulette Singley, Rodolphe El Khoury and Zvi Efrat, 38–123. New York: Princeton Architectural Press, 1994.

Mallgrave, Harry Francis. Introduction to *The Four Elements of Architecture and Other Writings*, by Gottfried Semper, 1–44. Cambridge. Cambridge University Press, 1989.

———. Introduction to *Style in the Technical and Tectonic Arts: or, Practical Aesthetics*, by Gottfried Semper, 1–67. Los Angeles: Getty Research Institute, 2004.

Malpas, Jeff. 'Heidegger in Benjamin's City', *Journal of Architecture* 12, no. 5 (2007): 489–97.

———. 'Repetitions'. In *Repetitions*. Exhibition Catalogue, 6–20. Hobart: Plimsoll Gallery, University of Tasmania, 2008.

Martin, Reinhold. 'Atrocities: or, Curtain Wall as Mass Medium', *Perspecta* 32 (2001): 67–75.

Papapetros, Spyros. 'World Ornament: The Legacy of Gottfried Semper's 1856 Lecture on Adornment', *Res: Journal of Anthropology and Aesthetics* 57/58 (2010): 309–29.

Poulet, Georges. *Proustian Space*. Translated by Elliott Coleman. Baltimore, MD: Johns Hopkins University Press, 1977.

Rohe, Ludwig Mies van der. 'Working Theses'. In *Programs and Manifestos on 20th-Century Architecture*. Edited by Ulrich Conrads, 74. Cambridge, MA: MIT Press, 1971.

Rykwert, Joseph. 'Gottfried Semper and the Conception of Style'. In *Gottfried Semper und die Mitte des 19. Jahrhunderts*. Conference Proceedings, 67–83. Basel: Birkhäuser, 1976.

———. *The Dancing Column: On Order in Architecture*. Cambridge, MA: MIT Press, 1996.

———. 'Architecture Is All on the Surface: Semper and *Bekleidung*', *Rassegna* 73 (1998): 20–9.

Schwartz, Frederic J. *Blind Spots: Critical Theory and the History of Art in Twentieth-Century Germany*. New Haven, CT: Yale University Press, 2005.

Semper, Gottfried. 'From "Concerning the Formal Principles of Ornament and Its Significance as Artistic Symbol"'. In *The Theory of Decorative Art: An Anthology of European and American Writings, 1740–1940*. Edited by Isabelle Frank and translated by David Britt, 91–115. New Haven, CT: Yale University Press, 2000.

———. *Style in the Technical and Tectonic Arts: or, Practical Aesthetics*. Translated by Harry Francis Mallgrave and Michael Robinson. Los Angeles: Getty Research Institute, 2004.

Simmel, Georg. 'Adornment'. In *The Sociology of Georg Simmel*. Edited and translated by Kurt H. Wolff, 338–44. Glencoe, IL: Free Press, 1950.

———. 'The Metropolis and Mental Life'. In *The Sociology of Georg Simmel*. Edited and translated by Kurt H. Wolff, 409–24. Glencoe, IL: Free Press, 1950.

Spelman, Elizabeth Rowe. *Gottfried Semper and the Profound Surface of Architecture*. Master's Thesis: Rice University, 1997.

Thompson, Francis. *Harris Tweed: The Story of a Hebridean Industry*. Newton Abbot: David and Charles, 1969.

van Zanten, David. *The Architectural Polychromy of the 1830's*. New York: Garland Publishing, 1977.

Vernant, Jean-Pierre and Françoise Frontisi-Ducroux. 'Features of the Mask in Ancient Greece'. In *Myth and Tragedy in Ancient Greece*. Edited by Jean-Pierre Vernant and Pierre Vidal-Naquet and translated by Janet Lloyd, 189–206. New York: Zone Books, 1990.

Wigley, Mark. *White Walls, Designer Dresses: The Fashioning of Modern Architecture*. Cambridge, MA: MIT Press, 2001.

Zaczek, Iain and Charles Phillips. *The Complete Book of Tartan: A Heritage Encyclopedia of over 400 Tartans and the Stories that Shaped Scottish History*. London: Hermes House, 2004.

Ritual

Figure 7.1 Walter Blaikie, *Waulking, Eriskay*, 1899.

Repetition

Figure 7.2 Anonymous, *Weaving Shed at the Baltic Works, Dundee*, late nineteenth century.

Every profound experience longs to be insatiable, longs for return and repletion until the end of time, and for the reinstatement of an original condition from which it sprang.

Walter Benjamin

For them there is no significance in life; they have no dancing, no Helicon, no Muse.

Anonymous

122 *Ritual | Repetition*

Until the early twentieth century in the Outer Hebrides, 'labour and song went hand in hand; labour gave rise to song and song lightened the labour', strain giving way through immersion in the rhythm, the burden of the task at hand mitigated, its measure not in hours, but in tune.[1] The milking of cows, the striking of oars against the sea, the harvesting of crops, the crooning of children and the waulking of the cloth, each form had its own repertoire,[2] varying from island to island and even in their breadth, from one end to the other, each task, regardless, following the direction of habit, *deiseil*, the coursing of the sun.[3] Through the waulking song in particular, a great oral tradition was perpetuated, as histories long past were given presence and were coupled with more prosaic and ribald verse, speculating on, indeed, if not celebrating, life contemporary to its singers, wherein the name of the one or the other and that of their purported lover was cited in song.[4]

Steeped in ritual the waulking was a festal affair, Thursday, the day of Columba, it is said, being the most auspicious day to undertake the task.[5] While no definitive account or classic form of waulking, as such, exists, typical to all performances was the structure wherein one woman sang the verse, the rest participating, joining in at the chorus, allowing the lead singer to draw breath in the refrain, surging forward again renewed then in song. Several bars before the singing began, thumping heralded the tune, the preliminary beating of the table establishing a 'pure rhythm [...] almost hypnotic in its insistence and excitement, accumulating in its intensity to the point when [...] it positively *demands* a song to go with it',[6] the tempo somatically engrained, its pulsations given form, and choreographed in the fulling of the cloth.

> The course of the web along the board describes a series of zigzags, each woman's movements forming the letter V, of which she herself is the base, and each point being marked by the loud thud of the cloth upon the board, always in four time. At *one* she receives the cloth from her neighbour on the right, leaning forward and throwing it down at arm's length; at *two* she draws herself upright and brings it down again immediately in front of her, twisting as she does so; at *three* she passes it, again at arm's length to her neighbour on the left; and at *four*, once more upright, she brings her hands again in front of her, still beating time, and is thus ready for one, *da capo*, for the rhythm is ceaseless.[7]

The movement of the body, the criss-crossing of the arms in the waulking mirrors the herringbone weave, patterns echoing across and between different modes, figures repeating, the practices of weaving also emulated in dance, the Hebridean Weaving Lilt a playful performance of its preparations and processes.[8] As a means of commemoration, waulking, dancing and the like were collective practices and participatory, participation and imitation chiasmatically entwined, their definition founded upon interaction, an exchange mutually derived.[9] The originary medium of imitation, we are told, was the body, with language and dance its means, the 'gestures of body and lips' vital in giving form to the immemorial through semblance and play, both 'interfolded' and proper to the realm of art and traditional aesthetics.[10] In ancient times, such performances were understood not as superficial impressions or meagre impersonations, but rather conveyed:

> the expression of feelings and the manifestation of experiences through movement, musical harmonies, and the rhythms of speech – an acknowledgement through the body's presence, of its intermediate location *between* Being and Becoming.[11]

'All true ritual', we are told, is 'sung, danced and played',[12] the word for 'play' in German, *Spiel*, originally meaning 'dance'.[13] With its steps and becks embodying and perpetuating cultural patterns through representation as a communal affair, the nature of an individual's sentiments is said to be of lesser import, though '[n]either the expressive function of dance nor the emotional outlet it gives to each [...] is denied',[14] one and all captivated by, and indeed at one with, its impetus. For the movement itself is momentous, the weaving motion of the body, the toing and froing a fundamental feature of play, participants losing all sense of self, freed from 'the burden of taking initiative', caught up in the activity, buoyed by a 'spontaneous tendency to repetition', the momentum a compulsive drive toward regeneration.[15]

Ritual, feast and game are bound by this rhythm, the mood permeating each and synchronic. But it is of another time that we speak, a lapsed time and labile, falling outside of the bounds of quotidian temporality, occurring in a place marked out through performance and so differentiated, place being hallowed in this way.[16] In the performance of rites ordinary life, it is said, comes to a standstill and 'is gleamed through',[17] a liminal domain emerging and established in an 'atemporal instant of primordial plenitude', experienced as a 'symbolic return',[18] a return founded upon perdurance.[19] For '[a]s long as it survives', ritual, we are told, 'retains its hold over the imaginations and the ways of thinking of the people who witness or practise it. [...] The rite is "truly" understood [only and so] long as it is practiced.'[20]

Through the intervention of ritual what returns moves toward us, facilitating an encounter, an active exchange with a history[21] that is thoroughly alive and ever-changeable, mutable and capable of being reshaped

124 *Ritual | Repetition*

through interpretation. 'Thus', in this manner, 'a potent yesterday', we are told, 'perpetually renews itself'.[22]

An event premised upon mediation,[23] ritual, it is said, is the '"reactualisation" of an act of cosmic creation', a cosmogonic feat repeated,[24] but this repetition is never 'the simple continuance of the self-identical', synonymous with lifelessness and death, but is rather an engagement with a tradition replete with potential, 'modification and innovation' inherent to it.[25] Repetition and recollection, it has been suggested, are one and the same movement, driven, however, toward opposite ends, 'for what is recollected has been, [and] is repeated backwards, whereas genuine repetition is recollected forward',[26] ritual, the weaving betwixt and between the past and the future and taking place in the 'the present of the commemorative act'.[27] Indeed:

> what is repeated is a process of becoming, a movement of differentiation and dispersion – and what is differentiated and dispersed is nothing other than time itself. There can be no passing moment that is not already both the past and the future: the moment must be simultaneously past, present, and future in order for it to pass at all. This is why this eternal repetition does not mean 'the return of the same' but rather the return of what is never simply itself. What returns is the movement through which something other is inscribed within the same which, now no longer the same, names what is always other than itself. If the eternal return therefore comes as the eternal repetition of alterity, we could say, somewhat elliptically, that this eternal return is the return of returning itself. It is the desire for things to return.[28]

For Semper, architecture subscribed to this cycling and was understood as the 'translation of ritual into tangible form',[29] reified and 'enshrined in monuments' anchored to the soil, establishing a 'physical presence',[30] the levity of music and dance embodied. In play and through it, architecture, along with the other arts, were to realise their primordial motive, not through imitation of the extant world but rather by falling in step with its rhythms, manifesting in all manner of compositions: a building, a wreath, a scroll, or a dance, all legitimately created, concordant with its laws,[31] poets, in this light, regardless of means, once said to be the world's 'unacknowledged legislators'.[32]

> Surrounded by a world full of wonder and forces whose laws we may divine, may wish to understand but will never decipher, that touch us only in a few fragmentary harmonies and suspend our souls in a continuous state of unresolved tension, we conjure up in play

the perfection that is lacking. We make for ourselves a tiny world in which the cosmic law is evident within the strictest limits, yet complete in itself and perfect in this respect. In such play we satisfy our cosmogonic instinct.[33]

In accordance with this impulse, architecture as a tradition was to find its origins not in the plastic arts nor in the disciplines of science, but rather in the performing arts, once referred to as cosmic, 'their laws of spatial harmony' said to be generative and 'immanently form giving'.[34] Architecture's practices therein were to rest 'on two analogies: of the building as a body, and of the design as a re-enactment of some primitive – or [...] archetypal action'.[35] Tradition, as such, operates as a form of transmission rather than as the sanctioning of mere conservation, the past grasped at in order to learn from it, not so that it might be simply replicated, but only insofar as it might be transformed, reordered and fashioned again.

In the wake of the Industrial Revolution, however, new means of technological reproducibility were to disengage the work of art 'from its [...] dependence on ritual',[36] and as a consequence its embeddedness and use in place, stripped of its authenticity through reproduction, all ties seemingly severed with tradition, the body no longer regarded as a meaningful locus. 'Soul, eye and hand [were thus] disjoint[ed]', the worker transformed into the labourer and deskilled, no longer wielding the tool but instead exercised by it, latched to the machine, his movements ordained by its 'uniform and unceasing motion', a 'dislocating rhythm to which he must react, [...] each act [...] an exact repetition of the last', devoid of any alternative extemporisation or improvisation.[37] The labouring life, as such, was inescapably subject to the 'homogenous time of manufacture',[38] unlike the product of work, of which, it is said, 'there exists no "natural" rhythm', being born instead of necessity, a matter of mindfulness and ministration.[39]

The abundance of objects produced by machines at an ever-quickening rate changed the character of the artefact, the artefact 'entirely determined by the categories of means and end', the processes and procedures engaged with in its making 'com[ing] to an end in it' and being the very 'means to produce this end'.[40] Fashioned by artisans or craftsmen, it was premised on a model, a paradigm, which operated as both its measure and was accordingly measured by it, an overarching image, a blueprint of sorts, guiding the fabrication process. This image, it is said, 'not only precedes' the work, but endures beyond the finished product, 'surviv[ing] intact', present to the infinite possibilities of its fabrication.[41] The potentiality of multiplication intrinsic to the artefact, as such, corresponds with a variable rhythm, one which drives a pattern of movement, each manifestation, we are told, a 'precious product', the result 'of a long chain of causes similar to one another'.[42] Such multiplication stands in marked distinction, however, from the deadening repetition innate to labour, answering, as it does, to the 'ever-recurrent needs of consumption' and the proclivities of fashion coveted by the masses. The commodity in usurping the artefact, once coveted and admired, however, was to 'lack the worldly permanence of a piece of work', free enterprise diminishing the 'difference between use and consumption, between the relative durability of use objects, [in] the swift coming and going of consumer goods'.[43]

Works of art were similarly subject to this change, having always been reproducible, this potential lying dormant and always inherent to the artwork itself, for '[m]anmade artefacts', it is said, 'could always be imitated by men'.[44] Indeed, Semper was to observe this phenomenon; changes in material, media, or *Stoffwechsel*, as he was to term it, if honourably and appropriately applied, continued to express the artistic motive and primeval type, carrying discernable of traces of its lineage.[45]

In the early years of the twentieth century, however, the internal movement native to the artwork, the work already at work within it accelerated with alacritous speed, the sheer intensity and prodigiousness of replication compounding. The photographic apparatus and its processes were emblematic of the transformation, new techniques of production progressively shaping and controlling the very make-up of the artwork, and by extension, our way of living.[46] 'For the first time in the process of pictorial reproduction', we are told, 'photography freed the hand of the most important artistic functions',[47] its powers by and large transferred by the touch of a finger, the focus now concentrated on the relationship between lens and eye, the surface of the print seemingly no longer handled in the manner of the painted surface, touched and retouched by the brush: an extension of the arm, mind and eyes.

Eschewing history and any sense of provenance, the significance of the artwork, as a consequence, was revolutionised, its value determined by the sheer spectacle of exhibition and pecuniary worth alone. While it was said that 'the work of art reproduced becomes the work of art designed for reproducibility',[48] the potential for imitation was capable of manifesting, however, only when an 'indifference to history' was to wane, opening up to and acknowledging the very possibility of transmission. For 'what is lost in the withering of semblance' of works of art as a result of the repetition of relationships that already exist, we are told, is 'gain[ed] in the scope [or room] for play [*Spiel-Raum*]',[49] the promise of which can never be entirely exhausted, by enabling media used for reproductive objectives to create new relationships in being put to productive ends.

Tradition, we might recall, is only realised through its transmission, with '[t]he phenomenon of translation', it is said, 'provid[ing] a model for the real nature of' it.[50] For translation is the very play of languages, in poetry's reinscription we are told that 'a poet's meaning progresses from words to words, metamorphosed from one language into another',[51] but this sense of relocation can never be absolute, for what reaches the new domain is 'that element in a translation which goes beyond transmittal of subject matter'.[52] Movement is nonetheless implicit within the concept, the origins of translation once pertaining to the passage from life to death, and so to redemption too, its processes integral and essential to becoming and change.[53]

Imbued with a sense of physicality, translation, it is said, conveys 'a change of condition or site', founded upon a relationship that suggests a 'geography of action', modifications and adjustments occurring *across* a domain, 'the sense of the physical or geographical separateness [...] still implicit and potent' despite the correlations and connections made. Through translation, a sense of transfer, of handling, is embedded and retained, for like tradition, something is handed on or down, in the conveyance of 'something [meaningful] from one person, [place], or condition' to the next, and so on, thereafter establishing a chain of exchanges, a lineage emerging and binding.[54]

In giving form to the expression of tradition in its continual translation realised through semblance and play, the presence of the hand is there, it is said, 'making its presence known', for 'the hand touches the world itself, feels it, lays hold of it', its dexterous manipulations enabling knowledge to be multiplied,[55] the apprehension of the world by touch a remedy, providing a means through which the recovery of experience is disclosed and capable again of being conveyed. For, '[s]alvation', we are told, 'includes [a] firm, [yet] apparently brutal grip', grasping, taking hold of what lies before us.[56]

The essence of the hand, however, can never be determined by its capacity to grasp, its significance lying in the fact that '[e]very motion of the hand in every one of its works carries itself through the element of thinking, every bearing of the hand bears itself in that element'.[57] Indeed, 'every contact [...] raises the question of an answer [and] the skin is asked to reply',[58] thinking and feeling, the very work of the hand, in alignment with psyche and eye. The hands together, we are told, are 'instruments of both poetry and industry',[59] their contact and conduct 'placing us "in the midst of the world"', indeed, in and amongst things.[60] For 'in taking a few shreds of the world', another world is thus able to be fashioned and contrived,[61] matter and material remoulded and reshaped, brought forth and in doing so bringing forth the place in which they are divined.[62]

In a shed in the Outer Hebrides lie photographs of Melbourne's curtain walls, once images in their architects' minds, translated into drawings, and translated again, reified in built form, only to be later inscribed onto a light-fixing substrate, waiting to be translated into Harris Tweed, their surfaces traced over, grids drawn up to scale for the making. Ossified and skeletal, the stripped and naked language of the curtain wall, it has been suggested, can conceivably only be redeemed when its language is transposed to another,[63] its glazing glossed over and given a sense of redress, for 'the language of the translation', we are told, is akin to dressing, an envelopment enshrouding 'its content like a royal robe', a re-covering replete 'with ample folds',[64] the interior of a camera once said to be similarly arrayed in a form of riddel.[65]

The fundamental purpose of translation, like remediation, 'the representation of one medium by another',[66] we are told, lies in the expression of the 'reciprocal relationships between languages', for, 'languages are not strangers to one another, but are [...] interrelated in what they want to express'.[67]

But is not enough to simply utter, write or inscribe, nor to produce or to make by any other means, for we must poetically dwell, fashioning a shell composed of language,[68] a text, whether woven of words, wool or stone, laden with impressions which bear the very marks of our being, and are given form in the weaving, in traversing 'the expanse of the leeway between earth and sky',[69] for '*only then*', it is said, '*can we build*'.[70]

Notes

1 'No one ever asks [...] "How long will it take?" but "How many songs will it take?"' The Gaelic scholar Reverend Kenneth MacLeod discussing the practice of waulking, quoted in Francis Thompson, *Harris Tweed: The Story of a Hebridean Industry* (Newton Abbot: David and Charles, 1969), 171. A very similar version of this essay, 'Ritual | Repetition', was published in *Textile: Journal of Cloth and Culture* 13, no. 1 (2015), © Taylor and Francis, available online: www.tandfonline.com/ DOI: 10.2752/ 175183515x14235680035386.

2 See Frances Tolmie, *One Hundred and Five Songs of Occupation from the Western Isles of Scotland* (Edinburgh: Llanerch Publishers, 1997).

3 Nan MacKinnon of Vatersay in 1964 noted of the waulking, that: 'They had a different way in every place, even in the island of Barra – the west and the east, and the north end.' Quoted in J. L. Campbell, 'The Waulking Pulse', in *Hebridean Folksongs: A Collection of Waulking Songs by Donald MacCormick in Kilphedir in South Uist in the Year 1863* (London: Oxford University Press, 1969), 221–2.

4 The waulking can be seen to embody the expression *die schöne Sittlichkeit* – literally 'the beautiful ethical life' which, as Gadamer notes, 'does not mean

that their ethical customs were full of beauty in the sense of being filled with pomp and ostentatious splendour. It means that the ethical life of the people found expression in all forms of communal life, giving shape to the whole and so allowing men to recognize themselves in their own world.' Hans-Georg Gadamer, 'The Relevance of the Beautiful: Art as Play, Symbol and Festival', in *The Relevance of the Beautiful and Other Essays*, ed. Robert Bernasconi and trans. Nicholas Walker (Cambridge: Cambridge University Press, 1986), 14.

5 Thursday was the day associated with St Columba (521–97 A.D.), the saint who christianised the Gaels and the Picts, the early inhabitants of the Highlands and the Isles. See Thompson, *Harris Tweed*, 170.

6 Campbell, 'The Waulking Pulse', 220.

7 Ada Goodrich Freer, *The Outer Isles*, quoted in Campbell, 'The Waulking Described', 9. To view a waulking where this zigzag phenomenon is particularly pronounced, see *Eriskay: A Poem of Remote Lives*, dir. Werner Kissling, http://movingimage.nls.uk/film/1701. Accessed 18 March 2016.

8 To view a performance of the 'Hebridean Weaving Lilt', see *Scotland Dances*, dir. Alan Harper (Edinburgh: Campbell Harper Films, 1957), http://movingimage.nls.uk/film/2224. Accessed 18 March 2016.

9 Leatherbarrow observes that: 'participation (*methexis* in Plato and *metalepsis* in Aristotle, or *proportione* in Cicero, in the sense of each having its due portion of the good) is exemplified in all cases of imitation or *mimesis*. [...] Because participation exists in number or measure and life or action it is the key to understanding their essential mutuality.' David Leatherbarrow, *The Roots of Architectural Invention: Site, Enclosure, Materials* (New York: Cambridge University Press, 1993), 87–8. Huizinga's view, however, is more limited, stating that the rite 'is *methetic* rather than *mimetic*'. Johan Huizinga, *Homo Ludens: A Study of the Play Element in Culture* (Boston, MA: Beacon Press, 1955), 15. Emphasis in Huizinga.

10 See Walter Benjamin, 'The Work of Art in the Age of Its Technological Reproducibility' (Second Version), in *The Work of Art in the Age of its Technological Reproducibility, and other Writings on Media*, ed. Michael W. Jennings, Brigid Doherty and Thomas Y. Levin (Cambridge, MA: Belknap Press of Harvard University Press, 2008), 48, n. 23.

11 With reference to ancient Greek theatre and the *choreia*, see Alberto Pérez-Gómez, 'The Space of Architectural Representation', in *Chora 1: Intervals in the Philosophy of Architecture*, ed. Alberto Pérez-Gómez and Stephen Parcell (Montreal: McGill University Press, 1994), 12. Emphasis in Pérez-Gómez. For a further discussion of the liminality of the body, see Jeff Malpas, 'The Threshold of the World', http://jeffmalpas.com/wp-content/uploads/2013/02/The-Threshold-of-the-World.pdf. Accessed 5 September 2013.

12 Huizinga, *Homo Ludens*, 158.

13 See Hans-Georg Gadamer, *Truth and Method*, 2nd ed. rev., trans. Joel Weinsheimer and Donald G. Marshall (London: Continuum, 2004), 104.

14 Alan Lomax, Irmgard Bartenieff and Forrestine Paulay, 'Dance Style and Culture', in *Folk Song Style and Culture*, ed. Alan Lomax (New Brunswick, NJ: Transaction Publishers, 1968), 223.

130   *Ritual | Repetition*

15 See Gadamer, *Truth and Method*, 104–5.
16 See Huizinga, *Homo Ludens*, 20–2.
17 Mari Hvattum, *Gottfried Semper and the Problem of Historicism* (Cambridge: Cambridge University Press, 2004), 66.
18 Mircea Eliade, *Myth of the Eternal Return*, quoted in Edward S. Casey, *Remembering: A Phenomenological Study*, 2nd ed. (Bloomington, IN: Indiana University Press, 2000), 231.
19 Casey notes that '[p]erdurance represents a via media between eternity and time', with ritual exhibiting 'perdurance as its […] main temporal mode'. Casey, *Remembering*, 217–18. Emphasis in Casey.
20 Joseph Rykwert, *The Idea of a Town: The Anthropology of Urban Form in Rome, Italy and the Ancient World* (London: Faber and Faber, 1976), 88.
21 Casey, *Remembering*, 228.
22 Henri Focillon, 'In Praise of Hands', trans. S. L. Faison Jnr, in *The Life of Forms in Art* (New York: George Wittenborn Shultz, 1948), 71.
23 Casey notes that 'in acts of commemoration remembering is intensified by taking place through the interposed agency of a text […] and in the setting of a social ritual, [they are] highly mediated affair[s]'. Casey, *Remembering*, 218. Emphasis in Casey.
24 With reference to Mircea Eliade's *Myth of the Eternal Return*, see Casey, *Remembering*, 231.
25 See Casey, *Remembering*, 229. Casey further clarifies aspects of 'ritual action' in terms of the ritual's relationship with representation, myth, drama and concepts pertaining to the sacred and profane, in Edward S. Casey, 'Reflections on Ritual', *Spring: An Annual of Archetypal and Jungian Thought* (1985): 102–9.
26 Søren Kierkegaard, *Fear and Trembling. Repetition*, quoted in Mikhail Iampolski, 'Translating Images …', *Res: Journal of Anthropology and Aesthetics* 32 (1997): 38.
27 Casey, *Remembering*, 229.
28 Eduardo Cadava, 'Sternphotographie: Benjamin, Blanqui, and the Mimesis of Stars', *Qui Parle* 9, no. 1 (1995): 15–16.
29 Hvattum, *Gottfried Semper*, 69.
30 Rykwert, *Idea of a Town*, 27.
31 See Harry Francis Mallgrave, introduction to *The Four Elements of Architecture and Other Writings*, by Gottfried Semper (Cambridge: Cambridge University Press, 1989), 35–6.
32 Percy Bysshe Shelley, *A Defence of Poetry* (Indianapolis, IN: Bobbs-Merrill Company, 1904), 90.
33 Gottfried Semper, *Style in the Technical and Tectonic Arts: or, Practical Aesthetics*, trans. Harry Francis Mallgrave and Michael Robinson (Los Angeles: Getty Research Institute, 2004), 82.
34 Mallgrave, introduction to *The Four Elements*, 33.
35 Joseph Rykwert, 'The École des Beaux-Arts and the Classical Tradition', in *The Beaux-Arts and Nineteenth-Century French Architecture*, ed. Robin Middleton (Cambridge, MA: MIT Press, 1982), 17.

Ritual | Repetition 131

36 Walter Benjamin, 'The Work of Art in the Age of Mechanical Reproduction', in *Illuminations: Essays and Reflections*, ed. Hannah Arendt and trans. Harry Zohn (New York: Schocken Books, 1969), 224.

37 See Esther Leslie, 'Walter Benjamin: Traces of Craft', *Journal of Design History* 11, no. 1 (1998): 7. Arendt's understanding of the differences between work and labour, between *homo faber* and *animal laborens*, departs from the physician and philosopher John Locke's (1632–1704) 'distinction between working hands and a labouring body'. She further observes that 'the Greek language distinguishes between *ponein* and *ergazethai*, the Latin between *laborare* and *facere* or *fabricari*, which have the same etymological root, the French between *travailler* and *ouvrer*, the German between *arbeiten* and *werken*. In all these cases, only the equivalents for 'labour' have an unequivocal connotation of pain and trouble.' Hannah Arendt, *The Human Condition* (Chicago: University of Chicago Press), 80, and 80, n. 3.

38 Leslie, 'Walter Benjamin', 7.

39 See Arendt, *Human Condition*, 145, n. 8. Sennett, in his discussion of skill, exposes the inextricable relationship between ritual and rhythm in its formation. See Richard Sennett, *Together: The Rituals, Pleasures and Politics of Co-Operation* (New Haven, CT: Yale University Press, 2012), 200–3.

40 See Arendt, *Human Condition*, 143. Here Gadamer concurs when he notes: 'The work is finished if it answers the purpose for which it is intended.' He goes on to suggest, however, that a work of art is never truly finished, only in its reception is something made of it. See Gadamer, *Truth and Method*, 81–2.

41 See Arendt, *Human Condition*, 141, and 104.

42 The poet Paul Valéry (1871–1945) describes nature thus, and is quoted in Walter Benjamin, 'The Storyteller: Reflections on the Work of Nikolai Leskov', in *Illuminations: Essays and Reflections*, ed. Hanna Arendt and trans. Harry Zohn (New York: Schocken Books, 1969), 92.

43 Arendt, *Human Condition*, 125.

44 Benjamin, 'Work of Art', 218.

45 See Semper, *Style*, 253

46 See Eduardo Cadava, *Words of Light: Theses on the Photography of History* (Princeton, NJ: Princeton University Press, 1997), 43.

47 See Benjamin, 'Work of Art', 219.

48 Benjamin, 'Work of Art', 224.

49 See Walter Benjamin, 'Work of Art' (SecondVersion), 48, n. 23.

50 Gadamer, 'Relevance of the Beautiful', 49.

51 Alberto Manguel, *A History of Reading* (London: Flamingo, 1997), 266.

52 Walter Benjamin, 'The Task of the Translator: An Introduction to the Translation of Baudelaire's *Tableaux Parisiens*', in *Illuminations: Essays and Reflections*, ed. Hannah Arendt and trans. Harry Zohn (New York: Schocken Books, 1969), 75.

53 As Sontag notes: 'Translation is about difference. [...] Originally (at least in English) translation was about the biggest difference of all: that between being alive and being dead. To translate is, etymologically, to transfer, to remove, to displace. To what end? In order to be rescued, from death or

132 Ritual | Repetition

extinction.' Susan Sontag, 'Being Translated', *Res: Journal of Anthropology and Aesthetics* 32 (1997): 15.
54 See Sontag, 'Being Translated', 15.
55 See Focillon, 'In Praise of Hands', 68–78.
56 Benjamin, Arcades Project, quoted in Leslie, 'Walter Benjamin', 6.
57 Martin Heidegger, 'What Calls for Thinking?', in *Basic Writings from 'Being in Time' (1927) to 'The Task of Thinking' (1964)*, ed. David Farrell Krell (San Francisco: Harper Collins, 1993), 381. For a further discussion of this concept, see Juhani Pallasmaa, *The Thinking Hand: Existential and Embodied Wisdom in Architecture* (Chichester: Wiley, 2009).
58 Roland Barthes, *A Lover's Discourse: Fragments*, trans. Richard Howard (London: Penguin Books, 1990), 67.
59 Focillon, 'In Praise of Hands', 70.
60 With reference to Maurice Merleau-Ponty, *The Visible and the Invisible*, see Edward S. Casey, *The Fate of Place: A Philosophical History* (Berkeley, CA: University of California Press, 1997), 236.
61 See Focillon, 'In Praise of Hands', 69.
62 With reference to the ancient Greek concept of *technē*, Heidegger was to comment that 'the erecting of buildings would not be suitably defined even if we were to think of it in the sense of the original Greek *technē* as solely a letting-appear, which brings something made, as something present, among the things that are already present', suggesting that the essential role of building, of making, is only achieved when locales are brought forth in their very joining with the object or construction of that making. See Martin Heidegger, 'Building Dwelling Thinking', in *Basic Writings from 'Being in Time' (1927) to 'The Task of Thinking' (1964)*, ed. David Farrell Krell (San Francisco: Harper Collins, 1993), 361. Emphasis in Heidegger.
63 As Gadamer observes: 'The ossified language of literature only becomes art when it becomes part of our own language. The same is true of the figurative arts and architecture as well.' Gadamer, 'Relevance of the Beautiful', 49.
64 Benjamin, 'Task of the Translator', 75.
65 The philosopher Gottfried Wilhelm Leibniz (1646–1716) once likened the brain to a room, its functioning remarkably prescient of the camera, stating that: 'To increase the resemblance we should have to postulate that there is a screen/canvas/curtain/membrane [*toile*] in the darkened room [...] to receive the species [...] and that it is not uniform but is diversified by folds [...] representing items of innate knowledge; and what is more, that this screen/canvas/curtain/membrane, being under tension, has a kind of elasticity or active force, and indeed that it acts (or reacts) in ways that are adapted both to past folds and to new ones coming from impressions of the species.' Gottfried Wilhelm Leibniz, *New Essays on Human Understanding*, quoted in Anthony Vidler, 'Skin and Bones: Folded Forms from Leibniz to Lynn', in *Warped Space: Art, Architecture, and Anxiety in Modern Culture* (Cambridge, MA: MIT Press, 2000), 221.
66 Jay David Bolter and Richard Grusin, *Remediation: Understanding New Media* (Cambridge, MA: MIT Press, 2000), 45.

67 Benjamin, 'Task of the Translator', 72. On this point, also refer to Alberto Pérez-Gómez, 'The Relevance of Beauty in Architecture', in *The Cultural Role of Architecture: Contemporary and Historical Perspectives*, ed. Paul Emmons, Jane Lomholt and John Hendrix (London: Routledge, 2012), 164–5.
68 As Heidegger notes: 'Language is the precinct [*templum*], i.e., the house of being.' Martin Heidegger, 'Why Poets?', quoted in Jeff Malpas, *Heidegger's Topology: Being, Place, World* (Cambridge, MA: MIT Press, 2008), 264. Rykwert also observes that Vitruvius, in the opening of his second book, describes '[t]he intimate connection between the invention of speech and of building'. Joseph Rykwert, 'Building as Gesture, Building as Argument', *Thesis: Wissenschaftliche Zeitschrift der Bauhaus-Universität Weimar* 3 (2003): 45.
69 Martin Heidegger, 'Hebel – Friend of the House', quoted in Malpas, *Heidegger's Topology*, 266.
70 Heidegger, 'Building Dwelling Thinking', 361. Emphasis in Heidegger.

Bibliography

Arendt, Hannah. *The Human Condition*. Chicago: University of Chicago Press, 1958.

Barthes, Roland. *A Lover's Discourse: Fragments*. Translated by Richard Howard. London: Penguin Books, 1990.

Benjamin, Walter. 'The Storyteller: Reflections on the Work of Nikolai Leskov'. In *Illuminations: Essays and Reflections*. Edited by Hanna Arendt and translated by Harry Zohn, 83–109. New York: Schocken Books, 1969.

———. 'The Task of the Translator: An Introduction to the Translation of Baudelaire's *Tableaux Parisiens*'. In *Illuminations: Essays and Reflections*. Edited by Hannah Arendt and translated by Harry Zohn, 69–82. New York: Schocken Books, 1969.

———. 'The Work of Art in the Age of Mechanical Reproduction'. In *Illuminations: Essays and Reflections*. Edited by Hannah Arendt and translated by Harry Zohn, 217–52. New York: Schocken Books, 1969.

———. 'The Work of Art in the Age of its Technological Reproducibility' (2nd Version). Translated by Edmund Jephcott and Harry Zohn. In *The Work of Art in the Age of its Technological Reproducibility, and other Writings on Media*. Edited by Michael W. Jennings, Brigid Doherty and Thomas Y. Levin, 19–55. Cambridge, MA: Belknap Press of Harvard University Press, 2008.

Bolter, Jay David and Richard Grusin. *Remediation: Understanding New Media*. Cambridge, MA: MIT Press, 2000.

Cadava, Eduardo. '*Sternphotographie*: Benjamin, Blanqui, and the Mimesis of Stars', *Qui Parle* 9, no. 1 (1995): 1–32.

———. *Words of Light: Theses on the Photography of History*. Princeton, NJ: Princeton University Press, 1997.

Campbell, J. L., ed. *Hebridean Folksongs: A Collection of Waulking Songs by Donald MacCormick in Kilphedir in South Uist in the Year 1863*. London: Oxford University Press, 1969.

Casey, Edward S. 'Reflections on Ritual', *Spring: An Annual of Archetypal and Jungian Thought* (1985): 102–9.

———. *The Fate of Place: A Philosophical History*. Berkeley: University of California Press, 1997.

———. *Remembering: A Phenomenological Study*, 2nd ed. Bloomington: Indiana University Press, 2000.

Eriskay: A Poem of Remote Lives. Directed by Werner Kissling, http://movingimage.nls.uk/film/1701. Accessed 18 March 2016.

Focillon, Henri. 'In Praise of Hands'. Translated by S. L. Faison Jnr. In *The Life of Forms in Art*, 65–78. New York: George Wittenborn Schultz, 1948.

Gadamer, Hans-Georg. 'The Relevance of the Beautiful: Art as Play, Symbol and Festival'. In *The Relevance of the Beautiful and Other Essays*. Edited by Robert Bernasconi and translated by Nicholas Walker, 1–53. Cambridge: Cambridge University Press, 1986.

———. *Truth and Method*, 2nd ed. rev. Translated by Joel Weinsheimer and Donald G. Marshall. London: Continuum, 2004.

Heidegger, Martin. 'Building Dwelling Thinking'. In *Basic Writings from "Being in Time" (1927) to "The Task of Thinking" (1964)*. Edited by David Farrell Krell, 343–64. San Francisco: Harper Collins, 1993.

———. 'What Calls for Thinking?'. In *Basic Writings from "Being in Time" (1927) to "The Task of Thinking" (1964)*. Edited by David Farrell Krell, 365–92. San Francisco: Harper Collins, 1993.

Huizinga, Johan. *Homo Ludens: A Study of the Play Element in Culture*. Boston, MA: Beacon Press, 1955.

Hvattum, Mari. *Gottfried Semper and the Problem of Historicism*. Cambridge: Cambridge University Press, 2004.

Iampolski, Mikhail. 'Translating Images …', *Res: Journal of Anthropology and Aesthetics* 32 (1997): 37–42.

Leatherbarrow, David. *The Roots of Architectural Invention: Site, Enclosure, Materials*. New York: Cambridge University Press, 1993.

Leslie, Esther. 'Walter Benjamin: Traces of Craft', *Journal of Design History* 11, no. 1 (1998): 5–13.

Lomax, Alan, Irmgard Bartenieff and Forrestine Paulay. 'Dance Style and Culture'. In *Folk Song Style and Culture*. Edited by Alan Lomax, 222–47. New Brunswick, NJ: Transaction Publishers, 1968.

Mallgrave, Harry Francis. Introduction to *The Four Elements of Architecture and Other Writings*, by Gottfried Semper, 1–44. Cambridge. Cambridge University Press, 1989.

Malpas, Jeff. *Heidegger's Topology: Being, Place, World*. Cambridge, MA: MIT Press, 2008.

———. 'The Threshold of the World', http://jeffmalpas.com/wp-content/uploads/2013/02/The-Threshold-of-the-World.pdf. Accessed 5 September 2013.

Manguel, Alberto. *A History of Reading*. London: Flamingo, 1997.

Pallasmaa, Juhani. *The Thinking Hand: Existential and Embodied Wisdom in Architecture*. Chichester: Wiley, 2009.

Pérez-Gómez, Alberto. 'The Space of Architectural Representation'. In *Chora 1: Intervals in the Philosophy of Architecture*. Edited by Alberto Pérez-Gómez and Stephen Parcell, 1–34. Montreal: McGill University Press, 1994.

———. 'The Relevance of Beauty in Architecture'. In *The Cultural Role of Architecture: Contemporary and Historical Perspectives*. Edited by Paul Emmons, Jane Lomholt and John Hendrix, 157–66. London: Routledge, 2012.

Rykwert, Joseph. *The Idea of a Town: The Anthropology of Urban Form in Rome, Italy and the Ancient World*. London: Faber and Faber, 1976.

———. 'The *Ecole des Beaux-Arts* and the Classical Tradition'. In *The Beaux-Arts and Nineteenth-Century French Architecture*. Edited by Robin Middleton, 8–17. Cambridge, MA: MIT Press, 1982.

———. 'Building as Gesture, Building as Argument', *Thesis: Wissenschaftliche Zeitschrift der Bauhaus-Universität Weimar* 3 (2003): 44–54.

Scotland Dances. Directed by Alan Harper. Edinburgh: Campbell Harper Films, 1957. http://movingimage.nls.uk/film/2224. Accessed 18 March 2016.

Semper, Gottfried. *Style in the Technical and Tectonic Arts: or, Practical Aesthetics*. Translated by Harry Francis Mallgrave and Michael Robinson. Los Angeles: Getty Research Institute, 2004.

Sennett, Richard. *Together: The Rituals, Pleasures and Politics of Co-Operation*. New Haven, CT: Yale University Press, 2012.

Shelley, Percy Bysshe. *A Defence of Poetry*. Indianapolis, IN: Bobbs Merrill Company, 1904.

Sontag, Susan. 'Being Translated', *Res: Journal of Anthropology and Aesthetics* 32 (1997): 13–18.

Thompson, Francis. *Harris Tweed: The Story of a Hebridean Industry*. Newton Abbot: David and Charles, 1969.

Tolmie, Frances. *One Hundred and Five Songs of Occupation from the Western Isles of Scotland*. Edinburgh: Llanerch Publishers, 1997.

Vidler, Anthony. 'Skin and Bones: Folded Forms from Leibniz to Lynn'. In *Warped Space: Art, Architecture, and Anxiety in Modern Culture*, 219–34. Cambridge, MA: MIT Press, 2000.

Text

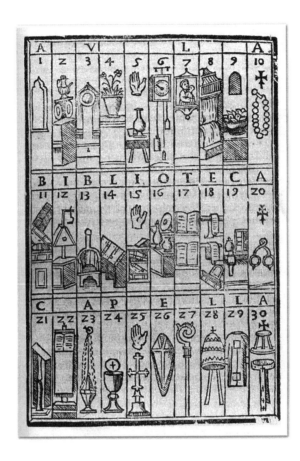

Figure 8.1 'The Abbey Memory System'. From Johann Horst von Romberch, *Congestorium artificiose memorie* (Venice: Melchiorre Sessa, 1533). By kind permission of Kislak Center for Special Collections, Rare Books and Manuscripts, University of Pennsylvania.

Memory

Figure 8.2 Ezra Stoller, *Seagram Building, Mies van der Rohe with Philip Johnson, New York, NY,* 1958.

Shadow solar ink
Handwriting of my light.

Guillaume Apollinaire

Environment and setting still have a great influence upon one; there is something about them which stamps itself firmly and deeply in the memory, or rather upon the whole soul, and which is therefore never forgotten.

Søren Kierkegaard

The buildings of the ancient Greeks, we are told, like those of other ancient civilisations,[1] were once brightly coloured, stuccoes tinted with mineral ochres, ground stones and various dyes coating their revetments; their surfaces figuring now though as a *tabula rasa* bearing only vestiges of colour, and like the mystic writing pad, of lettering and inscriptions too, their role integral in the crafting of civic space, the concept of memory central to it.[2]

In the sixth century B.C., the physical act of writing in ancient Greece was performed as a continuous flow, from left to right then right to left, and so on, being read also in this way. Its passage was likened to that of an ox ploughing a field, from whence it gets its name, *boustrophēdon*. While meaning and sense were inscribed so too was another pattern, that of the figuring of the text, its skew acknowledging the change in course, evidenced in the slant of the inscription of alternate lines, bequeathing upon the script an aesthetic dimension, beyond the hand, a grain. This alt was to persist, even when this style of writing was replaced by the left-to-right standard some hundred years later, the inflection of the script now regular, the pattern instead accentuated by colour, black and red ink marking every other line. It has been said that the Greeks did not borrow this form of writing from any other culture,[3] but perhaps, it might be suggested, its inspiration was closer to hand, drawing from the plying of the loom, that symbol of hearth and home.[4]

In the Outer Hebrides, not the isolated weaver's hut, but villages resounded not so long ago with the clickety-clack of the looms. The shuttle passing over and under the warp threads created a shed in the loom, the lifting and lowering of the heddles enabling the weft to amount in a to-and-fro fashion, writing, so to speak, the surface of the cloth, the herringbone pattern, with the one colour in the warp and the other in the weft, viewed across the loom rather than from its seat, reminiscent of the pre-classical Greek text.

The web of cloth, the Harris Tweed, is conceivably doubly woven, if not more so, sometimes crooned over by the weaver, and not so long ago incanted over in the waulking, its songs part of a great oral tradition, whose composer is long since forgotten, the singers' roles recalling that of the ancient Greek *rhapsōidos*, the 'one who resews the song', song itself understood then as a fabric.[5]

In the Hebrides there is no handbook of weaving, no series of instructions written down, no standard way prescribed in text of its making. Harris Tweed is steeped in oral tradition; children playing around the loom soon learned to wind bobbins, watching as their mother or father peddled the loom, assisting with other tasks as they grew, imbibing its laws, taking note of its patterns, though not in a studied way, but rather amidst the distraction of daily activities and the changing light, experienced in the shifting colours of land, sea and sky. The tweed is inextricably bound with the Gaelic language, the one re-enforcing the other,[6] the cloth still somehow resonant with the resounding rhythms of the waulking, ancient narratives impressed upon it by the chevronned interweaving of hands in its finishing.[7]

For until the eighteenth century, Gaelic was by and large not written, and when poems were thence collected and transcribed, it was the chorus of vocables of the air to which they were sung that proved to be more powerful, acting as a mnemonic,[8] orality and memory inextricably bound, performance and participation 'keeping an entire body of collectively held lore alive'.[9] Stories thus accompanied the hand at work, history and lore, spoken, sung and heard, accent betraying the place of one's birth.[10] For, '[o]nly the spoken word', it is said, 'is not sealed, folded, occult or undemocratic'.[11]

The transcribing of verses and poems, a movement from oral accounts and recitations to written speech, signalled, we are told, 'a shift' from the aural realm to the domain of visual space, the relationship established between printing and writing, containing within it at its outset, nonetheless, the residues of orality.[12] A surface or substrate was necessarily required, and on this basis the image, then, whether etched out in lettering or figured as any kind gained pre-eminence as memory's agent, whether triggered by sight, touch, scent, taste or sound, for all amounted to image, the image memory's *aides-mémoire* and means of mediation.[13]

The invention of writing along with the secularisation of memory, it is said, gave rise in the ancient world to mnemotechnology,[14] the art of memory, or place system as it is sometimes called,[15] a method founded upon two sets of images, their layout instigating correlations between image and place, conceived of as an 'elective affinity', place and memory '[n]ot only [...] suited to [each] other', but 'each call[ing] for the other',[16] images adherent, nonetheless, the one to the other, taken to heart and fixed in mind. The first set of images, a series of places, *loci* in Latin, or *topoi* in Greek, we are told, were serially arranged, providing the background, a structure reminiscent of a street; the second comprised of another set bound to them, images of words (*memoria verborum*) or things (*memoria rerum*)[17] symbolising the points of a speech later to be recalled and declaimed, the deployment of these techniques famously portrayed in the tale of Simonides (c. 556–468 B.C.), he who once declared that 'the word is a picture of things'.[18]

This public intellectual, the first purported, a poet who was paid, was once commissioned to recite an *epinikion*, an ode to victory, during the course of a feast in honour of a Thessalian prince. This piece was excessively devoted, or so his patron thought, to the praise of the godly brothers Kastor and Polydeukes, together strangely graced, so much so that he paid him only half his agreed fee, suggesting that its balance be paid by them.[19] Answering a call to the door to address the Dioskouroi, or so it would later seem, he excused himself from the feast, arriving to find no one there, the roof of the banquet hall caving in on his absence. His fellow diners were crushed and killed, their bodies mangled and malformed, so much so that their identities were no longer discernable. Simonides remembering each guest and their seating enabled the bodies of the deceased to be returned to their respective families for proper burial and mourning.[20] As a result of this tragedy, we are told, he was credited with devising the 'art of memory' or the art of recollection, as it might well be called, premised on the remembrance of images and their order, the distinction between places and the images associated with them also ascribed to him.[21] Such recall, then, was understood to be not a passive act but active, premised upon rehearsal and retrieval.

Memoria as an art was further developed during the course of antiquity, with significant developments occurring subsequently in the first century B.C. and the following century A.D.,[22] when its practices were referred to and coined 'artificial'.[23] Rhetoric then, we are told, was the 'fashioning [of] a good speech',[24] reaching its apotheosis during the Middle Ages, when it was the soul that was furnished, while giving shape to civic life through the exercise of jurisprudence, later to assume an occult dimension during the course of the Renaissance, 'its thrust diverted, definitively if not totally, from oral performance to [the practices of] writing' with the onset of the Age of Romanticism.[25] Memory, moreover its art, we are told, was thus understood and deployed as a device for the 'invention and retention of knowledge',[26] the recounting of it, whether planned or at a whim, an integral facet of rhetoric, its 'noblest' aspect, and, as some have said, the very basis of it.[27]

During the Middle Ages, the superimposition of images, the one upon the other, was reliant on two models, memory as a book and as an architectural edifice,[28] pages or *mise-en-scènes* composed, surfaces binding and bound, 'recollection occur[ing] consciously [nonetheless] through association'.[29] Each archetype, it is said, was to draw from different texts, Quintilian's *Institutio Oratoria* and the *Rhetorica ad Herennium* respectively, these two versions, however, were said to be by no means 'radically separate'.[30]

Since ancient times, memory has been conceived of as a surface, a wax tablet inscribed, or alternatively impressed upon with a seal, a mark incising and entombing a sign, place corresponding to the waxen block, the letters or glyphs to the images, these marks capable of being erased when no longer relevant or useful, but the tablet like place remaining fast and enduring.[31] Indeed, it was said that:

memory ... is in a manner the twin sister of written speech [*litteratura*] and is completely similar [*persimilis*] to it, [though] in a dissimilar medium. For just as script consists of marks indicating letters and of the material on which those marks are imprinted, so the structure of memory, like a wax tablet, employs places [*loci*] and in these gathers together [*collocat*] images like letters.[32]

Quintilian's memory system, a legatee of the *tabula memoriae* tradition,[33] was premised upon the 'act of reading', with his prescriptions adhering to the page and nearly concomitant with the emergence of the codex, precursor to the book, competing with and soon to usurp antiquity's scrolls of parchment and papyrus. Stipulating that the same manuscript be used, the text was to be columniated and divided, with words or images placed in the margins of the page in order to prompt the memory in the reclamation and pronouncement of a 'text's content and meaning'.[34]

Rhetoric, it has been suggested, however, owes its origins to architecture more so than to the book, 'the image of a building, both in plan and volume' said to be the very 'place or *topos* of any discourse',[35] the *thesaurus* or 'storage room', a 'treasure-house of found things',[36] as it has been variously called, a vital image and edifying, one amongst many engaged by the learned mind, the formulation of such images encapsulating both the place and the ordered manner of a speech or knowledge's archiving.[37]

The *Ad Herennium*, written in the first century B.C., so called in honour of the 'Roman citizen to whom it was dedicated',[38] provided 'the main source of the tradition', and was conceived of as an 'inner writing', indeed, it might be said, a design.[39] For the construction of a mental edifice, its premise, whether real or imaginary, we are told, was to take the form of 'a house, an inter-columnar space, a recess, an arch, or the like',[40] through which a series of interconnected architectural spaces was to be composed, these 'places [...] designed to receive whatever memory object [was] to be housed by them'. Every route through the edifice was to be committed to memory and known by heart prior to the imposition of images, their depositing signalling 'what is to be remembered along' the way, so that upon return, a journey undertaken through it enabled the retrieval of the information so placed, its recovery easily facilitated.[41]

This guide prepared for the student of rhetoric, it is said, was a highly regulated affair, conditions specified at length and in some detail for both images and places in order to achieve the desired effect: correspondences clinging and lastingly so in memory.

In brief, it is said that the places or backgrounds, as they are otherwise called, must be 'complete and conspicuous',[42] scenes within themselves, and largely vacated of human presence so as not to 'distract[] from the memory figures placed within them'.[43] These backdrops, further, 'must [also] be varied, of medium size [and] well-li[t]',[44] their arrangement sequential and set,[45] with their positioning occurring at regular intervals.[46] Images, by comparison, were to be conceived of as 'a figure, [a] mark, or [a] portrait',[47] corresponding to what one must remember, operating as *agentes*, such pictures 'simultaneously striking, emotionally moving, and active', while always involving the placement of human figures.[48]

Performative, the practice of memory, as such, was likened to 'a mental journey', a venture undertaken 'through [a] series of rooms or places, [each] containing [a] striking tableau', conveying 'incidents of particular violence, ugliness, or ridiculousness or, alternatively', portraying striking events of significant 'nobility or beauty'. These sorties, it could be said, were episodic, their plotting reminiscent of the dramatic structure of a play, composed of acts with scenes contained within, 'each scene serv[ing] to recall a [...] concept or word', each act embodying a broader mood or theme. The settings, as such, were to take on a resemblance to a stage in both 'the local and theatrical sense of the word',[49] their spectacular nature calling to mind the theatre's ancient association with *theoria*, the theatre itself taking on a leading role during the course of the Renaissance.[50]

The design of the background was of special note in the place system, whether a page or a wall, the grid a guiding principle, this means for extension and subdivision gaining prominence during the Middle Ages, when 'memory [was] treated as though it were a flat area and divided linearly',[51] like an architectural drawing composed or the format of a page diagrammed and delineated, these surfaces reminiscent of raiments, fabrics and landscapes. For 'the flat, patterned backgrounds', we are told, were:

> like tiles and shingles, or tapestries, or a field changing its colour and texture through the various seasons, [and] are located in relation to one another like small rooms (*cellae*) in a rectangular grid, pages (as it were) of the book of memory. The active images placed in these locations inhabit a shallow stage without much distance imagined between fore- and background.[52]

In the twelfth century, it is said, this overarching grid system was dimensionalised, acquiring a more pronounced depth of field, the 'images part of a larger structure', placed within a church or cloister, the revival of monumental art then coextensive with a renewed interest in the *Herennian* model. 'A new relationship between architecture and images', we are told, 'emerged', the sculptural programmes of the Romanesque period and their transition to the Gothic advancing and endorsing 'a newly active

[…] architectural setting', developments in the arts of memory coincident with transformations in the concept of place, affecting, it is said, the nature of painting in Italy in the late thirteenth century.[53]

For by the end of the thirteenth century, the monumental art of the Gothic period was supplanted by the fresco, '*memoria* and *renovatio Romae*' combining, the architecture durable, the images placed within them and lining their walls more ephemeral, these surfaces whitewashed and erased when the message was no longer serving, 'the difference between stable memory *loci* and transient memory images', it is said, accordingly re-enacted. Prefigured in the *duecento* by pronounced links to antiquity in Rome, the deployment of the art of memory in religious practices continued to prevail, further influencing the nature of public images, patrons and painters participants in both realms, the mix of civic and Christian art demanding it. The array of narrative bands which came to adorn public and religious buildings in the *trecento* thus recalled a strange mix of 'Roman and early Christian [painted] compositional schemes' and the tenets of Gothic monumental sculpture, their strapping revealing 'a succession of rectangles and squares display[ing] discrete episodes […] or concepts' within a larger edifice, their organisation conceivably varied, but always in accordance with the *Herennian* scheme.[54]

These frames, we are told, were open and receptive, each with a distinct scene encased within, housed in a *Raumkasten*, a 'local box', reminiscent of a *conditorium*, as some have called it, the setting adorned with figures, with architecture drawn from the contemporary urban environment, the architecture, however, repoussoired, pushed back while pulling the eye in, these buildings not to scale nor in accord with a unified point of view, the relationship between foreground and background contracted, 'the construction of place', its staging 'catalys[ing] [a] new [kind of] pictorial' order, 'a spacious place […] represented within the pictorial field' though 'not identical with it'. The story contained within these surrounds, we are told, was thus able to unfold not in accordance with a single point of view, the arrangement, nonetheless, enabling the viewer also enclosed to discern the figures contained therein, further distinguishing between the different places also bounded in a play between surfaces: the city, its architecture and its scenic renditions.[55]

Spaciousness, it is said, is a condition of narrative, a feature of its structure, the interplay between depth and volume in *memoria*'s scenes enabling the story to take place,[56] the nature of the epic tale, in distinction from the climactic linear plot, also composed in this manner, a series of 'boxes within boxes created by thematic recurrences'.[57] Memory, conceived of as a 'nesting', recalls this structure,[58] happenings occurring long ago circumscribed by larger occasions, as places are similarly situated amidst broader domains, the method of the *loci* similarly arrayed

146 *Text | Memory*

and appropriating this patterning. A sense of passage, of permeability, nonetheless, is necessary for the movement in between, '"spacing" and "imaging" [...] the "media" of memory', such means amassing meaning only when emplaced.[59]

'To portray a city', one's own city, to tell its story, it is said, 'a native must have other deeper motives – motives of one who travels into the past instead of into the distance. A native's book about his city will always be related to memoirs; the writer has not spent his childhood there in vain.' Such 'superficial inducements' are, however, a call to venture not only into the distance but into the past as well, 'for without [such] distance[s] there can be no description, except that of mere *reportage*'.[60]

In wanderings through the streets of Melbourne, another landscape was disclosed, the consequences of a tarrying in step with 'the footsteps of a hermetic tradition',[61] an archaeology of memory unearthed, not from the trodden bitumen and bluestone, but dislodged from the very drapery replete and adorning its walls.[62]

The camera, it is said, is a 'metaphorical tomb',[63] a little box, a prosthetic room obscured and on occasion illuminated, the camera's own internal curtaining reflecting that of an urban interior, its lining illumining architecture's textile origins and, in doing so, bringing backgrounds to the fore, reverberations felt in these chequered sites of encounter, oscillating between curtain wall and Harris Tweed, the recordings of these appearances, a script of light, 'encumber[ing] [the body] with innumerable negatives',[64] a lapse in time, a certain distancing, necessary for their development. For in these images, memory surfaces as 'traces of a mnemonics forgotten',[65] still legible when brought to light, revealing not transient figures familiar or otherwise, nor any other cipher, but rather the very places of the showing, screens revealed, *scrinia* exposed, their surfaces once again receptive through their photographic disinterment.

'[T]he city', we are told, 'is the artisan of [...] "hidden [...] interweavings"',[66] weaving a fabric out of the threads of our existence, strands of memories composed, 'remembrance [...] the woof [...] forgetting the weft',[67] epiphanies an unveiling, the perdurance of place disclosed. But it is only in the movement from place to place, it is said, that the gift of sentience is bestowed.

Notes

1 The other ancient civilisations that coloured their buildings include: Roman, Mesopotamian, Sumerian, Babylonian, Egyptian and Assyrian. See Joseph Rykwert, *The Dancing Column: On Order in Architecture* (Cambridge, MA: MIT Press, 1996), 232.

2 As Le Goff has noted: 'the great period of inscriptions was that of ancient Greece and Rome, about which Louis Robert has said, "one could call the

Greek and Roman countries a civilisation of epigraphy." In temples, cemeteries, public squares and avenues along roads and even "deep in the mountains, in the greatest solitude," inscriptions accumulated and encumbered the Greco-Roman world with an extraordinary effort of commemoration and perpetuation of memory. Stone, usually marble, served as a support for an overload of memory. These "stone archives" added to the function of archives proper the character of an insistent publicity, wagering on the ostentation and durability of the lapidary and marmoreal memory.' Jacques Le Goff, *History and Memory*, trans. Steven Rendall and Elizabeth Claman (New York: Columbia University Press, 1992), 59.

3 Anne Carson, *Eros the Bittersweet* (Champaign, MA: Dalkey Archive Press, 1998), 58–9.

4 'An essential constituent of the Greek household (*oikos*) as its hearth (*hestia*) was its loom (*histon*).' Indra Kagis McEwen, *Socrates' Ancestor: An Essay in Architectural Beginnings* (Cambridge, MA: MIT Press, 1993), 107.

5 See John Scheid and Jesper Svenbro, *The Craft of Zeus: Myths of Weaving and Fabric*, trans. Carol Volk (Cambridge, MA: Harvard University Press, 1996), 112. In ancient Greece, weaving was closely linked to song and the Greek lyric poets engaged metaphors from weaving, their own art referred to as a 'web of song'. See Jane McIntosh Snyder, 'The Web of Song: Weaving Imagery in Homer and the Lyric Poets', *The Classical Journal* 76, no. 3 (1981): 193.

6 Former C.E.O. of the Harris Tweed Authority, Ian Angus MacKenzie in a radio documentary stressed the interrelationship between Harris Tweed and the Gaelic language in *The Battle of the Tweed* (Glasgow: BBC4, 6 February 2009).

7 In Kissling's *Eriskay: A Poem of Remote Lives*, the herringbone pattern of the arms of the women as they waulk the cloth is clearly pronounced. See *Eriskay: A Poem of Remote Lives*, dir. Werner Kissling, http://movingimage.nls.uk/film/1701. Accessed 18 March 2016.

8 As Campbell remarks: 'when Scottish Gaelic poetry first began to appear in print in the eighteenth century, and the authors or collectors wished to indicate to readers to what airs the poems were sung, they needed to do no more than to give the (usually meaningless words of the chorus as the "tune") […] In earlier times readers who happened to be unacquainted with the airs could get a good idea of their rhythmic patterns from their meaningless refrains. This is all the *notational* value such refrains could be said to possess; their real value was *mnemonic*, as the great majority of traditional singers, especially waulking women, could not read Gaelic in any case.' See J. L. Campbell, ed., *Hebridean Folksongs: A Collection of Waulking Songs by Donald MacCormick in Kilphedir in South Uist in the Year 1863* (London: Oxford University Press, 1969), 236–7.

9 Edward S. Casey, *Remembering: A Phenomenological Study*, 2nd ed. (Bloomington, IN: Indiana University Press, 2000), 11.

10 Many of the Hebrideans could neither read nor write, but held nonetheless an immense knowledge in their heads and hearts. With scant exception, no books existed in Scottish Gaelic until the publication of Knox's *Liturgy* in 1567, and only a few books of poetry transcribed from the bardic tradition

remain. In truth, it was not until after the Jacobite uprising of 1745 that Gaelic literature appeared in print. See Lucy E. Broadwood, introduction to *One Hundred and Five Songs of Occupation from the Western Isles of Scotland* by Frances Tolmie (Edinburgh: Llanerch Publishers, 1997), viii. For a discussion of the relationship between oral traditions and writing in light of memory, see Le Goff, *History and Memory*, 58–68; and Walther J. Ong, *Orality and Literacy: The Technologizing of the Word* (London: Routledge, 2002), 95–100.

11 Carson, *Eros the Bittersweet*, 100. McQuire also notes that: 'Ong proposes a notion of "secondary orality" in which new technologies such as telephone, radio and television are able to "maintain" oral cultures without the disruptive shifts which marked the transition to literacy.' Scott McQuire, *Visions of Modernity: Representation, Memory, Time and Space in the Age of the Camera* (London: Sage Publications, 1998), 48, n. 13.

12 See Ong, *Orality and Literacy*, 11.

13 Carruthers observes, with reference to Aristotle, that: 'whether its origin be visual or auditory, tactile or olfactory, [e]very sort of sense perception ends up in the form of a phantasm in memory'. Carruthers, *The Book of Memory*, 16–17. For an elegant and concise account of ancient memory, see Casey, *Remembering*, 11–16.

14 See Le Goff, *History and Memory*, 65.

15 As Yates has observed: 'The art of memory is an invisible art; it reflects real places [and also imaginary ones] but is about, not the places themselves, but the reflection of these within the imagination.' Frances A. Yates, 'Architecture and the Art of Memory', *Architecture Association Quarterly* 12, no. 4 (1980): 5.

16 Edward S. Casey, *Remembering*, quoted in J. E. Malpas, *Place and Experience: A Philosophical Topography* (Cambridge: Cambridge University Press, 1999), 106.

17 See Mary Carruthers, *The Book of Memory: A Study of Memory in Medieval Culture* (Cambridge: Cambridge University Press, 1990), 73.

18 Simonides of Keos, 'Fragment 821', quoted in Anne Carson, *Economy of the Unlost (Reading Simonides of Keos with Paul Celan)* (Princeton, NJ: Princeton University Press, 1999), 47. The concept of seating relates to Quintilian's discussion of commonplaces, or *loci communes*, which can be conceived of as abstract headings as well as 'collections of sayings', which as Ong notes, 'could be worked into one's own speech-making or writing. In this sense the *loci communes* can be styled "cumulative commonplaces" [...] ke[eping] alive the old oral feeling for thought and expression [...] inherited from the past.' Ong, *Orality and Literacy*, 108. Here Benjamin's discussion of the storyteller is recalled, when he observes that '[t]he storyteller takes what he tells from experience – his own or that reported by others. And he in turn makes it the experience of those who are listening to his tale.' Walter Benjamin, 'The Storyteller: Reflections on the Work of Nikolai Leskov', in *Illuminations: Essays and Reflections*, ed. Hannah Arendt and trans. Harry Zohn (New York: Schocken Books, 1969), 87.

19 Kastor and Polydeukes, known together as the Dioskouri, were brothers, one mortal, the other undying, their bond so close, it is said, that they could not bear to be separated by death, dividing, as Carson notes, 'a single eternity between them, spending alternate days on and under the earth'. Carson, *Economy of the Unlost*, 40.

20 While the tale of Simonides features in numerous texts on memory, this account draws in particular from that found in Carson, *Economy of the Unlost*, 38–40.

21 See Le Goff, *History and Memory*, 66. As Carson notes, however, unlike the later practices of mnemonics, this experience was very much lived by the poet. See Carson, *Economy of the Unlost*, 43.

22 Three Latin texts formed the basis of the classical art of memory: the *Ad C. Herennium Libri IV* or *Rhetorica Ad Herennium* (c. 86–82 B.C.); Cicero's *De Oratore* (55 B.C.); and Quintilian's *Institutio Oratoria* (end of the first century A.D.). For an introduction to these texts see, for example, Francis A. Yates, *The Art of Memory* (London: Pimlico, 2006), 17–41.

23 *Ad C. Herennium de Ratione Dicendi*, trans. Harry Caplan (Cambridge, MA: Harvard University Press, 1954), III, xvi, 28.

24 Mary Carruthers and Jan M. Ziolkowski, 'General Introduction', in *The Medieval Craft of Memory: An Anthology of Texts and Pictures*, ed. Mary Carruthers and Jan M. Ziolkowski (Philadelphia, PA: University of Pennsylvania Press, 2002), 28.

25 See Ong, *Orality and Literacy*, 109–10.

26 Jean-Philippe Antoine, 'Memory, Places, and Spatial Invention', *Any* 15 (1996): 18.

27 See Carruthers, *Book of Memory*, 9. In discussing the relationship between hermeneutics and rhetoric, Gadamer observes that '[h]ermeneutical theory orientated itself to the task of interpreting expressions of life that are fixed in writing. [...] Rhetoric, on the other hand, concerned itself with the impact of speaking in all its immediacy.' Hans-Georg Gadamer, 'On the Scope and Function of Hermeneutical Reflection', trans. G. B. Hess and R. E. Palmer, in *Philosophical Hermeneutics*, ed. and trans. David E. Linge (Berkeley, CA: University of California Press, 2008), 23.

28 As Antoine notes with reference to the medieval period: 'Up until the 11th century, reading and the circumstances of reading took precedence in the practice of the art of memory; a strong architectural bent emerged in the 12th century.' See Antoine, 'Memory, Places, and Spatial Invention', 18. Here it is perhaps interesting to note the portrayal of St Jerome in Masaccio's *St Jerome and St John the Baptist* (1428), both hands occupied, the one holding a book, the other a model of a small building.

29 Carruthers, *Book of Memory*, 20.

30 Here the Utrecht Psalter (ninth century) is provided as an example. See Antoine, 'Memory, Places and Spatial Invention', 18.

31 As Carruthers notes: 'The metaphor of memory as a written surface is so ancient and so persistent in all Western cultures that it must [...] be seen as a governing model or "cognitive archetype," in Max Black's phrase.'

150   Text | Memory

Carruthers, *The Book of Memory*, 16. Plato, in developing an image implicit in Homer, it is said, was the first to use the metaphor of memory as a waxed surface in *Theaetetus*, and for Aristotle, the forming of mental images, differing from sense images, was likened to the movement wherein a signet ring was impressed upon a surface. See Carruthers, *The Book of Memory*, 21; Yates, *The Art of Memory*, 47–50, and Richard Sorabji, *Aristotle on Memory* (Providence, RI: Brown University Press, 1972), 50. For a further discussion on the difference between the various types of images referred to in the writings of Aristotle, see Sorabji, *Aristotle on Memory*, 11–12, noting 12, n. 4.

32 Cicero, *Partitiones oratoriae*, quoted in Carruthers, *Book of Memory*, 16.
33 For a further discussion of the *tabula memoriae* tradition, see Carruthers, *Book of Memory*, 16–32.
34 See Antoine, 'Memory, Places and Spatial Invention', 18, and Yates, *Art of Memory*, 40.
35 Joseph Rykwert, 'Building as Gesture, Building as Argument', *Thesis: Wissenschaftliche Zeitschrift der Bauhaus-Universität Weimar* 3 (2003): 45.
36 With reference to the *Ad Herennium*, III, xvi, 28, see Carruthers, *Book of Memory*, 34.
37 See Carruthers, *Book of Memory*, 33. Carruthers further notes that *cellula*, *arca*, *sacculus*, *scrinium* and *male* are synonymous with *thesaurus*, with pigeon coops, dove cotes and beehives also operating as models, these domiciles for winged creatures recalling that images of birds and bees have been variously associated with the soul, memory and thought. The compartmentalisation of a classical house along with the biblical Ark were also significant archetypes. For a further discussion of architectural models, see Carruthers, *The Book of Memory*, 33–45; Frances A. Yates, 'Architecture and the Art of Memory', *Architecture Association Quarterly* 12, no. 4 (1980): 4–13, and Frances A. Yates, 'Architectural Themes', *AA Files* 1 (1981): 29–53.
38 See Antoine, 'Memory, Places and Spatial Invention', 18.
39 Yates, *Art of Memory*, 21. Yates further notes that '[e]very [subsequent] *Ars memorativa* treatise [...] is repeating the plan, the subject matter, and as often as not the actual words of the *Ad Herennium*'.
40 *Ad Herennium*, III, xvi, 29.
41 See Antoine, 'Memory, Places and Spatial Invention', 18–19.
42 *Ad Herennium*, III, xvi, 29.
43 With reference to the *Ad Herennium*, III, xvii, 31, see Antoine, 'Memory, Places and Spatial Invention', 18.
44 With reference to the *Ad Herennium*, III, xix, 31–2, see Antoine, 'Memory, Places and Spatial Invention', 18.
45 See *Ad Herennium*, III, xvi, 30, 209.
46 With reference to the *Ad Herennium*, see Antoine, 'Memory, Places and Spatial Invention', 18.
47 *Ad Herennium*, III, xvi, 29.
48 With reference to the *Ad Herennium*, see Antoine, 'Memory, Places and Spatial Invention', 18.

49 With reference to the *Ad Herennium*, see Antoine, 'Memory, Places and Spatial Invention', 18.
50 For a discussion of this relationship see, for example, Rodolphe Gasché, 'Theatrum Theoreticum', in *The Honor of Thinking* (Stanford, CA: Stanford University Press, 2007), 188–208. The memory theatre of the Italian philosopher Giulio Camillo (1480–1544) is one example of the theatre as a model, its deployment by the English Paracelsian physician Robert Fludd (1574–1637), another. For a further discussion, see Yates, *Art of Memory*, 135–74 and 310–29.
51 Carruthers, *Book of Memory*, 129.
52 Thomas Bradwardine, 'On Acquiring a Trained Memory', trans. Mary Carruthers, in *The Medieval Craft of Memory: An Anthology of Texts and Pictures*, ed. Mary Carruthers and Jan M. Ziolowski (Philadelphia, PA: University of Pennsylvania Press, 2002), 206.
53 See Antoine, 'Memory, Places, and Spatial Invention', 19.
54 Antoine, 'Memory, Places, and Spatial Invention', 19–20.
55 Antoine appropriates the term *Raumkästen*, 'local boxes', from the art historian Erwin Panofsky (1892–1968), and his *Perspective as Symbolic Form*. But unlike Panofsky's version, it 'denotes a three-dimensional finite scene, not a fragment, chosen by the painter's eye, or infinite space. It does not imply a [perspectival or] mathematically unified point of view.' See Antoine, 'Memory, Place and Spatial Invention', 20, and 20, n. 5.
56 See Antoine, 'Memory, Place and Spatial Invention', 21.
57 With reference to Homer's *Iliad* and Cedric M. Whitman's chart of its narrative organisation, see Ong, *Orality and Literacy*, 141.
58 The psychologist Ulric Neisser (1928–2012) places special emphasis on the 'nested' character of memory, and draws from the work of J. J. Gibson's psychological studies in which a subject's embeddedness within an environment is deemed to be crucial. For a further discussion of the nested nature of memory in relationship to place, and the work of Neisser and Gibson, see Malpas, *Place and Experience*, 101–6.
59 With reference to Panofsky, see Anselm Haverkamp, 'Ghost Machine or Embedded Intelligence: Architexture and Mnemotechnique', *Any* 15 (1996): 12.
60 See Peter Szondi, 'Walter Benjamin's City Portraits', trans. Harvey Mendelsohn, in *On Walter Benjamin: Critical Essays and Reflections*, ed. Gary Smith (Cambridge, MA: MIT Press, 1988), 19. Emphasis in Szondi.
61 Walter Benjamin, 'Berlin Chronicle', trans. Edmund Jephcott, in *Selected Writings*, Volume 2, Part 2: *1931–1934*, ed. Michael W. Jennings, Howard Eiland and Gary Smith (Cambridge, MA: Belknap Press of Harvard University Press, 2005), 598.
62 As Leslie notes: 'The German word for "in the earth" is *Erdinnern*, which is very close to the word *erinnern*, to remember.' Esther Leslie, 'Souvenirs and Forgetting: Walter Benjamin's Memory-Work', in *Material Memories: Design and Evocation*, ed. Marius Kwint, Jeremy Aynsley and Christopher Breward (Oxford: Berg, 1999), 108, n. 5.

63 Salvatore Puglia, 'Abstracts of Abstracts of Anamnesis', *Any* 15 (1996): 56.
64 Marcel Proust, *Remembrance of Things Past*, quoted in Eduardo Cadava, *Words of Light: Theses on the Photography of History* (Princeton, NJ: Princeton University Press, 1997), 76.
65 Anselm Haverkamp, 'The Scene of Memory: Names and Places, the Means of Translation, A Response to Carol Jacobs', *Any* 15 (1996): 41.
66 With reference to Benjamin's 'Berlin Chronicle', see Carol Jacobs, 'Walter Benjamin: Topographically Speaking', *Studies in Romanticism* 31, no. 4 (1992): 508.
67 Walter Benjamin, 'The Image of Proust', in *Illuminations: Essays and Reflections*, ed. Hannah Arendt and trans. Harry Zohn (New York: Schocken Books, 1969), 202.

Bibliography

Ad C. Herennium de Ratione Dicendi. Translated by Harry Caplan. Cambridge, MA: Harvard University Press, 1954.
Antoine, Jean-Philippe. 'Memory, Places, and Spatial Invention', *Any* 15 (1996): 18–21.
The Battle of the Tweed. Glasgow: BBC Radio 4. 6 February 2009.
Benjamin, Walter. 'The Image of Proust'. In *Illuminations: Essays and Reflections*. Edited by Hannah Arendt and translated by Harry Zohn, 201–15. New York: Schocken Books, 1969.
———. 'The Storyteller: Reflections on the Work of Nikolai Leskov'. In *Illuminations: Essays and Reflections*. Edited by Hannah Arendt and translated by Harry Zohn, 83–109. New York: Schocken Books, 1969.
———. 'Berlin Chronicle'. Translated by Edmund Jephcott. In *Selected Writings*, Volume 2, Part 2: *1931–1934*. Edited by Michael W. Jennings, Howard Eiland and Gary Smith, 595–637. Cambridge, MA: Belknap Press of Harvard University Press, 2005.
Bradwardine, Thomas, 'On Acquiring a Trained Memory'. Translated by Mary Carruthers. In *The Medieval Craft of Memory: An Anthology of Texts and Pictures*. Edited by Mary Carruthers and Jan M. Ziolowski, 205–14. Philadelphia, PA: University of Pennsylvania Press, 2002.
Broadwood, Lucy E. Introduction to *One Hundred and Five Songs of Occupation from the Western Isles of Scotland*, by Frances Tolmie, v–xiv. Edinburgh: Llanerch Publishers, 1997.
Cadava, Eduardo. *Words of Light: Theses on the Photography of History*. Princeton, NJ: Princeton University Press, 1997.
Campbell, J. L., ed. *Hebridean Folksongs: A Collection of Waulking Songs by Donald MacCormick in Kilphedir in South Uist in the Year 1863*. London: Oxford University Press, 1969.
Carruthers, Mary. *The Book of Memory: A Study of Memory in Medieval Culture*. Cambridge: Cambridge University Press, 1990.
——— and Jan M. Ziolowski, eds. *The Medieval Craft of Memory: An Anthology of Texts and Pictures*. Philadelphia, PA: University of Pennsylvania Press, 2002.

Carson, Anne. *Eros the Bittersweet*. Champaign, MA: Dalkey Archive Press, 1998.

———. *Economy of the Unlost (Reading Simonides of Keos with Paul Celan)*. Princeton, NJ: Princeton University Press, 1999.

Eriskay: A Poem of Remote Lives. Directed by Werner Kissling, http://movingimage.nls.uk/ film/1701. Accessed 18 March 2016.

Gadamer, Hans-Georg. 'On the Scope and Function of Hermeneutical Reflection'. Translated by G. B. Hess and R. E. Palmer. In *Philosophical Hermeneutics*. Edited and translated by David E. Linge, 18–43. Berkeley, CA: University of California Press, 2008.

Gasché, Rodolphe. 'Theatrum Theoreticum'. In *The Honor of Thinking*, 188–208. Stanford, CA: Stanford University Press, 2007.

Haverkamp, Anselm. 'The Scene of Memory: Names and Places, the Means of Translation, a Response to Carol Jacobs', *Any* 15 (1996): 41–8.

Jacobs, Carol. 'Walter Benjamin: Topographically Speaking', *Studies in Romanticism* 31, no. 4 (1992): 501–24.

Le Goff, Jacques. *History and Memory*. Translated by Steven Rendall and Elizabeth Claman. New York: Columbia University Press, 1992.

Leslie, Esther. 'Souvenirs and Forgetting: Walter Benjamin's Memory-Work'. In *Material Memories: Design and Evocation*. Edited by Marius Kwint, Jeremy Aynsley and Christopher Breward, 107–22. Oxford: Berg, 1999.

McEwen, Indra Kagis. *Socrates' Ancestor: An Essay in Architectural Beginnings*. Cambridge, MA: MIT Press, 1993.

McQuire, Scott. *Visions of Modernity: Representation, Memory, Time and Space in the Age of the Camera*. London: Sage Publications, 1998.

Malpas, J. E. *Place and Experience: A Philosophical Topography*. Cambridge: Cambridge University Press, 1999.

Ong, Walther J. *Orality and Literacy: The Technologizing of the Word*. London: Routledge, 1991.

Puglia, Salvatore. 'Abstracts of Abstracts of Anamnesis', *Any* 15 (1996): 55–7.

Rykwert, Joseph. *The Dancing Column: On Order in Architecture*. Cambridge, MA: MIT Press, 1996.

———. 'Building as Gesture, Building as Argument', *Thesis: Wissenschaftliche Zeitschrift der Bauhaus-Universität Weimar* 3 (2003): 44–54.

Scheid, John and Jesper Svenbro. *The Craft of Zeus: Myths of Weaving and Fabric*. Translated by Carol Volk. Cambridge, MA: Harvard University Press, 1996.

Snyder, Jane McIntosh. 'The Web of Song: Weaving Imagery in Homer and the Lyric Poets', *The Classical Journal* 76, no. 3 (1981): 193–6.

Sorabji, Richard. *Aristotle on Memory*. Providence, RI: Brown University Press, 1972.

Yates, Frances A. 'Architecture and the Art of Memory', *Architecture Association Quarterly* 12, no. 4 (1980): 4–13.

———. 'Architectural Themes', *AA Files* 1 (1981): 29–53.

———. *The Art of Memory*. London: Pimlico, 2006.

On

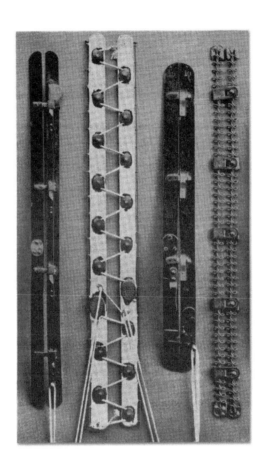

Figure 9.1 Anonymous, *Corset Hardware*, nineteenth century.

Closing

Figure 9.2 Bill Brandt, *Shad Thames*, 1939.

What is the material and subject matter of all artistic endeavour? I believe it is man in all his relations and connections to the world.

Gottfried Semper

At such moments it seems to me I see why these images exert such a powerful fascination over the mind; I seem to detect the underlying reasons for the unwearying and irrational zeal that makes man give a meaning to all appearances devoid of it, to look for parallels everywhere, and to create them where they do not already exist. I see the origin of the irresistible attraction of metaphor and analogy, the explanation of our strange and permanent need to find similarities in things. I can scarcely refrain from suspecting some ancient, diffused magnetism; a call from the centre of things; a dim, almost lost memory, or perhaps a presentiment [...] of a universal syntax.

Roger Caillois

It is said that 'only in visibly impressing [a] path into the surface of the earth' are 'places [...] objectively connected', but this, of course, is not the only way of journeying.[1] Like Walter Benjamin, whose history of photography relied on travels across collections of images bound,[2] other excursions have here ensued, marking paths across photographs, descendents of those heliographs once paved in bitumen,[3] from architecture to textile realms once unknown, toing and froing across plates of captured light, charting traces in between, further to be lured again to the very place, the situatedness of the cloth and its making, to witness the shuttle's course across the loom, to hear again the chant of the waulking, to make friends, and to return with tweeds and more images, mediators and mementos of the experience: surface appearings.

Walking, 'to go about', we are told, originates from waulking, the fulling and thickening of the cloth, the cloth having been cut from the loom, in need of finishing, so that it may be tailored and worn. To walk, it is said, refers to the Old English *wealcan*, 'to roll' or 'to toss', and the Old High German *walchan*, 'to full' or 'to cudgel', a lineage which suggests that 'to walk' derives from 'waulking', and not the other way round.[4] Waulking transforms the tweed cut from the loom into cloth that is wearable, and in walking the streets or alternatively the moors and mountainsides, or shorelines and coves, the body, it is said, 'bring[s] forth places',[5] lived places, experienced in and through their traversal, the body and its surrounds enlivened through motility. Experiences such as those revealed through the act of walking are, it is said, 'born of wisdom, and practical knowledge', and in German experience is designated by the term *Erfahrung*, its foundation explicit in *fahren*, the word for travel.[6] Benjamin once noted that an old German proverb stated that the traveller had stories to tell,[7] and nowadays such tales are often accompanied by photographs, an album of sorts to share and to show, containing a series of aspects, coinciding, and at times overlapping, which seek to enrich the telling, lending a certain cohesiveness to the whole. And so for now, my story is told, but what are we to make of this journey and the accounts and images here relayed?

Perhaps, we might surmise, it was only in the placing of photographs, an image of a curtain wall and a swatch of Harris Tweed, the one beside the other, that this story was able to come to light, images juxtaposed, their surfaces so arrayed in such a way as to allow each to come into focus the one in the other, both beholden and held in exquisite tension, equipoised. These adjacencies were manipulated, the images handled, as much by the hands, if not more so by the eyes, their iridescent touch exposing seemingly happenstance connections, latent images lying in wait, covalencies developing over time.[8] For in a web woven according to saccadic rhythms, reading between the images, across the grain and amidst the lines, other images appeared, 'loosened and lure[d] [...] from their familiar context[s]',[9] drawn nigh and similarly arranged, a concatenation of associations, image worlds, materialising.

The photograph, we are told, is an 'image that is always traversed by the "thesis of existence"',[10] and though sundered and sequestered from the different times and places of their taking, the arrangement of these images, nonetheless, exposed a unity and plurality at play, a fabric of sense emerging, the result of recontextualisations, new emplacements and various coursings in between. The reading of images, we might recall, was once considered an endangered art and is still conceivably so, its demise foreshadowed in a prophecy which claimed that the illiteracy of the future would pertain to photography even more so than to writing.[11] 'Reading with understanding', however, it is said, 'is always a kind of reproduction, [a] performance, [an] interpretation',[12] and so in part here an attempt has been made to give the reading of images some sense of redress, foregrounding this practice as a means of passage, a form of access. For in the taking of photographs, in their reading and the subsequent writings, thinking and weaving the while,[13] what has been revealed as foremost, and has been disclosed and made known again and again, is the very interconnectedness of things, of their entwinement, presented in the intermittent manifestations of surfaces and the multitudinous patternations lying immanent amongst and between things. For 'the poet was right', we are told,

> when he spoke of the "mysterious threads" which are broken by life. But the truth, even more, is that life is perpetually weaving fresh threads which link one individual and one event to another, and that these threads are crossed and recrossed, doubled and redoubled to thicken the web, so that between any slightest point of our past and all the others, a rich network of memories gives an almost infinite variety of communicating paths to choose from.[14]

In the forays here undertaken, in the study of surfaces and their photographic mediation, what has emerged is conceivably that which appears and appears to have waned, only to recur again, reflected in the relationship between the curtain wall and Harris Tweed, calling us to consider how we might come to view differently the surfaces of the city and their means of fabrication, while acknowledging the seemingly forgotten, or at least overlooked, legacy of a time-honoured textile, Harris Tweed. In considering the embedded nature of Hebridean check counterpoised with the dispersed and disconnected qualities of the curtain wall, the nature of place and its surfacing has naturally arisen, a fabric spanning the in between and partaken of, revealing the very enigma of place, of one's often unspoken communication with another, and with others, a tacit network in operation disclosed, 'each place, each name, holding [within] a secret history', even so.[15]

Facilitated by photography and the various passages it has forged, the significance of metaphor has also increasingly come to the fore, this trope 'originat[ing] in the belief that the world is built up of correspondences'.[16] And the task that lies before us, it would seem, is to be '[o]pen [to those] confidences […] being made every day', to see them, engaging with them without any sense of 'prejudice or restraint'.[17] For it is said that 'there cannot be any architecture without metaphor',[18] nor anything else which is truly meaning-full besides, without a bridge availed, one which enables us 'to cross from the minor truth of the seen to the major truth, […] unseen' yet always abiding.[19]

'[T]he very nature of appearance', we are told, is 'to reveal *and to conceal*',[20] and while this study's questioning and rejoinders have been revealed in the working through, a number of other issues have, nonetheless, been purposely left aside, kept under wraps so to speak, that are worthy of consideration too. And these pertain largely to how these findings might be applied: how architects, artists and designers might gain from this study and put it to use; how a return to the textile nature of the surface, architectural or conceivably otherwise, might reinvest their designs with a more meaningful and context-driven approach; how it might also activate the unforeseen potential of Harris Tweed; how the weavers' knowledge of colour and pattern might be otherwise engaged with and brought into play; calling into question how else might the cloth be deployed, and how traditional forms of knowledge might be further validated and learned from, while also being supported, invested in and revitalised at the same time.[21]

It has always been my intention following the installation of *Urban Fabric: Greige* to have these images of curtain walls translated into Harris Tweed, and to invite various Melbourne art, architecture, craft and design practitioners to engage with the surfaces of their city, refashioning it anew, a community gathered in order to celebrate the role of the crafts in the design and fabrication of the metropolis while giving voice to the *clò mhòr* and its various traditions. And this quest continues, for it was once said that 'our capacity to preserve and maintain, the capacity that supports human culture, rests in turn upon the fact that we must always order anew what threatens to dissolve before us'.[22] Or perhaps to put it another way, we might say that the task of finishing is never finished.

Notes

1 Georg Simmel, 'Bridge and Door', trans. Mark Ritter, *Theory, Culture & Society* 11, no. 5 (1994): 6.

2 See Mary Price, *The Photograph: A Strange Confined Space* (Stanford, CA: Stanford University Press, 1994), 60.
3 The heliographs produced by Joseph Nicéphore Niépce (1765–1833) at the birth of photography relied on varying substrates coated in light-sensitive bitumen of Judea. See Michel Frizot, 'Light Machines: On the Threshold of Invention', in *A New History of Photography*, ed. Michel Frizot (Cologne: Könemann, 1998), 19–20.
4 See J. L. Campbell, 'Waulking Described', in *Hebridean Folksongs: A Collection of Waulking Songs by Donald MacCormick in Kilphedir in South Uist in the Year 1863*, ed. J. L. Campbell (London: Oxford University Press, 1969), 3, n. 1. Campbell also notes that '[t]he usual Gaelic term, *luadhadh*, means to roll or toss'.
5 Edward S. Casey, *The Fate of Place: A Philosophical History* (Berkeley: University of California Press, 1997), 236.
6 See Esther Leslie, 'Walter Benjamin: Traces of Craft', *Journal of Design History* 11, no. 1 (1998): 5.
7 Walter Benjamin, 'The Storyteller: Reflections on the Work of Nikolai Leskov', in *Illuminations: Essays and Reflections*, ed. Hannah Arendt and trans. Harry Zohn (New York: Schocken Books, 1969), 84.
8 Malpas describes the 'happening of the world' as an '"iridescence" in which things constantly shine out in different ways'. For a further discussion see Jeff Malpas, *Heidegger's Topology: Being, Place, World* (Cambridge, MA: MIT Press, 2008), 249–50.
9 Herman Schweppenhäuser, 'Propaedeutics of Profane Illumination', trans. Lloyd Spencer, Stephan Jost and Gary Smith, in *On Walter Benjamin: Critical Essays and Recollections*, ed. Gary Smith (Cambridge, MA: MIT Press, 1988), 43.
10 With reference to Jean-Marie Schaeffer, *L'Image Précaire*, see Luc Lang, 'The Photographer's Hand: Phenomenology in Politics', trans. Elizabeth Hamilton, in *Gerhard Richter* (Paris: Dis Voir, 1995), 36.
11 Echoing László Moholy-Nagy, although he is not explicitly cited, see Walter Benjamin, 'Little History of Photography', trans. Edmund Jephcott and Kingsley Shorter, in *Selected Writings, Volume 2, Part 2: 1931—1934*, ed. Michael W. Jennings, Howard Eiland and Gary Smith (Cambridge, MA: Belknap Press of Harvard University Press, 2005), 527.
12 Hans-Georg Gadamer, *Truth and Method*, 2nd ed. rev., trans. Joel Weinsheimer and Donald G. Marshall (London: Continuum, 1989), 153.
13 Arendt was to observe of the relationship between weaving and thinking that: 'the business of thinking is like Penelope's web; it undoes every morning what it has finished the night before. For the need to think can never be stilled by allegedly definite insights of "wise men"; it can be satisfied only through thinking, and the thoughts I had yesterday will satisfy this need today only to the extent that I want and am able to think them anew.' Hannah Arendt, *The Life of the Mind* (San Diego, CA: Harcourt, 1978), 88.
14 Marcel Proust, 'Time Regained'. In *In Search of Lost Time*, vol. 6, trans. Andreas Mayor and Terence Kilmartin, rev. D. J. Enright (New York: Modern Library, 1999), 504.

162 On | Closing

15 Jeff Malpas, 'Repetitions', in *Repetitions*, Exhibition Catalogue (Hobart: Plimsoll Gallery, University of Tasmania, 2008), 14.
16 Peter Szondi, 'Walter Benjamin's City Portraits', trans. Harvey Mendelsohn, in *On Walter Benjamin: Critical Essays and Reflections*, ed. Gary Smith (Cambridge, MA: MIT Press, 1988), 30.
17 Man Ray, 'The Age of Light', in *Man Ray: Photographs 1920–1934* (New York: East River Press, 1975), n.p.
18 Joseph Rykwert, *The Dancing Column: On Order in Architecture* (Cambridge, MA: MIT Press, 1996), 383.
19 Ernest Fenollosa, 'The Chinese Written Character as a Medium for Poetry', quoted in Arendt, *Life of the Mind*, 106.
20 With reference to Maurice Merleau-Ponty, *The Visible and the Invisible*, see Arendt, *Life of the Mind*, 54. Emphasis in Arendt.
21 On this matter, also see Alberto Pérez-Gómez, 'The Relevance of Beauty in Architecture', in *The Cultural Role of Architecture: Contemporary and Historical Perspectives*, ed. Paul Emmons, Jane Lomholt and John Hendrix (London: Routledge, 2012), 165.
22 Hans-Georg Gadamer, 'Art and Imitation', in *The Relevance of the Beautiful and Other Essays*, ed. Robert Bernasconi and trans. Nicholas Walker (London: Cambridge University Press, 1986), 104.

Bibliography

Arendt, Hannah. *The Life of the Mind*. San Diego, CA: Harcourt, 1978.
Benjamin, Walter. 'The Storyteller: Reflections on the Work of Nikolai Leskov'. In *Illuminations: Essays and Reflections*, edited by Hanna Arendt and translated by Harry Zohn, 83–109. New York: Schocken Books, 1969.
———. 'Little History of Photography'. Translated by Edmund Jephcott and Kingsley Shorter. In *Selected Writings*, Volume 2, Part 2: *1931–1934*. Edited by Michael W. Jennings, Howard Eiland and Gary Smith, 505–30. Cambridge, MA: Belknap Press of Harvard University Press, 2005.
Casey, Edward S. *The Fate of Place: A Philosophical History*. Berkeley: University of California Press, 1997.
Frizot, Michel. 'Light Machines: On the Threshold of Invention'. In *A New History of Photography*. Edited by Michel Frizot, 15–21. Cologne: Könemann, 1998.
Gadamer, Hans-Georg. 'Art and Imitation'. In *The Relevance of the Beautiful and Other Essays*. Edited by Robert Bernasconi and translated by Nicholas Walker, 92–104. London: Cambridge University Press, 1986.
———. *Truth and Method*, 2nd ed. rev. Translated by Joel Weinsheimer and Donald G. Marshall. London: Continuum, 1989.
Hebridean Folksongs: A Collection of Waulking Songs by Donald MacCormick in Kilphedir in South Uist in the Year 1863. Edited by J. L. Campbell. London: Oxford University Press, 1969.
Lang, Luc. 'The Photographer's Hand: Phenomenology in Politics'. Translated by Elizabeth Hamilton. In *Gerhard Richter*, 29–52. Paris: Dis Voir, 1995.

Leslie, Esther. 'Walter Benjamin: Traces of Craft', *Journal of Design History* 11, no. 1 (1998): 5–13.

Malpas, Jeff. *Heidegger's Topology: Being, Place, World*. Cambridge, MA: MIT Press, 2008.

———. 'Repetitions'. In *Repetitions*, Exhibition Catalogue, 6–20. Hobart: Plimsoll Gallery, University of Tasmania, 2008.

Man Ray. 'The Age of Light'. In *Man Ray: Photographs 1920–1934*, n.p. New York: East River Press, 1975.

Pérez-Gómez, Alberto. 'The Relevance of Beauty in Architecture'. In *The Cultural Role of Architecture: Contemporary and Historical Perspectives*. Edited by Paul Emmons, Jane Lomholt and John Hendrix, 157–66. London: Routledge, 2012.

Price, Mary. *The Photograph: A Strange Confined Space*. Stanford, CA: Stanford University Press, 1994.

Proust, Marcel. 'Time Regained'. In *In Search of Lost Time*, vol. 6. Translated by Andreas Mayor and Terence Kilmartin, revised by D. J. Enright. New York: Modern Library, 1999.

Rykwert, Joseph. *The Dancing Column: On Order in Architecture*. Cambridge, MA: MIT Press, 1996.

Schweppenhäuser, Herman. 'Propaedeutics of Profane Illumination'. Translated by Lloyd Spencer, Stephan Jost and Gary Smith. In *On Walter Benjamin: Critical Essays and Recollections*. Edited by Gary Smith, 33–50. Cambridge, MA: MIT Press, 1988.

Simmel, Georg. 'Bridge and Door', trans. Mark Ritter, *Theory, Culture & Society* 11, no. 5 (1994): 5–10.

Szondi, Peter. 'Walter Benjamin's City Portraits'. Translated by Harvey Mendelsohn. In *On Walter Benjamin: Critical Essays and Reflections*. Edited by Gary Smith, 18–32. Cambridge, MA: MIT Press, 1988.

Names

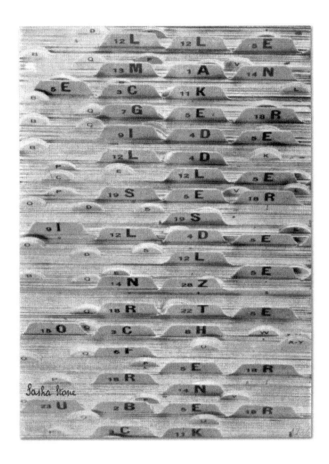

Figure I.1 Sasha Stone, *Kartei* (Files), c. 1925–6.

Topics

Figure I.2 I. G. Farbenindustrie, *Am Strande (Sur la Plage, Strand)*, before 1929.

Names from which the thinking process starts are unreliable.
Hannah Arendt

Images shelter contents that arrange themselves into systematic themes.

Edward S. Casey

Index

'The Abbey Memory System' 136
Achilles, shield of 32n11
Acropolis 48
Aeschylus 102
agora (public meeting place) 27, 48
Albers, Anni 16n47, 16n48
Alberti, Leon Battista 10, 15n39; *On the Art of Building in Ten Books* 49
Anaximander 32n11
ancient Greece: buildings and colour 140; *dēmioergoi* (craftsmen) 24, 26; *kosmos* (order) 103; religion 24; theatre 48–9; women and veils 48; writing and memory 140; *xenia* (guest-friendship) 69
Anderson, Fiona 14n24
Antoine, Jean-Philippe 149n28, 151n55
apertio (opening) 49
apertionis mysterium see baptism
Apollinaire, Guillaume 136
Architectural Review 87
architecture parlante 51, 58n41
Arendt, Hannah 35n42, 55n6, 76n27, 76n28, 94n52, 131n37, 161n13, 164
Aretino, Pietro 57n29
Aristotle 51, 57n38, 75n16, 94n50, 112n53, 129n9, 150n31
arts and crafts, rift between 27
Asman, Carrie 109n11
Athena 25

Babbage, Charles 38n78
baptism, *apertionis mysterium* 49
Barasch, Moshe 57n31
Barber, E. J. W. 14n24, 38n89
Barthes, Roland 59n64
Barvas, Isle of Lewis 26
Baudelaire, Charles 37n76, 103
Beckett, Samuel 44

Bédard, Jean-François 57n40, 58n43, 58n48
Belting, Hans 12n2, 38n98
Benjamin, Andrew 55n6
Benjamin, Walter: on city architecture 112n59; on dwelling 113n64; on *epiphora* 75n18; 'Experience and Poverty' 113n70; on the face 59n56; on furniture 93n46; image and 8, 13n21, 65, 76n31, 77n36, 77n38, 77n42, 77n47; on industrialisation 37n62; and Linfert 112n59; "phantasmagoria" 35n46; on photography 38n81, 58n53; on physiognomics 58n52; on repetition 118; on *Schwelle* 75n18; on storytellers 148n18; on travelling 6, 158; 'Work of Art' 131n47
Bérard, Claude 33n19
Berlin 6
Blaikie, Walter, *Waulking, Eriskay* 118
Bocchi, Franscesco 57n31
Borges, Jorge Luis 39n99
boustrophēdon (act of writing) 140
Bradwardine, Thomas 151n52
Brandt, Bill, *Shad Thames* 155
Brecht, Bertolt 113n67
Breitschmid, Markus 94n54
Bruno, Giuliana 113n66
Buchanan, George 109n8
Burnham, Dan 9
Burt, Edward, *Men Attired in the Feileadh Mhor* 98

Cadava, Eduardo 13n19, 77n40, 130n28
Caillois, Roger 155
calanas (wool-work), book as 11
Camillo, Giulio 151n50
Campbell, J. L. 147n8
Carlin, Peta: *Swatch of Harris Tweed* 5; *Untitled* 4; *Urban Fabric: Greige* 7

Carlyle, Thomas 35n48, 110n17
carpet 84–5, 90; hanging 85–6, 89
Carruthers, Mary 148n13, 149n31, 150n37, 151n51
Carson, Anne 54n1, 148n11, 149n19, 149n21
Cartesianism 51, 52
Casey, Edward S.: on *dēmios* 31n1; on images 165; on landscape 56n13; on memory 59n59, 130n19, 130n23, 130n25; on Philoponus 38n88; on Plato 60n65
Celts 8
Chevreul, Michel-Eugène 34n38; 'Law of Simultaneous Colour Contrasts' 35n54; *The Principles of Harmony and Contrast of Colours and their Application to the Arts* 86
Chicago Frame 37n64
chiton (piece of clothing) 102
chōra (place) 25–6, 89–90
Cicero 129n9, 150n32; *De Oratore* 149n22
cinema 29
cities: and dressing 107, 108; memory and 145, 146; modern 27; *polis* 24–7, 48, 89, 106; walls 48, 89, 106
clò mhòr (big cloth) 8, 26, 74, 160
clothing and place 102–8
Coleridge, Samuel Taylor 76n19
Colomina, Beatriz 113n69
colour: ancient Greece 140; Chevreul on 34n38, 36n54, 86; *chōra* 26; grid and 87, 88; Harris Tweed 26, 86, 102, 103, 109n8; Le Corbusier and 88–9; photography and 6, 30; and place 108; polychromy 7, 9, 25–6, 84, 88–9, 93n47, 104; primary 88; Semper on 7, 104
Corset Hardware (anon) *154*
Crystal Palace 27, 86
cultivation 26
curtain walls 28–31; Chicago School 37n64; and city architecture 106, 159; and façadism 52–3; first 9; Lever House, New York 35n49; Melbourne 31, 53, 128; metaphoric potential 70, 72–3; photography and 53, 128, 146, 158; surface and 87, 113n73; veiling 48

Daedalus 24, 25
Daguerre, Louis-Jacques-Mandé 91n19
daidalon (well-crafted article) 24–5
dance 25, 106, 122–4; Hebridean Weaving Lilt 122
Danto, Arthur C. 13n14

De Stijl movement 88
della Porta, Giambattista, *De Humana Physiognomonia* 51
dēmioergoi (craftsmen) 24, 26
Didi-Huberman, Georges 38n85
doorways 48–50
dromos (course of pageant) 84
Durand, Jean-Louis-Nicolas 52
dyes 8, 102–3

efficiency 52
eidolon, Epicurean (image) 15n35, 73
Elkins, James 15n35
enantiomorph (mirror image) 38n84
Engels, Friedrich 27
epiphaneia (visible surface) 25, 103
eurhythmy 49
Evans, Robin 92n36

fabrica (artefact and its place of making) 50
façades 9, 29–31, 49–50, 52–4, 58n47, 70, 87
feileadh mhor (ancient Hebridean clothing) 89, 102
fenestra locutaria (window spoken through) 52
flatness 84, 87–8
Focillon, Henri 59n61, 93n42, 93n42, 130n22
formalism 9, 87, 108
Forster, Kurt W. 15n34
frames 9, 49, 85–6, 89, 145
Frampton, Kenneth 112n54
fresco 145
Frontisi-Ducroux, Françoise 59n57, 59n59
functionalism 29, 52, 72

Gadamer, Hans-Georg 60n68, 75n13, 91n11, 128n4, 131n40, 132n63, 149n27
Gaelic language 26, 141, 147n6, 147n10
Gesamtkunstwerk (synthesis of arts) 104
Gibson, Ralph, *Overtones: Diptychs and Proportions* 66, 67
Giedion, Sigfried 92n34
Goodrich Freer, Ada 74n4, 129n7
Gorgon iconography 59n57
Gothic art 142, 143
Great Exhibition (1851) 27
Greenberg, Clement 80
Grid Photo, Grand Theatre of Liceu (anon) *20*
grids: architectural 25, 28, 29, 52, 128; Chicago frame 37n64; and corporate

style 28–9; and fabric 31; and memory 144; Modernism 9; pattern 86–8, 108; in Pollock 34n37

habit 107
Hajek-Halke, Heinz, *Erotik—Ganz Groß! (Erotic— In a Big Way!)* 45
hanging carpets 85–6, 89
Hardy, Thomas 94n55
Harries, Karsten 16n54
Harris Tweed: as 'big cloth' (*clò mhòr*) 8, 26, 74, 160; colours 26, 86; curtain walls and 31, 53, 70, 73, 128, 158–9; defined by Act of Parliament 8; and dressing 102–3; first commission 86; forgery 68; gestening 69; Great Exhibition 27; incantations and waulking 140; mechanisation 35n49; patterns 86; peat smoke and 34n39; photography 53; and place 26, 102; polychromy 26; trademark 68; woven surface 26
Harris Tweed Association 68
Harris Tweed Authority 14n27, 34n34
Hattersley loom 35n49
Hebridean Isles 11, 74, 89, 102, 106; Outer Hebrides 8, 27, 31, 122, 128, 140
Hebridean Weaving Lilt 122
Heidegger, Martin 132n62, 133n68
heliographs 158
Hephaestus 32n11
Herbert, Catherine, Lady Dunmore 8, 9
Hermes 32n6
Hesiod 24
Hestia 32n6
Höfer, Albert 111n35
Homer 7, 24, 54n1, 54n3, 150n31
horizontality *see* flatness
Hubbard, Thomas K. 16n53
Huizinga, Johan 129n9

I. G. Farbenindustrie, *Am Strande (Sur la Plage, Strand)* 165
Industrial Revolution 125
Isle of Lewis 26

Jacquard loom 29, 38n78
Jauss, Hans Robert 36n58
Johnston, Annie 74n5
Jones, Owen 36n54

kairos (target) 54, 59n64, 60n69
Kierkegaard, Søren 130n26, 137
Kissling, Werner 147n7

Knossos 24
Kohane, Peter and Hill, Michael 57n27
kosmos (order) 103
Kracauer, Siegfried 76n29
Krauss, Rosalind 92n32
krēdemnon (female head-binding) 48

Lawson, Bill 14n26
Le Corbusier 88, 93n47, 94n49
Le Goff, Jacques 146n2
Leatherbarrow, David 15n43, 56n16, 58n47, 74n3, 77n39, 111n37, 129n9
Leeds 27
Leibniz, Gottfried Wilhelm 132n65
Leslie, Esther 151n62
Lever, William Hesketh, 1st Viscount Leverhulme 35n49
Linfert, Carl 112n59
Locke, John 131n37
Lucretius 38n88

MacKenzie, Ian Angus 147n6
MacKenzie, Kenneth 35n49
MacKinnon, Nan 128n3
MacLeod, Kenneth 128n1
Mallgrave, Harry Francis 15n41, 130n34
Malpas, J. E. 13n15, 13n17, 15n45, 56n14, 77n46, 92n31, 114n78, 161n8
Man, Paul de 58n50
Manchester 27
maquillage 103
Marcus Vitruvius Pollio *see* Vitruvius
Martin, Reinhold 37n72, 37n75, 92n28
masks 52, 53, 105
McCann, Colum 35n43
McEwen, Indra Kagis 16n52, 21, 33n18, 33n19, 147n4
McQuire, Scott 148n11
mechanisation 28, 35n49
Melbourne 6, 30–1, 128, 146
memory 6, 53, 71, 73, 107, 136–46
memory theatre 151n50
Merwood, Joanna 14n30
metaphor: camera and 146; curtain wall and 29; eye and window 57n27; importance of 160; memory 149n31; and place 90; Semper on 7; of weaving 11, 25, 87, 147n5; words 69–73
metropolis 27, 160
mirrors 26, 30, 38n84
mnemotechnology 141
Modernism 9, 108
Mòds 26
money 71–2
movement 158

murals 88–9
Murray tartan 9
Muybridge, Eadweard, *Animal Locomotion* 99

Neisser, Ulric 151n58
Neo-Platonism 38n88
Newall, S. A. 35n49; *Men Stretching and Rolling Up a Length of Harris Tweed* 80
Niépce, Joseph Nicéphore 161n3
Nietzsche, Friedrich 81, 112n43

O'Doherty, Brian 34n37
Ong, Walther J. 148n18
openings 49–50, 52–4, 86
orality 102, 122, 140–2, 148n11, 148n18
the Orb 68
Outer Hebrides 8, 27, 31, 122, 128, 140

Panofsky, Erwin 60n69, 151n55
Papapetros, Spyros 109n11, 112n47
pattern 81–90; of movement 122, 123, 125, 147n7; and photography 72; of textile 8, 21, 25–6, 29–30, 103; of writing 140, 144, 146
Pérez-Gómez, Alberto 33n17, 55n12
Petrarch 50
"phantasmagoria" 35n46
Philoponus 38n88
photography: Belting on 12n2, 39n98; Benjamin and 8, 58n53, 158; façadism 9, 52–4; and Great Exhibition 27; hyphantic potential 8, 54; interconnectedness 71, 73–4, 159; invention announced 86; *kairos* and 54; Kracauer 58n51; memory and 6, 146; metaphoric potential 72–3; pattern 87; reproducibility 126; Tiedemann on 38n87
physiognomics 31, 51, 53, 58n52
place 10, 98–108; connectedness 158–60; horizontality 84; memory 141–6; pattern 89–1; photography and 73–4; repetition 123–4; weaving 25–31
Plato 129n9, 150n31
polis (city-state) 24–7, 48, 89, 106
Pollock, Jackson 34n37, 92n38
polychromy 7, 9, 25–6, 84, 88–9, 93n47, 104
Poulet, Georges 12n3, 98, 113n77
Proust, Marcel 76n23, 161n14
psychoanalysis 53
pteron (colonnade) 11, 25
punctum (Barthes) 59n64

Quintilian 143, 148n18; *Institutio Oratoria* 142, 149n22

Raumkasten ('local box') 145
Renaissance 50–1, 142, 144
repetition 49, 87, 107, 122–4
reproducibility 28, 71, 125, 126
rhapsōidos (singer) 140
rhetoric 142–3
Rhetorica ad Herennium 142, 149n22
Richter, Gerhard, *Spiegel, Grau* 37n61
Rilke, Rainer Maria 64
ritual 25, 28, 72, 105, 122–8
Robert, Louis 146n2
Romberch, Johann Horst von, *Congestorium artificiose memorie* 136
Root, John Welbourn and Burnham, Dan, *Reliance Building* 9
Roth, H. Ling 92n29
Ruskin, John 55n3, 103
Rykwert, Joseph 14n31, 38n86, 57n39, 58n45, 130n20, 133n68

Sachlichkeit (objectivity) 27
Schwartz, Frederick J. 35n46, 112n59
Sebald, W. G. 5
Secondat, Charles-Louis de, Baron de La Brède et de Montesquieu 55n6
Semper, Gottfried 6–10, 154; on carpet 84, 91n14; on Chevreul 110n12; exhibition design 35n50; on festivals 49; *Gesamtkunstwerk* 110n23; on Indian architecture 111n28; influence on Le Corbusier 88; *kosmos* 109n11; on patterns 29; *On Polychromy* 5; on ritual 124, 125, 126; on surface 15n40, 16n46, 56n20, 90n10, 91n15; theatre and performing arts 105–6; theory of dressing 103–5; theory of formal beauty 103; word-plays 104
senses, hierarchical order of 56n22
Sert, Jose Luis 37n74
Shuttle Coursing across a Loom (anon) 21
Simmel, Georg 33n35, 36n60, 45, 76n24, 76n30, 76n32, 99, 110n24, 113n60
Simonides of Keos 141–2
Sontag, Susan 131n53
Spencer, John R. 15n38
St Columba 129n5
Stephen, Ian 4
Stoller, Ezra, *Seagram Building, Mies van der Rohe with Philip Johnson, New York, NY* 137
Stone, Sasha, *Kartei* (Files) 164

surface: in art and architecture 10, 49, 159, 160; dressing 103–8; memory 140, 142, 144–6, 149n31, 150n31; pattern 88; photography 159; walking 158; weaving 25, 70
symbolon (keepsake) 61

tableau (surface) 85, 86
tableaux vivants 88
tabula memoriae 142
tapestry 86, 88–9, 108
Taut, Bruno 58n46
Taylor, Mark C. 14n32
Taylorism 29
theatre 48–50, 60n68, 105–6, 125, 144
'This Morning I Have Risen Early' (waulking song) 102
Thompson, Francis 74n7
Tiedemann, Rolf 13n18, 59n61
topos (place) 25, 38n86, 143
toreutics 32n11, 104
tradition 125–7
tragedy, ancient 48–9

Valéry, Paul 76n28, 131n42
van Doesburg, Theo 93n39
van Zanten, David 33n15
veiling 10, 48, 105
Venturi, Robert 14n32

Vernant, Jean-Pierre 32n3, 59n57
vestiary arts (*Bekleidung*) 7, 103
Vitruvius (Marcus Vitruvius Pollio) 7, 51, 103, 133n68
Vogler, Gisela, *Marion Campbell, Hanging Tweeds Out to Dry* 81

Wagner, Richard 110n23
Warburg, Aby 9
Ward, Janet 15n40
waulking 26, 34n34, 68, 102, 122, 141, 158
Wauters, Émile, *Cairo and the Banks of the Nile* 44
weaving 7–11, 21–31; and dressing 102–4, 108; *kairos* 54; and memory 140–1; pattern 86–7; repetition 122–4; Sebald on 5
Weaving Shed at the Baltic Works, Dundee (anon) 119
Weber, Samuel 75n18, 77n43
West, Martin 31n2
Whitehead, Alfred North 20
Wigley, Mark 93n39, 93n44, 93n47, 112n46
windows 47–8, 52, 57n27

xenia (guest-friendship) 69

Yates, Frances A. 148n15, 150n39

End Image Peta Carlin, *Urban Fabric*, Proposed Installation View without Artefacts. Drawing Letó Tsolakis and Tina Atic, 2013.